J. J. BLUNT'S
UNDESIGNED
SCRIPTURAL
COINCIDENCES
The Proof of Truth

BY ERIC LOUNSBERY

PRESS

J. J. BLUNT'S UNDESIGNED SCRIPTURAL COINCIDENCES
by Eric Lounsbery

Printed in the United States of America

ISBN 1-59781-274-9

Unless otherwise indicated, Bible quotations are taken from the King James Version of the Bible.

www.xulonpress.com

BLUNT, JOHN JAMES: English theologian; b. at Newcastle-under-Lyme (15 m. n.n.w. of Stafford), Staffordshire, 1794; d. at Cambridge June 18, 1856. He studied at St. John's College, Cambridge (B.A., and fellow, 1816; M.A., 1819; B.D., 1826); traveled in Italy and Sicily; became curate to Reginald Heber at Hodnet, Shropshire, in 1821; rector of Great Oakley, Essex, 1834; Lady Margaret professor of divinity at Cambridge 1839. He wrote many books and contributed much to the periodical press; some of his works have passed through many editions. They include *A Sketch of the Reformation in England* (London, 1832); *Undesigned Coincidences in the Writings both of the Old Testament and New Testament an Argument for their Veracity* (1847); *A History of the Christian Church during the First Three Centuries* (1856); *The Duties of the Parish Priest* (1856); *Two Introductory Lectures on the Study of the Early Fathers* (with memoir, Cambridge, 1856).

CONTENTS

INTRODUCTION

In just a few weeks I will be representing the Christian faith in a debate with Monty Gaither, the Director of Arizona's Division of American Atheists, the organization started by the late Madalyn Murray O'Hair. The topic of the debate is "Christianity or Atheism, Where Does the Evidence Point?" In the past two years I have also debated two of the nation's most noted atheists, Dan Barker, and Reginald Finley (a.k.a. The Infidel Guy). As a Christian since July 1, 1979, I have always had a strong interest in apologetics. I have listened to numerous debates as well as read practically everything I could find on defending the Christian faith. Yet, it was in preparation for my first debate with Dan Barker that I initially came across J. J. Blunt's book. The copy I have is the seventeenth edition of "*Undesigned Coincidences in the Writings both of the Old and New Testament, an Argument of Their Veracity*". The book is dated, 1897.

With new books on apologetics coming off the press seemingly every day that contain the latest information on Bible archeology, intelligent design, as well as sophisticated philosophical arguments pertaining to the existence of God, miracles, the spiritual realm, etc., why would anyone want to reprint an apologetic book written over one hundred years ago?

The only answer I can give is that when a great treasure has been "buried", it is a time of incredible celebration for all who get to share the treasure when it is "dug up". J. J. Blunt's *Undesigned Scriptural Coincidences* is such a treasure.

Herein you will find what I believe are the strongest arguments for the veracity of the Scriptures found in any book in print. That is a huge claim in light of the scholarly works written by my "heroes": Norman Geisler, John Warwick Montgomery, William Lane Craig, Gary Habermas, Josh McDowell, and too many others to name here. The reason I make this claim is because Blunt's unique apologetic approach exposes facts in the Scriptures whose presence can only be explained if the Scriptures are true.

I have made two minor changes to Blunt's material: One, I have included headings at the beginning of each argument. Two, I have used today's common method of noting Biblical passages as opposed to the Roman Numeral system used by Blunt. The rest of the material is as it appeared over one hundred years ago, that includes spelling and grammar.

My prayer is that God will be glorified as a result of the impact of this material upon your life.

Eric Lounsbery
Pastor, Family Christian Fellowship
Mesa, Arizona
March 15, 2005

PREFACE

The present Volume is a republication, with corrections and large additions, of several short Works which I printed a few years ago separately; and which, having passed through more or fewer editions, have become out of print: I have thus been furnished with an opportunity of revising and consolidating them. These words were: "The Veracity of the Books of Moses;" "The Veracity of the Historical Scriptures of the Old Testament;" and " The Veracity of the Gospels and Acts," argued from undersigned coincidences to be found in them when compared in their several parts; and in the last instance, when compared also with the writings of Josephus. They were all of them originally the substance of Sermons delivered before the University, some in a Course of Hulsean Lectures, others on various occasions. And though two of them, The Veracity of the Books of Moses, and The Veracity of the Gospels and Acts, were divested of the form of Sermons before publication, the third, The Veracity of the Historical Scriptures of the Old Testament (which constituted the Hulsean Lectures), still retained it. I have thought that by reducing this to the same shape as the rest, and combining it with them, the whole would present a continued argument, or rather a continued series of independent arguments, for the Veracity of the Scriptures, of which the effect would be greater than that of the separate works could be, which might be read perhaps out of the natural order, and which were not altogether uniform in their plan. But as this test of veracity proved applicable, though in a less degree, for reasons I have assigned elsewhere, to the Prophetical Scriptures also, I have introduced into the present Volume, in its proper place, evidence of the same kind which had been long lying by me, for the Veracity of some of those Writings; thus employing one and the same touchstone of truth, to verify successively the Books of Moses, the Historical Scriptures of the Old Testament, the Prophetical, and the Gospels and Acts, in their order.

The argument, as my readers will of course be aware, is an extension of that of the *Horæ Paulinæ,* and which originated, as was generally supposed, with Dr. Paley. But Dr. Turton, the present Bishop of Ely, has rendered the claims of Dr. Paley to the first conception of it doubtful, by producing a passage from the conclusion of Dr. Doddridge's Introduction to his Paraphrase and Notes on the First Epistle to the Thessalonians, to the following effect:-

"Whoever reads over St. Paul's Epistles with attention will discern such intrinsic characters in their genuineness, and the divine authority of the doctrines they contain, as will perhaps produce in him a stronger conviction than all the external evidence with which they are attended. To which we may add, that the exact coincidence observable between the many *allusions* to particular facts, in this, as well as in other *Epistles*, and the account of the facts themselves as they are recorded in the History of the *Acts*, is a remarkable confirmation of the truth of each."

Be this, however, as it may, Dr. Paley first brought the argument fully to light in support of the Epistles of St. Paul; and I am not aware that it has since been deliberately applied to any other of the sacred books, except by Dr. Graves, in two of his Lectures on the Pentateuch, to that portion of holy writ. Much, however, of the same kind of testimony I have no doubt has escaped all of us; and still remains to be detected by future writers on the Evidences. For myself, though I may not lay claim to the merit (whatever it may be) of actually discovering all the examples of consistency without contrivance, which I shall bring forward in this volume,—indeed, I could not myself now trace to their beginnings thoughts which have progressively accumulated—and though in many cases, where the detection was my own, I may have found, on examination, that there were others who had forestalled me, *qui nostra ante nos*, yet most of them I have not seen noticed by commentators at all, and scarcely any of them in that light in which only I regard them, as *grounds of Evidence*. It is to this application, therefore, of expositions, often in themselves sufficiently familiar, that I have to beg the candid attention of my readers; and if I shall frequently bring out of the treasures of God's word, or of the interpretation of God's word, "thing old, " the use that I make of them may not perhaps be thought so.

As the argument for the Veracity of the Gospels and Acts, derived from undersigned coincidences, discoverable between them and the Writings of Josephus, does not fall within the general design of this work, as now constructed, and yet is related to it, and important in itself, I have thought it best not to suppress, but to throw it into an Appendix.

Cambridge, May 3, 1847

ADVERTISMENT TO THE THIRD EDITION

In this Edition I have corrected a few errors overlooked in the former, chiefly in the references; strengthened several of the arguments; and supplied one or two other—a proof of the truth of the remark made in the foregoing Preface, that the subject was still (and probably, it may be added, ever will be) open to further enlargement.

With respect to the origin of the *Horæ Paulinæ* itself, another point there adverted to, I would suggest, that the twelfth chapter of Mr. Biscoe's "History of the Acts of the Holy Apostles," considered as evidence of the truth of Christianity,—a chapter in which the author "would further observe the agreement there is between the Acts and the Epistles in the names and descriptions of St. Paul's fellow-labourers and converts,"—might perhaps be as likely as the passage in Dr. Doddridge, to have put Dr. Paley on the plan of his Work: not to say that Mr. Biscoe's Work appeared whilst Dr. Doddridge's Commentary was in progress. Certain it is, that in the course of the details by which Mr. Biscoe supports his proposition, more than one coincidences of the *Horæ Paulinæ* are touched.
Cambridge, Jan. 1, 1850

Part I

The Veracity of the Books of Moses

It is my intention to argue in the following pages the Veracity of the Books of Scripture, from the instances they contain of *coincidence without design*, in their several parts. On the nature of this argument I shall not much enlarge, but refer my readers for a general view of it to the short dissertation prefixed to the *Horæ Paulinæ* of Dr. Paley, a work where it is employed as a test of the veracity of St. Paul's Epistles with singular felicity and force, and for which suitable incidents were certainly much more abundant than those which any other portion of Scripture of the same extent provides; still, however, if the instances which I can offer, gathered from the remainder of Holy Writ, are so numerous, and of such a kind as to preclude the possibility of their being the effect of accident, it is enough. It does not require many circumstantial coincidences to determine the mind of a jury as to the credibility of a witness in our courts, even where the life of a fellow-creature is at stake. I say this, not as a matter of charge, but as a matter of fact, indicating the authority which attaches to this species of evidence, and the confidence universally entertained that it cannot deceive. Neither should it be forgotten, that an argument thus popular, thus applicable to the affairs of common life as a test of truth, derives no small value when enlisted in the cause of Revelation, from the readiness with which it is apprehended and admitted by mankind at large, and from the simplicity of the nature of its appeal; for it springs out of the documents the truth of which it is intended to sustain, and terminates in them; so that he who has these, has the defense of them.

2. Nor is this all. The argument deduced from coincidence without design has further claims, because, if well made out, it establishes the authors of the several books of Scripture as *independent* witnesses to the facts they relate; and this, whether they consulted each other's writings or not; for the coincidences, if good for anything, are such as *could not* result

from combination, mutual understanding, or arrangement. If any which I may bring forward may seem to be such as might have so arisen, they are only to be reckoned ill chosen, and dismissed; for it is no small merit of this argument, that it consists of parts, one or more of which (if they be thought unsound) may be detached without any dissolution of the reasoning as a whole. *Undesignedness* must be apparent in the coincidences, or they are not to the purpose. In our argument we defy people to set down together, or transmit their writings one to another, and produce the like. Truths known independently to each of them, must be at the bottom of documents having such discrepancies and such agreements as these in question. The point, therefore, whether the authors of the books of Scripture have or have not copied from one another, which in the case of some of them has been so much labored, is thus rendered a matter of comparative indifference. Let them have so done, still by our argument their independence would be secured, and the nature of their testimony be shown to be such as could only result from their separate knowledge of substantial facts.

3. I will add another consideration which seems to me to deserve serious attention: that in several instances the probable truth of a *miracle* is involved in the coincidence. This is a point which we should distinguish from the general drift of the argument itself. The general drift of our argument is this, that when we see the writers of the Scriptures clearly telling the truth in those cases where we have the means of *checking* their accounts,—when we see that they are artless, consistent, veracious writers, where we have the opportunity of examining the fact,—it is reasonable to believe that they are telling the truth in those cases where we have not the means of checking them,—that they are veracious where we have not the means of putting them to proof. But the argument I am now pressing is distinct from this. We are hereby called upon, not merely to assent that Moses and the author of the Book of Joshua, for example, or Isaiah and the author of the Book of Kings, or St. Matthew and St. Luke, speak the truth when they record a miracle, because we know them to speak the truth in many other matters (though this would be only reasonable where there is no impeachment of their veracity whatever), but we are called upon to believe a *particular miracle, because the very circumstances which attend it furnish the coincidence.* I look upon this as a point of very great importance. I do not say that the coincidence in such a case establishes the miracle, but that, by establishing the truth of ordinary incidents which involve the miracle, which compass the miracle round about, and which cannot be separated from the miracle without the utter laceration of the history itself, it goes very near to establish it.

4. On the whole, it is surely a striking fact, and one that could scarcely happen in any continuous fable, however cunningly devised, that annals written by so *many hands*, embracing so many generations of men, relating to so many different states of society, abounding in supernatural incidents throughout, when brought to this same touchstone of truth, *undesignedness*, should still not flinch from it; and surely the character of a history, like the character of an individual, when attested by vouchers not of one family, or of one place, or of one date only, but by such as speak to it under various relations, in different situations, and at divers periods of time, can scarcely deceive us.

Perhaps I may add, that the turn which biblical criticism has of late years taken, gives the peculiar argument here employed the advantage of being the word in season; and whilst the articulation of Scripture (so to speak), occupied with its component parts, may possibly cause it to be less regarded than it should be in the mass and as a whole, the effect of this argument is to establish the general truth of Scripture, and with that to content itself—its *general* truth, I mean, considered with a reference to all practical purposes, which is our chief concern—and thus to pluck the sting out of those critical difficulties, however numerous and however minute, which in themselves have a tendency to excite our suspicion and trouble our peace. Its effect, I say, is to establish the *general* truth of Scripture, because by this investigation I find occasional tokens of veracity, such as cannot, I think, mislead us, breaking out, as the volume is unrolled,—unconnected, unconcerted, unlooked for; tokens which I hail as guarantees for more facts than they actually cover; as spots which truth has singled out whereon to set her seal, in testimony that the whole document, of which they are a part, is her own act and deed; as pass-words, with which the Providence of God has taken care to furnish his ambassadors, which, though often trifling in themselves, and having no proportion (it may be) to the length or importance of the tidings they accompany, are still enough to prove the bearers to be in the confidence of their Almighty Sovereign, and to be qualified to execute the general commission with which they are charged under his authority.

I shall produce the instances of coincidence without design which I have to offer, in the order of the Books of Scripture that supply them, beginning with the Books of Moses. But before I proceed to individual cases, I will endeavor to develop a principle upon which the Book of Genesis goes *as a whole*, for this is in itself an example of *consistency*.

I. THE PATRIARCHAL CHURCH

There may be those who look upon the Book of Genesis as an epitome of the *general* history of the world in its early ages, and of the *private* history of certain families more distinguished than the rest. And so it is, and on a first view it may seem to be little else; but if we consider it more closely, I think we may convince ourselves of the truth of this proposition: that it contains *fragments (as it were) of the fabric of a Patriarchal Church*—fragments scattered, indeed, and imperfect, but capable of combination, and, when combined, *consistent as a whole*. Now it is not easy to imagine that any impostor would set himself to compose a book upon a plan so recondite; nor, if he did, would it be possible for him to execute it as it is executed here. For the incidents which go to prove this proposition are to be picked out from among many others, and on being brought together by ourselves, they are found to agree together as *parts of a system*, though they are not contemplated as such, or at least are not produced as such, by the author himself.

I am aware that, whilst we are endeavoring to obtain a view of such a Patriarchal Church by the *glimpses* afforded us in Genesis, there is a danger of our theology becoming visionary: it is a search upon which the imagination enters with alacrity, and readily breaks its bounds—it has done so in former times and in our own. Still the principle of such investigation is good; for out of God's book, as out of God's world, more may be often concluded than our philosophy at first suspects. The principle is good, for it is sanctioned by our Lord himself, who reproaches the Sadducees with not *knowing* those Scriptures which they received, because they had not *deduced* the doctrine of a future state from the words of Moses, "I am the God of Abraham, and the God of Isaac, and the God of Jacob," though the doctrine was there if they would but have sought it out. One consideration, however, we must take along with us in this inquiry, that the Books of Moses are in most cases a very *incomplete* history of facts—telling something and leaving a great deal untold—abounding in chasms which cannot be filled up—not, therefore, to be lightly esteemed even in their *hints*, for *hints* are often all that they offer.

The proofs of this are numberless; but as it is important to my argument that the thing itself should be distinctly borne in mind, I will name a few. Thus if we read the history of Joseph as it is given in the 37th chapter of Genesis, where his brethren first put him into the pit and then sell him to the Ishmaelites, we might conclude that he was himself quite *passive* in the whole transaction. Yet when the brothers happen to talk together upon this same subject many years afterwards in Egypt, they say one to another,

"We are verily guilty concerning our brother, in that we saw the *anguish of his soul when he besought us*, and we would not hear." [Gen. 42:21.] All these fervent entreaties are sunk in the direct history of the event, and only come out by accident after all. As another instance. The simple account of Jacob's reluctance to part with Benjamin would lead us to suppose that it was expressed and overcome in a short time, and with no great effort. Yet we incidentally hear from Judah that this family struggle (for such it seems to have been) had occupied as much time as would have sufficed for a journey to Egypt and back [Gen. 43:10.] . As a third instance. The several blessings which Jacob bestows on his sons have probably a reference to the *past* as well as to the *future* fortunes of each. In the case of Reuben the allusion happens to be a circumstance in his life with which we are already acquainted; here, therefore, we understand the old man's address [Gen. 49:4.] ; but in the case of several at least of his other sons, where there are probably similar allusions to events in their lives too, which have not, however, been left on record, there is much that is obscure; the brevity of the previous narrative not supplying us with the proper key to the blessing. Of this nature, perhaps, is the clause respecting Simeon and Levi, "In their anger they slew a man, and in their self-will they digged down a wall." [Gen. 49:6.] As another instance. The address of Jacob on his death-bed to Reuben, to which I have just referred, shows how deeply Jacob resented the wrong done him by this son many years before, and proves what a breach it must have made between them at the moment; yet all that is said of it in the Mosaic history is, "and Israel heard it," [Gen. 35:22.] —not a syllable more. Again, of Anah it is said [Gen. 36:24.] , "This was that Allah that found the mules in the wilderness, as he fed the asses of Zibeon his father:" an allusion to some incident apparently very well known, but of which we have no trace in the previous narrative. Once more. The manner in which Joshua is mentioned for the first time, clearly shows how conspicuous a character he already was amongst the Israelites; and how much previous history respecting him has been suppressed. "And Moses said unto Joshua, choose us out men, and go out, fight with Amalek." [Exod. 17:9.] And the same remark applies to Hur, in an ensuing sentence, "And Moses, Aaron, and Hur went up to the top of the hill:" the Jewish tradition being that Hur was the husband of Miriam. Again, it is said, "that Jethro, Moses' father-in-law, took Zipporah, Moses' wife, after he *had sent her back*." [Exod. 18:2.] The latter clause refers to some transaction, familiar, no doubt, to the historian, but of which no previous mention had been made. It is needless to multiply instances; all that I Wish to impress is this, that in the Book of Genesis a *hint* is not to be wasted, but *improved;* and that he who expects every probable deduction from Scripture to be made out complete in all its parts before he will admit it, expects more than he will in many cases meet with, and will learn much less than he might otherwise learn.

Having made these preliminary remarks, I shall now proceed to collect the detached incidents in Genesis which appear to point out the existence of a *Patriarchal Church*. And the circumstance of so many incidents tending to this one centre, though evidently without being marshaled or arranged, implies veracity in the record itself; for it is a very comprehensive instance of *coincidence without design* in the several parts of that record.

1. First, then, the Patriarchs seem to have had *places* set apart for the worship of God, consecrated, as it were, especially to his service. To do things "*before the Lord*" is a phrase not unfrequently occurring, and generally in a local sense. Cain and Abel appear to have brought their offerings to the *same* spot, it might be (as some have thought) [Hooker, Eccl. Pol. b. v. § 11. Vide Mr. Faber's Three Dispensations, Vol. i. p. 8; and comp. Wisdom ix. 9.] , to the East of the Garden, where the symbols of God's presence were displayed; and when Cain is banished from his first dwelling, and driven to wander upon the earth, he is said to have "gone out from the *presence of the Lord;*" [Gen. 4:16.] as though, in the land where he was henceforward to live, he would no longer have access to the spot where God had more especially set his name: or it might be a sacred tent, for it is told Cain, "if thou doest not well, sin (i.e. a sin-offering) lieth at the *door:*" [Gen. 4:7.] and we know that the sacrifices were constantly brought to the door of the Tabernacle, in later times [See Lightfoot, i. 3.] . Again, when the angels had left Abraham, and were gone towards Sodom, "Abraham," we read, "stood yet *before the Lord,*" [Gen. 18:22.] i.e., he staid to plead with God for Sodom in the place best suited to such a service, the place where prayer was wont to be made; and accordingly it follows immediately after, "and Abraham *drew near* and said;" [Gen. 18:23.] and again, the next day, "Abraham gat up early in the morning," (probably his usual hour of prayer), "to the place where he stood *before the Lord,*" [Gen. 19:27.] the same where he had put up his intercessions to God the day before; in short, the place where he "built an altar unto the Lord" when he first came to dwell in the plain of Mamre [Gen. 13:18.] , for that was still the scene of this transaction. Again, of Rebekah we read, that when. the children struggled within her, "she *went* to inquire of the Lord," and an answer was received prophetic of the different fortunes of those children [Gen. 25:22.] . And when Isaac contemplated blessing his son, which was a *religious* act, a solemn appeal to God to remember his covenant unto Abraham, it was to be done

22

"before the Lord." [Gen. 27:7.] The *place* might be, as I have just said, an altar such as was put up by Abraham at Hebron, by Isaac at Beer-sheba, or by Jacob at Beth-el, where they respectively dwelt [See Gen. 13:18; 26:25; 35:6.] ; it might be, as I have also suggested, a separate tent, and a tent actually was set apart by Moses outside the camp, before the Tabernacle was erected, where every one repaired who *sought the Lord* [Exod. 33:7.] ; or it might be a separate part of a chamber of the tent; but however that was, the expression is a definite one, and relates to some appointed quarter to which the family resorted for purposes of devotion. Accordingly the very same expression is used in after-times, when the Tabernacle had been set up, *confessedly* as the place where the people were to assemble for prayer and sacrifice. "He shall offer it of his own voluntary will at the door of the Tabernacle of the congregation *before the Lord*, and he shall kill the bullock *before the Lord*." [Lev. 1:3.] "Three times in the year shall all thy males appear *before the Lord* thy God in the place which he shall choose." [Deut. 16:16.] Here there can be no question as to the meaning of the phrase; it occurs, indeed, some five-and-thirty times in the last four books of Moses, and in *all* as significant of the place set apart for the worship of God. I conclude therefore, that in those passages of Genesis which I have quoted, Moses employs the same expression in the same sense.

Such are some of the *hints* which seem to point to *places* of *patriarchal worship*.

2. In like manner, and by evidence of the same indirect and imperfect kind, I gather that there were *persons* whose business it was to perform the rites of that worship—not perhaps their sole business, but their appropriate business. Whether the *first-born* was by right of birth the *priest* also, has been doubted; at the same time it is obvious that this circumstance would often, perhaps generally where there was no impediment, point him out as the fit person to keep alive in his own household the fear of that God who alone could make it to prosper. Persons, however, invested with the sacerdotal office there undoubtedly were; such was Melchizedek "the Priest of the Most High God," as he is expressly called [Gen. 14:18.] , and the functions of his ministry he publicly performs towards Abraham, blessing him as God's servant, as the instrument by which His arm had overthrown the confederate kings, and receiving from Abraham a tenth of the spoil, which could be nothing but a religious offering, and which indeed, as such, is the ground of St. Paul's argument for the superiority of Christ's priesthood over the Levitical. *Tithes*, therefore, were already paid [Heb. 7:9.] . Such probably was Jethro "the Priest of Midian." [Exod. 2:16.] Moreover, we find the *priests* expressly mentioned

as a body of functionaries existing amongst the Israelites even before the consecration of Aaron and his sons [Exod. 19:22.] ; the "young men," who offered burnt-offerings, spoken of Exod. 24:5, being the same under a different name, probably the first-born. Then if we read of Patriarchal *Priests*, so do we of Patriarchal "*Preachers* of Righteousness," as in Noah [2 Pet. 2:5.] . So do we of Patriarchal *Prophets*, as in Abraham [Gen. 20:7.] , as in Balaam, as in Job, as in Enoch. All these are *hints* of a Patriarchal Church, differing perhaps less in its construction and in the manner in which God was pleased to use it, as the means of keeping Himself in remembrance amongst men, from the churches which have succeeded, than may be at first imagined.

3. Pursue we the inquiry, and I think a *hint* may be discovered of a peculiar *dress* assigned to the Patriarchal Priest when he officiated; for Jacob, being already possessed of the birthright, and probably, in this instance, of the priesthood with it, since Esau by surrendering the birth-right became "*profane,* " [Heb. 12:16.] goes in to Isaac to receive the blessing, a religious act, as I have already said, to be done *before the Lord.* Now on this occasion, Rebekah took "*goodly raiment*" (such is our translation) "of her *eldest* son Esau, which were with her in the house, and put them upon Jacob her younger son." [Gen. 27:15.] Were these the *sacerdotal robes* of the firstborn? It occurred to me that they might be so; and on reference I find that the Jews themselves so interpreted them [Vide Patrick in loc.] , an interpretation which has been treated by Dr. Patrick more contemptuously than it deserved to be [More especially as he quotes in another place (on Exod. 28:2) an opinion of the Hebrew Doctors, that vestments were inseparable from the priesthood, so that Adam, Abel, and Cain, did not sacrifice without them; see Gen. 3:22: and again (on Exod. 28:35), a maxim among the Jews, that when the priests were clothed with their garments they were priests; when they were not so clothed, they were not priests.]; for I look upon it as a trifle indeed, but still as a trifle which is a component part of the system I am endeavoring to trace out: had it stood alone it would have been fruitless perhaps to have hazarded a word upon it; as it stands in conjunction with so many other indications of a Patriarchal Church it has its weight. Now I do not say that the Hebrew expression [beged:H899] here rendered "raiment" (for of the epithet "goodly" I will speak by and by) is exclusively confined to the garments of a priest; it is certainly a term of considerable latitude, and is by no means to be so restricted; still, when the priest's garments are to be expressed by any general term at all, it is always by the one in question. Yet there is another term in the Hebrew [salmah:H8008] , perhaps of as frequent occurrence, and also a comprehensive term; but whilst this latter

is constantly applied to the dress of other individuals of both sexes, I do not find it ever applied to the dress of the priests. The distinction and the argument will be best illustrated by examples:—Thus we read in Leviticus [Chap. 21:10.] , according to our version, "the high-priest that is consecrated to put on the *garments*, shall not uncover his head, nor rend his *clothes*." The word here translated "garments" in the one clause, and "clothes" in the other, is in the Hebrew in both clauses the same—is the word in question—is the *raiment* of Esau which Rebekah took, and in both clauses the priests' dress is meant, and no other. So again, what are called [Exod. 35:19.] "the *clothes* of service," is still the same word, as implying *Aaron's* clothes, or those of his sons, and no other. And again, Moses says [Lev. 10:6.] , "uncover not your heads, neither rend your *clothes*, lest ye die;" still the word is the same, for he is there speaking to Aaron and his sons, and to none other. But when he says [Deut. 29:5.] , "your *clothes* are not waxed old," the Hebrew word is no longer the same, though the English word is, but is the other word of which I spoke [salmah:H8008] ; for the *clothes* of the *people* are here signified, and not of the priests.

This, therefore, is all that can be maintained, that the term used to express the "*raiment*" which Rebekah brought out for Jacob, is the term which would express *appropriately* the dress of the priest, though it certainly would not express it *exclusively*. But again, the epithet "*goodly*" (or "*desirable*" [chamad:H2530] as the margin renders it more closely) annexed to the raiment is still in favour of our interpretation, though neither is this word, any more than the other, conclusive of the question. Certain, however, it is, that though the word translated "goodly" is not restricted to *sacred things*, it does so happen that to *sacred things* it is attached in very many instances, if not in a majority of instances, where it occurs in Holy Writ. Thus the utensils of the Temple which Nebuchadnezzar carried away are called in the Book of Chronicles [2 Chron. 36:10.] "the *goodly* vessels of the House of the Lord." And Isaiah writes, "all our *pleasant* things are laid waste," [Isa. 64:11.] meaning the Temple—the word here rendered "pleasant," being the same as that in the former passages rendered "goodly;" and in the Lamentations [Lam. 1:10.] we read, "the adversary hath spread out his hand upon all our *pleasant* things," where the Temple is again understood, as the context proves; and in Genesis [Gen. 3:6.] , "a tree to be *desired* to make one wise," the term perhaps meant to convey a hint of violated *sanctity* as entering into the offence of our first parents. In other places it occurs in a bad sense, as relating to what was held *sacred* by heathens only, but still what was held sacred—"The oaks which ye have *desired*;" [Isa. 1:29.]

"all *pleasant* pictures," [Isa. 2:16.] objects of idolatry, as the tenour of the passage indicates; "their *delectable* things shall not profit," [Isa. 44:9.] that is, their idols. I may add too, that the στολη of the Septuagint (for this answers to the "raiment" of our version), though not limited to the robe of the altar, is the term used in the Greek as the appropriate one for the robe of Aaron; and finally, that the care with which this vesture had been kept by Rebekah, and the perfumes with which it was imbued when Jacob wore it (for Isaac "smelled the smell of his raiment"), savour of things pertaining unto God. Indeed we read in the Law [Exod. 37:29.] of particular drugs which were appropriated to compose the incense used in the service of God.

Again, it seems to be by no means improbable that "*the coat of many colours*," (χιτωνα ποικιλον, as the LXX understands it [Gen. 37:3.]) which Jacob made for Joseph, was a *sacerdotal* garment. It figures very largely in a very short history. It appears to have been viewed with great jealousy by his brothers; far greater than an ordinary dress, which merely bespoke a certain partiality on the part of a parent, would have been likely to inspire. They strip him of it, when they put him in the pit; they dip it in the blood of the goat, when they want to persuade Jacob that a wild beast had devoured him. Reuben, Jacob's first-born, and naturally therefore the Priest of the family, had forfeited his father's affection and disgraced his station by his conduct towards Bilhah. Jacob might feel that the priesthood was open under the circumstances; and his fondness for Joseph might suggest to him, that he might in justice be considered his first-born; for that he supposed Rachel, Joseph's mother, to be his wife, when Leah, Reuben's mother, had been deceitfully substituted for her. He might give him, therefore, "this coat of many colours" as a token of his future office. Hannah brought Samuel "a little coat" from year to year, when she came up with her husband to offer his yearly sacrifice [1 Sam. 2:19.] : and, though Aaron's coat is not called a coat of many colours, it was so in fact; "and of the *blue* and *purple* and *scarlet* they made cloths of service, to do service in the holy place, and made the holy garments for Aaron." [Exod. 39:1.] On the whole, therefore, I think there was a meaning in this "coat of many colours" beyond the obvious one; and that it was emblematical of priestly functions which Jacob was anxious to devolve upon Joseph.

4. Furthermore, the Patriarchal Church seems not to have been without its *forms*. Thus Jacob consecrates the foundation of a place of worship with oil [Gen. 28:18.] ; the incident here alluded to being apparently a much more detailed and emphatic one than it seems at first sight: for we find him, by anticipation, calling "this the house of God, and this the gate of heaven," [Gen. 28:17.] and promising eventually to endow it with tithes

[Gen. 28:22.] : and we hear God reminding him of this solemn act long afterwards, when he was in Syria, and appropriating to Himself the very title of this Temple: "I am the God of Bethel, where thou anointedst the pillar, and where thou vowedst a vow unto me." [Gen. 31:13.] And accordingly we are told at much length, and with several of the circumstances of the case described, that Jacob, after his return from Haran, actually fulfilled his pious intentions, and "built an altar," and "set up a pillar," and "poured a drink-offering thereon." [Gen. 35:1. 15.]

Then there appears to have been the rite of imposition of hands existing in the Patriarchal Church; and when Jacob blessed Joseph's children, he is very careful about the due observance of it; the narrative, succinct as on the whole it is, dwelling upon this point with much amplification [Gen. 48:13–19.] .

Again, the shoes of those who trod upon holy ground, or who entered consecrated places, were to be put off their feet; the injunction to this effect, of which we read in the case of Moses at the bush, implies a usage already established [Exod. 3:5.] ; and this usage, though nowhere expressly commanded in the Levitical Law, appears to have continued amongst the Israelites by tradition from the Patriarchal times; and is that which a passage in Ecclesiastes [Eccles. 5:1.] probably contemplates in its primary sense, "Look to thy *foot* when thou comest to the House of God." [See Mede's Works, b. ii. p. 340 et seq.] And finally the Patriarchal Church had its posture of worship, and men bowed themselves to the ground when they addressed God [Gen. 24:26–52; Exod. 4:31; 12:27.] .

But if there were Patriarchal *Places* for worship—if there were *Priests* to conduct the worship—if there were *Tithes* paid them—if there were decent *Robes* wherein those priests ministered at the worship—if there were *Forms* connected with that worship—so do I think there were stated *Seasons* set apart for it; though here again we have nothing but *hints* to guide us to a conclusion.

5. I confess that the Divine institution of the Sabbath as a day of religious duties, seems to me to have been from the beginning; and though we have but *glimpses* of such a fact, still to my eye they present themselves as parts of that one harmonious whole which I am now endeavouring to develope and draw out—even of a Patriarchal Church, whereof we see scarcely anything but by glimpse.

"And it came to pass that on the sixth day they gathered twice as much bread, two omers for one man and all the rulers of the congregation came, and told Moses. And he said unto them, This is that which the Lord *hath said*, To-morrow is the rest of the Holy Sabbath unto the Lord. Six days ye shall gather it; but on the seventh day, which is the Sabbath, in it there shall be none." [Exod. 16:22.] And again, in a few verses after, "And the Lord said unto Moses, How long refuse ye to keep my commandments and my laws? See, for that the Lord *hath given* you the Sabbath, therefore he giveth you on the sixth day the bread of two days." Now the transaction here recorded is by some argued to be the first institution of the Sabbath. The inference I draw from it, I confess, is different; I see in it, that a Sabbath had already been appointed—that the Lord had already given it; and that, in accommodation to that institution already understood, He had doubled the manna on the sixth day. But even supposing the Institution of the Sabbath to be here formally *proclaimed*, or supposing (as others would have it, and as the Jews themselves pretend), that it was not now promulgated, strictly speaking, but was actually one of the two precepts given a little earlier at Marah [Exod. 15:25, and compare Deut. 5:12.] , still it is not uncommon in the writings of Moses, nor indeed in other parts of Scripture, for an event to be mentioned as then occurring for the first time, which had in fact occurred, and which had been reported to have occurred, long before. For instance, Isaac and Abimelech meet, and swear to do each other no injury. "And it came to pass the same day, that Isaac's servants came and told him concerning the well which they had digged, and said unto him, We have found water: and he called it Shebah; therefore the *name of the city is Beer-Sheba unto this day.*" [Gen. 26:32.] Now who would not say that the name was then given to the place by Isaac, and for the first time? Yet it had been undoubtedly given by Abraham long before, in commemoration of a similar covenant which he had struck with the Abimelech of *his* day. "These seven ewe-lambs," said he to that Prince, "shalt thou take at my hand, that they may be a witness unto thee that I have digged this well; *wherefore he called the place Beer-Sheba*, because they sware both of them." [Gen. 21:31.] Again, "So Jacob came to Luz, which is in the land of Canaan, that is, Beth-el, he and all his people that were with him. And he built there an altar, and called the place *El-Beth-el*, because there God appeared unto him when he fled from the face of his brother." [Gen. 35:6, 7.] Who would not conclude that the new name was given to Luz now for the first time? Yet Jacob had in fact changed the name a great many years before, when he was on his journey to Haran. "And Jacob rose up early in the morning, and took the stone that he had put for his pillows, and set it up for a pillar, and poured oil upon the top of it. And he called the name of that place *Bethel:* but the name of the city was called Luz at the first." [Gen. 28:18, 19.] Or, as another instance:—"And God appeared unto Jacob again when he came out of Parian-Aram, and blessed him: and God said unto him, Thy name is Jacob, thy name shall not be called any more Jacob, but *Israel* shall be thy name, and he called his name *Israel*." [Gen. 35:10.] Who would not suppose that the name of Israel was now given to Jacob for the first time? Yet, several chapters before this, when Jacob had wrestled with the angel (not at Beth-el, which was the former scene, but at Peniel), we read, that "the *angel* said, What is thy name? and he said, Jacob: and he said, Thy name shall be called no more Jacob, but *Israel;* for as a prince hast thou power with God, and with man, and hast prevailed." [Gen. 32:28.] Thus again, to add one example more, we are told in the Book of Judges [Judges 10:4.] , that a certain *Jair*, a Gileadite, a successor of Abimelech in the government of Israel, "had thirty sons that rode on thirty ass-colts, and they had thirty cities, which are called *Havoth-Jair* unto this day, which are in the land of Gilead." Who would not conclude that the cities were then called by this name for the first time, and that this *Jair* was the person from whom they derived it? Yet we read in the Book of Numbers [Num. 32:41] , that another *Jair*, who lived nearly three hundred years earlier, "went and took the small towns of Gilead" (apparently these very same), "and called them *Havoth-Jair*." So that the name had been given nearly three centuries already. Why, then, should it be thought strange that the institution of the Sabbath should be mentioned as if for the first time in the 16th chapter of Exodus, and yet that it should have been in fact founded at the creation of the world, as the language of the 2nd chapter of Genesis [Gen. 2:3.] , taken in its obvious meaning, implies; and as St. Paul's argument in the 4th chapter of the Epistle to the Hebrews (I think) requires it to have been?—Nor is such a case without a parallel. *"Moses* gave unto you circumcision," says our Lord; yet there is added, "not because it is of Moses, but of the *Fathers;*" [John 7:22.] —and the like may be said of the Sabbath; that *Moses* gave it, and yet that it was of the *Fathers.* And surely such observance of the Sabbath from the *beginning* is in accordance with many hints which are conveyed to us of some distinction or other belonging to that day from the *beginning*—as when Noah sends forth the dove three times successively at intervals of *seven* days: as when Laban invites Jacob to "fulfil his *week,* " after the marriage of Leah; the nuptial festivities being probably terminated by the arrival of the Sabbath [Gen. 29:27.] : as when Joseph makes a mourning for his father of *seven* days [Gen. 1:10.] ; the lamentation most likely ceasing with the return of that festival: these and other hints of the same kind being, as appears to me, pregnant with meaning, and intended to be so, in a history of the rapid and desultory nature of that of Moses. Neither is there much difficulty in the passage of Ezekiel [Ezek. 20:10, 11, 12.] , with which those, who maintain the Sabbath to have been for the first time enjoined in the wilderness, support themselves. "Wherefore," says that Prophet, "I caused them to go forth out of the land of Egypt, and brought them into the wilderness—and I gave them my *statutes*, and showed them my *judgments*, which if a man do, he shall even live in them—moreover also I gave them my *Sabbaths*." Here, then, it is alleged, Ezekiel affirms, or seems to affirm, that the Almighty gave the Israelites his Sabbaths when He was leading them out of Egypt, and that He had not given them till then. Yet his *statutes* and *judgments* are also spoken of as given at the same time, whereas very many of those had *surely* been given long before. It would be very untrue to assert, that, until the Israelites were led forth from Egypt, no *statutes* or *judgments* of the same kind had been ever given: it was in the wilderness that the law respecting clean and unclean beasts was promulgated, yet that law had certainly been published long before [Gen. 7:2.] ; and the same may be said of many others, which I will not enumerate here, because I shall have occasion to do it by and by. My argument, then, is briefly this:—that as Ezekiel speaks of *statutes* and *judgments* given to the Israelites in the wilderness, some of which were certainly old statutes and judgments repeated and enforced, so when he says that the *Sabbaths* were given to the Israelites in the wilderness, he cannot be fairly accounted to assert that the Sabbaths had never been given till then. The fact indeed probably was, that they had been neglected and half forgotten during the long bondage in Egypt (slavery being unfavourable to morals), and that the observance of them was re-asserted and renewed at the time of the promulgation of the Law in the Desert. In this sense, therefore, the Prophet might well declare, that on that occasion God gave the Israelites his Sabbaths. It is true, that in addition to the motive for the observance of the Sabbath (hinted in the 2nd chapter of Genesis, and more fully expressed in the 20th of Exodus), which is of *universal* obligation, other motives were urged upon the Israelites *specially* applicable to them—as that "the day should be a sign between God and them" [Exod. 31:17.] —as that it should be a remembrance of their having been made to rest from the yoke of the Egyptians [Deut. 5:15.] . Yet such *supplementary* sanctions to the performance of a duty (however well adapted to secure the obedience of the Israelites) are quite consistent with a previous command addressed to all, and upon a principle binding on all [Justin Martyr, it is true, frequently speaks of the Patriarchs as observing no Sabbaths (See, *e.g.*, Dial. § 23); but it is certain that his meaning was, that the Patriarchs did not observe the Sabbaths *according to the peculiar rites of the Jewish Law;* his use of the word σαββατιζειν has always a reference to that Law; and by no means that they kept no Sabbaths at all].

I have now attempted to show, but very briefly, lest otherwise the scope of my argument should be lost sight of, that there were among the Patriarchs *places* set apart for worship—*persons* to officiate—a decent *ceremonial*—an appointed *season* for holy things; I will now suggest in very few words (still gathering my information from such *hints* as the Book of Genesis supplies from time to time,) something of the *duties* and *doctrines* which were taught in that ancient Church: and here, I think, it will appear, that the Law and the Prophets of the next Dispensation had their prototypes in that of the Patriarchs—that the Second Temple was greater indeed in glory than the First, but was nevertheless built up out of the First, the one body "not unclothed," but the other rather "clothed upon."

6. In this primitive Church, then, the distinction of clean and unclean is already known, and known as much in detail as under the Levitical Law, every animal being arranged by Noah in one class or the other [Gen. 7:2.] ; and the clean being exclusively used by him for sacrifice [Gen. 8:20.] . The blood, which is the life of the animal, is already withheld as food [Gen. 9:4.] . Murder is already denounced as demanding death for its punishment [Gen. 9:6; 42:22.] . Adultery is already forbidden, as we learn from the cases of Pharaoh and Abimelech [Gen. 12:18; 26:10.] , of Reuben [Gen. 49:4] , and Joseph [Gen. 39:9.] , Oaths are already binding [Gen. 26:28.] . Vows were already made [Gen. 28:20; 31:13.] . Fornication is already condemned, as in the case of Shechem, who is said "to have wrought folly in Israel, which thing ought not to be done." [Gen. 34:7.] Marriage with the uncircumcised or idolater is already prohibited [Gen. 34:14, and comp. Exod. 34:16, and Dr. Patrick's Comment.] . A curse is already denounced on him that setteth light by his father or his mother [Gen. 9:25, and comp. Deut. 27:16.] . Purifications are already enjoined those who approach a holy place, for Jacob bids his people "be clean and change their garments" before they present themselves at Bethel [Gen. 35:2.] . The eldest son had already a birthright [Gen. 25:31; and comp. Exod. 22:29; and Deut. 21:17.] . The brother is already commanded to marry the brother's widow, and to raise up seed unto his brother [Gen. 38:8.] . The daughter of the Priest (if Judah as the head of his own family may be considered in that character) is already to be brought forth and burned, if she played the harlot [Gen. 38:24.] . These laws, afterwards incorporated in the Levitical, are here brought together and reviewed at a glance; but as they occur in the book of Genesis, be it remembered, they drop out incidentally, one by one, as the course of the narrative happens to turn them up. They are therefore to be reckoned fragments of a more full and complete code, which was the groundwork, in all probability, of the Levitical code itself; for it is difficult to suppose that where there were these, there were not others like to them. But this is not

all—the Patriarchs had their *sacrifices*, that great and leading rite of the Church of Aaron; the subjects of those sacrifices fixed; useless without the shedding of blood; for what but the violation of an express command full of meaning, could have constituted the sin of Cain [See Gen. 3:21; 4:4, 5. 7.] ? Their sacrifices, how far regulated in their details by the injunctions of God himself, we cannot determine; yet it is impossible to read in the 15th chapter of Genesis the particulars of Abraham's offering of the heifer, the goat, the ram, the turtle-dove, and the pigeon—their ages, their sex, the circumspection with which he dissects and disposes them—whether all this be done in act or in vision, without feeling assured that very minute directions upon all these points were vouchsafed to the *Patriarchal Church*. And as that Church had her rite of *sacrifice*, so had she her rite of *circumcision:* and accordingly she had her *Sacraments*.

Then as she had her *sacraments*, so had she her *types*—types which in number scarcely yield to those of the Levitical Law, in precision and interest perhaps exceed them. For we meet with them in the names and fortunes of individuals whom the Almighty Disposer of events, without doing violence to the natural order of things, exhibits as pages of a *living* book in which the *Promise* is to be read—as characters expressing his counsels and covenants writ by his own finger—as actors, whereby He holds up to a world, not yet prepared for less gross and sensible impressions, scenes to come. It would lead me far beyond the limits of my argument were I to touch upon the multitude of instances, which will crowd, however, I doubt not, upon the minds of my readers. I might tell of Adam, whom St. Paul himself calls "the figure" or type "of Him that was to come." [Rom. 5:14; 1 Cor. 15:45.] I might tell of the sacrifice of Isaac (though not altogether after him whose vision upon this subject, always bright though often baseless, would alone have immortalized his name)— of that Isaac whose birth was preceded by an annunciation to his mother [Gen. 18:10.] —whose conception was miraculous [Gen. 18:14.] —who was named of the angel before he was conceived in the womb [Gen. 17:19.] , and Joy, or Laughter, or Rejoicing was that name [Gen. 21:6.] — who was, in its primary sense, the seed in which all the nations of the earth were to be blessed [Gen. 22:18.] —whose projected death was a rehearsal (as it were), almost two thousand years beforehand, of the great offering of all—the very mountain, Moriah, not chosen by chance, not chosen for convenience, for it was three days' journey from Abraham's dwelling-place, but no doubt appointed of God as the future scene of a Saviour's passion too [Gen. 22:2; 2 Chron. 3:1.] —a son, an only son the victim—the very instruments of the oblation, the *wood*, not carried by the young men, not carried by the ass which they had brought with them, but laid on the shoulders of him who was to die, as the *cross* was borne up that same ascent of Him who, in the fulness of time, was destined to expire upon it. But indeed I see the *Promise* all Genesis through, so that our Lord might well begin with *Moses* in expounding the things concerning Himself [Luke 24:27.] ; and well might Philip say, "We have found Him of whom Moses in the Law did write." [John 1:45.] I see the *Promise* all Genesis through, and if I have constructed a rude and imperfect Temple of Patriarchal worship out of the fragments which offer themselves to our hands in that history, the Messiah to come is the spirit that must fill that Temple with His all-pervading presence,—none other than He must be the Shekinah of the Tabernacle we have reared. For I confess myself wholly at a loss to explain the nature of that Book on any other principle, or to unlock its mysteries by any other key. Couple it with this consideration, and I see the scheme of Revelation, like the physical scheme, proceeding with beautiful *uniformity*—an unity of plan connecting (as it has been well said by Paley) the chicken roosting upon its perch with the spheres revolving in the firmament; and an unity of plan connecting in like manner the meanest accidents of a household with the most illustrious visions of a prophet. Abstracted from this consideration, I see in it details of actions, some trifling, some even offensive, pursued at a length (when compared with the whole) singularly disproportionate; while things which the angels would desire to look into are passed over and forgotten. But this principle once admitted, and all is consecrated— all assumes a new aspect—trifles that seem at first not bigger than a man's hand, occupy the heavens; and wherefore Sarah *laughed*, for instance, at the prospect of a son, and wherefore that *laugh* was rendered immortal in his name, and wherefore the sacred historian dwells on a matter so trivial, whilst the world and its vast concerns were lying at his feet, I can fully understand. For then I see the hand of God shaping everything to his own ends, and in an event thus casual, thus easy, thus unimportant, telling forth his mighty design of Salvation to the world, and working it up into the web of his noble prospective counsels [Gen. 21:6.] . I see that nothing is great or little before Him who can bend to his purposes whatever He willeth, and convert the light-hearted and thoughtless mockery of an aged woman into an instrument of his glory, effectual as the tongue of the seer which He touched with living coals from the altar. Bearing this master-key in my hand, I can interpret the scenes of domestic mirth, of domestic stratagem, or of domestic wickedness, with which the history of Moses abounds. The Seed of the Woman, that was to bruise the Serpent's head [Gen. 3:15.] , however indistinctly understood (and probably it was understood very indistinctly), was the one thing longed for in the families

of old, was "the *desire* of all nations," as the Prophet Haggai expressly
calls it [Hag. 2:7.] ; and provided they could accomplish this desire, they
(like others when urged by an overpowering motive) were often reckless
of the means, and rushed upon deeds which they could not defend. Then
did the wife forget her jealousy, and provoke, instead of resenting, the
faithlessness of her husband [Gen. 16:2; 30:3; 30:9.] ; then did the mother
forget a mother's part, and teach her own child treachery and deceit [Gen.
25:23; 27:13.]; then did daughters turn the instincts of nature backward,
and deliberately work their own and their father's shame [Gen. 19:31.] ;
then did the daughter-in-law veil her face, and court the incestuous bed
[Gen. 38:14.] ; and to be childless was to be a bye-word [Gen. 16:5; 30:1.]
; and to refuse to raise up seed to a brother was to be spit upon [Gen.
38:26; Deut. 25:9.] ; and the prospect of the *Promise*, like the fulfilment
of it, did not send peace into families, but a sword, and three were set
against two, and two against three [Gen. 27:41.] ; and the elder, who
would be promoted unto honour, was set against the younger, whom God
would promote [Gen. 4:5; 27:41.] , and national differences were engendered by it, as individuals grew into nations [Gen. 19:37; 26:35.] ; and
even the foulest of idolatries may be traced, perhaps, to this hallowed
source; for the corruption of the best is the worst corruption of all [Numb.
25:1, 2, 3.] . It is upon this principle of interpretation, and I know not
upon what other so well, that we may put to silence the ignorance of foolish men, who have made those parts of the Mosaic History a stumbling-
block to many, which, if rightly understood, are the very testimony of the
covenant; and a principle, which is thus extensive in its application and
successful in its results, which explains so much that is difficult, and
answers so much that is objected against, has, from this circumstance
alone, strong presumption in its favour, strong claims upon our sober
regard [See Allix, "Reflections on the Books of Holy Scripture," where
this interesting subject is most ingeniously pursued.] .

Such is the structure that appears to me to unfold itself, if we do but bring
together the scattered materials of which it is composed. The *place* of
worship—the *priest* to minister—the *tithes* to support him—the sacerdotal
dress—the ceremonial *forms*—the appointed *seasons* for holy things—
preachers—*prophets*—a code of *laws*—*sacrifices*—*sacraments*—*types* —
and a *Messiah* in prospect, as leading a feature of the whole scheme, as He
now is in retrospect of a scheme which has succeeded it. Complete the
building is not, but still there is symmetry in its component parts, and unity
in its whole. Yet Moses was certainly not contemplating any description of
a *Patriarchal Church*. He had other matters in his thoughts: he was the
mediator not of this system, but of another, which he was now to set forth in

all its details, even of the *Levitical*. Hints, however, of a former dispensation he does inadvertently let fall, and these we find, on collecting and comparing them, to be, as far as they go, harmonious.

Upon this *general* view of the Book of Genesis, then, I found my first proof of *consistency without design* in the writings of Moses, and my first argument for their veracity—for such consistency is too uniform to be *accidental*, and too unobtrusive to have been *studied*. Such a view is, doubtless, important, as far as regards the doctrines of Scripture; I, however, only urge it as far as regards the *evidences*. I shall now enter more into detail, and bring forward such *specific coincidences* amongst independent passages of the Mosaic writings, as tend to prove that in them we have the Word of Truth, that in them we may put our trust with faith unfeigned.

II. ABRAHAM'S INTERCESSION FOR SODOM

In the 18th chapter of Genesis we find recorded a very singular conversation which Abraham is reported to have held with a superior Being, there called the Lord. It pleased God on this occasion to communicate to the Father of the Faithful his intention to destroy forthwith the cities of Sodom and Gomorrah, of which the cry was great, and the sin very grievous. Now the manner in which Abraham is said to have received the sad tidings is remarkable. He does not bow to the high behest in helpless acquiescence—the Lord do what seemeth good in his sight—but, with feelings at once excited to the uttermost, he pleads for the guilty city, he implores the Lord not to slay *the righteous with the wicked;* and when he feels himself permitted to speak with all boldness, he first entreats that fifty good men may purchase the city's safety, and, still encouraged by the success of a series of petitions, he rises in his merciful demands, till at last it is promised that even if *ten* should be found in it, it should not be destroyed for ten's sake.

Now was there no motive beyond that of *general humanity* which urged Abraham to entreaties so importunate, so reiterated? None is named— perhaps such general motive will be thought enough—I do not say that it was not; yet I think we may discover a special and appropriate one, which was likely to act upon the mind of Abraham with still greater effect, though we are left entirely to detect it for ourselves. For may we not imagine, that no sooner was the intelligence sounded in Abraham's ears, than he called to mind that *Lot his nephew, with all his family*, was dwelling in this accursed town [Gen. 14:12.] , and that this consideration both prompted and quickened his prayer? For while he thus made his supplication for Sodom, I do not read that *Gomorrah and the other cities of the plain* [Gen. 19:28; Jude 7.] shared his intercession, though they stood in the same need of it—and why not? except that in them he had not the same deep interest. It may be argued too, and without any undue refinement, that in his repeated reduction of the number which was to save the place, he was governed by the hope that the single family of Lot (for he had sons-in-law who had married his daughters, and daughters unmarried, and servants,) would in itself have supplied so many individuals at least as would fulfil the last condition—*ten* righteous persons who might turn away the wrath of God, nor suffer his whole displeasure to arise.

Surely nothing could be more natural than that anxiety for the welfare of relatives so near to him should be felt by Abraham—nothing more natural than that he should make an effort for their escape, as he had done on a former occasion at his own risk, when he rescued this very Lot from the kings who had taken him captive—nothing more natural than that his family feeling should discover themselves in the earnestness of his entreaties—yet we have to collect all this for our-selves. The whole chapter might be read without our gathering from it a single hint that he had any relative within ten days' journey of the place. All we know is, that Abraham entreated for it with great passion—that he entreated for no other place, though others were in the same peril—that he endeavoured to obtain such terms as seemed likely to be fulfilled if a single righteous family could be found there. And then we know, from what is elsewhere disclosed, that the family of Lot did actually dwell there at that time, a family that Abraham might well have reckoned on being more prolific in virtue than it proved.

Surely, then, a coincidence between the zeal of the *uncle* and the danger of the *brother's son* is here detailed, though it is not expressed; and so utterly undesigned is this coincidence, that the history might be read many times over, and this feature of truth in it never happen to present itself.

And here let me observe, (an observation which will be very often forced upon our notice in the prosecution of this argument,) that this sign of truth (whatever may be the importance attached to it) offers itself in the midst of an incident in a great measure *miraculous:* and though it cannot be said that such indications of veracity in the *natural* parts of a story *prove* those parts of it to be true which are *supernatural;* yet where the natural and supernatural are in close combination, the truth of the former must at least be thought to add to the credibility of the latter; and they who are disposed to believe, from the coincidence in question, that the petition of Abraham in behalf of Sodom was a real petition, as it is described by Moses, and no fiction, will have some difficulty in separating it from the miraculous circumstances connected with it—the visit of the angel—the prophetic information he conveyed—and the terrible vengeance with which he was proceeding to smite that adulterous and sinful generation.

III. ISAAC AND REBEKAH

The 24th chapter of Genesis contains a very beautiful and primitive picture of Eastern manners, in the mission of Abraham's trusty servant to Mesopotamia, to procure a wife for Isaac from the daughters of that branch of the Patriarch's family which continued to dwell in Haran. He came nigh to the city of Nahor—it was the hour when the people were going to draw water. He entreated God to give him a token whereby he might know which of the damsels of the place He had appointed to Isaac for a wife. "And it came to pass that behold Rebekah came out, who was born to Bethuel, son of Milcah, the wife of Nahor, Abraham's brother, with her pitcher upon her shoulder"—"Drink, my lord," was her greeting, "and I will draw water for thy camels also." This was the simple token which the servant had sought at the hands of God; and accordingly he proceeds to impart his commission to herself and her friends. To read is to believe this story. But the point in it to which I beg the attention of my readers is this, that Rebekah is said to be *"the daughter of Bethuel, the son of Milcah, which she bare unto Nahor."* It appears, therefore, that the *grand-daughter* of Abraham's brother is to be the wife of Abraham's *son*—i. e. that a person of the *third* generation on Nahor's side is found of suitable years for one of the *second* generation on Abraham's side. Now what could harmonize more remarkably with a fact elsewhere asserted, though here not even touched upon, that Sarah the wife of Abraham was for a long time barren, and *had no child till she was stricken in years* [Gen. 18:12.] ? Thus it was that a generation on Abraham's side was lost, and the grand-children of his brother in Haran were the coevals of his own child in Canaan. I must say that this trifling instance of minute consistency gives me very great confidence in the veracity of the historian. It is an *incidental* point in the narrative—most easily overlooked—I am free to confess, never observed by myself till I examined the Pentateuch with a view to this species of internal evidence. It is a point on which he might have spoken differently, and yet not have excited the smallest suspicion that he was speaking inaccurately. Suppose he had said that Abraham's son had taken for a wife the *daughter* of Nahor, instead of the *grand-daughter*, who would have seen in this anything improbable? and to a mere inventor would not that alliance have been much the more likely to suggest itself?

Now here, again, the ordinary and extraordinary are so closely united, that it is extremely difficult indeed to put them asunder. If, then, the *ordinary* circumstances of the narrative have the impress of truth, the *extraordinary* have a very valid right to challenge our serious consideration too. If the coincidence almost establishes this as a certain fact, which I think it does, that Sarah did not bear Isaac while she was young, agreeably to what Moses affirms; is it not probable that the same historian is telling the truth when he says, that Isaac was born when Sarah was too old to bear him at all except by miracle?—when he says, that the Lord announced his future birth, and ushered him into the world by giving him a name foretelling the *joy* he should be to the nations; changing the names of both his parents with a prophetic reference to the high destinies this son was appointed to fulfil?

Indeed the more attentively and scrupulously we examine the Scriptures, the more shall we be (in my opinion) convinced, that the natural and supernatural events recorded in them must stand or fall together. The spirit of miracles possesses the entire body of the Bible, and cannot be cast out without rending in pieces the whole frame of the history itself, merely considered as a history.

IV. BETHUEL AND REBEKAH

There is another indication of truth in this same portion of patriarchal story. It is this—*The consistent insignificance of Bethuel in this whole affair.* Yet he was alive, and as the father of Rebekah was likely, it might have been thought, to have been a conspicuous person in this contract of his daughter's marriage. For there was nothing in the *custom of the country* to warrant the apparent indifference in the party most nearly concerned, which we observe in Bethuel. Laban was of the same country and placed in circumstances some-what similar; he, too, had to dispose of a daughter in marriage, and that daughter also, like Rebekah, had brothers [Gen. 31:1.]; yet in this case the terms of the contract were stipulated, as was reasonable, by the *father* alone; he was the active person throughout. But mark the difference in the instance of Bethuel—whether he was incapable from years or imbecility to manage his own affairs, it is of course impossible to say, but something of this kind seems to be implied in all that relates to him. Thus, when Abraham's servant meets with Rebekah at the well, he inquires of her, "whose daughter art thou? tell me I pray thee, is there room in thy *father's* house for us to lodge in?" [Gen. 24:23.] She answers, that she is the daughter of Bethuel, and that there is room; and when he thereupon declared who he was and whence he came; "the damsel ran and told them of her *mother's* house" (not of her *father's* house, as Rachel did when Jacob introduced himself [Gen. 29:12.]) "these things." This might be accident; but "Rebekah had a *brother*," the history continues, and "his name was Laban, and *Laban* ran out unto the man, and invited him in [Gen. 24:29.] . Still we have no mention of Bethuel. The servant now explains the nature of his errand, and in this instance it is said, that Laban and *Bethuel* answered [Gen. 24:50.]; Bethuel being here in this passage, which constitutes the sole proof of his being alive, coupled with his son as the spokesman. It is agreed, that she shall go with the man, and he now makes his presents, but to whom? "Jewels of silver, and jewels of gold, and raiment, he gave to *Rebekah*." He also gave, we are told, "to her *brother* and to her *mother* precious things;" [Gen. 24:53.] but not, it seems, to her father; still Bethuel is over-looked, and *he alone*. It is proposed that she shall tarry a few days before she departs. And by whom is this proposal made? Not by her father, the most natural person surely to have been the principal throughout this whole affair; but "by her *brother* and her *mother*." [Gen. 24:55.] In the next generation, when Jacob, the fruit of this marriage, flies to his mother's country at the counsel of Rebekah, to hide himself from the anger of Esau, and to procure for himself a wife, and when he comes to Haran and inquires of the shepherds after his kindred in that place, how does he express himself? "Know ye," says he, "Laban the *son of Nahor?*" [Gen. 29:5.] This is more marked than even the former instances, for Laban was the *son* of Bethuel, and only the *grandson* of Nahor; yet still we see Bethuel is passed over as a person of no note in his own family, and Laban his own child designated by the title of his grandfather, instead of his father.

   This is consistent—and the consistency is too much of one piece throughout, and marked by too many particulars to be accidental. It is the consistency of a man who knew more about Bethuel than we do or than he happened to let drop from his pen. It is of a kind, perhaps, the most satis-factory of all for the purpose I use it, because the least liable to suspicion of all. The uniformity of expressive silence—repeated *omissions* that have a meaning—no agreement in a positive fact, for nothing is asserted; yet a presumption of the fact conveyed by mere negative evidence. It is like the death of Joseph in the New Testament, which none of the Evangelists affirm to have taken place before the Crucifixion, though all imply it. This kind of consistency I look upon as beyond the reach of the most subtle contriver in the world.

V. ISAAC'S COMFORT

On the return of this servant of Abraham, his embassy fulfilled, and Rebekah in his company, he discovers Isaac at a distance, who was gone out (as our translation has it) "to *meditate*," or (as the margin has it) "to *pray* in the field at eventide." [Gen. 24:63.]

Now in this subordinate incident in the narrative there are marks of truth, (very slight indeed it may be,) but still, I think, if not obvious, not difficult to be perceived, and not unworthy to be mentioned. Isaac went out to *meditate* or to *pray*—but the Hebrew word does not relate to religious meditation *exclusively*, still less *exclusively* to direct prayer. Neither does the corresponding expression in the Septuagint (αδολεσχησαι) convey either of these senses exclusively, the latter of the two perhaps not at all. The leading idea suggested seems to be an anxious, a reverential, a painful, a *depressed* state of mind—"out of the abundance of my *complaint*" (or *meditation*, for the word is the same here, only in the form of a substantive), "out of the abundance of my *meditation* and *grief* have I spoken," are the words of Hannah to Eli [1 Sam. 1:16.] . "Who hath woe, who hath sorrow, who hath contentions, who hath *babbling*, (the word is here still the same, and evidently might be rendered with more propriety *melancholy*,) who hath wounds without cause, who hath redness of eyes?" [Prov. 23:29.] Isaac therefore went out into the field, not directly to *pray*, but to give ease to *a wounded spirit in solitude*. Now the occasion of this his trouble of mind is not pointed out, and the passage indeed has been usually explained without any reference to such a feeling, and merely as an instance of religious contemplation in Isaac worthy of imitation by all. But one of the last things that is recorded to have happened before the servant went to Haran, whence he was now returning, is the *death and burial of Sarah*, no doubt a tender mother (as she proved herself a jealous one) to the child of her old age and her only child. What more likely than that her loss was the subject of Isaac's mournful meditation on this occasion? But this conjecture is reduced almost to certainty by a few words incidentally dropped at the end of the chapter; for having lifted up his eyes and beheld the camels coming, and the servant, and the maiden, Isaac "brought her into his *mother Sarah's* tent, and took Rebekah and she became his wife; and he loved her, and *was comforted after his mother's death."* [Gen. 24:67.]

The agreement of this latter incident with what had gone before is not set forth in our version, and a scene of very touching and picturesque beauty impaired, if not destroyed.

VI. ISAAC'S LIFE EXTENDED

We have now to contemplate Isaac in a different scene, and to remove with him (after the fashion of this earthly pilgrimage) from an occasion of mirth to one of mourning.

Being now grown old, as he says, and "not knowing *the day of his death,"* he prepares to bless his first-born son *"before he dies."* [Gen. 27:2.4.] So spake the Patriarch. This looks very like one of the last acts of a life which time and natural decay had brought near its close; yet it is certain that Isaac continued to live a great many years after this, nay, that probably a fourth part of his whole life yet remained to him—for he was still alive when Jacob returned from Mesopotamia; when even many of Jacob's sons were grown up to manhood who were as yet in the loins of their father [Gen. 34:5.] ; and even after that Patriarch had repeatedly migrated from dwelling-place to dwelling-place in the land of Canaan. For "Jacob," we read when all these other events had been related in their order, "came unto *Isaac his father*, unto Mamre, unto the city of Arbah, which is Hebron, where Abraham and Isaac sojourned." [Gen. 35:27.]

How, then, is this seeming discrepancy to be got over? I mean the discrepancy between Isaac's anxiety to bless his son *before he died*, and the fact of his being found alive perhaps forty or fifty years afterwards? My answer is this—that it was probably at a moment of dangerous sickness when he bethought himself of imparting the blessing—and I feel my conjecture supported by the following *minute coincidences*. That Isaac was then desirous to have "*savoury meat* such as he loved," as though he loathed his ordinary food: that Jacob bade him "*arise and sit* that he might eat of his venison," as though he was at the time stretched upon his bed; that he "*trembled very exceedingly,"* when Esau came in and he was apprized of his mistake, as though he was very weak; that the words of Esau, when he said in his heart "the days of *mourning* for my father are at hand," are as though he was thought sick unto death; and that those of Rebekah, when she said unto Jacob "should I be deprived of you *both* in one day," are as though she supposed the time of her widowhood to be near.

I will add that the prolongation of Isaac's life *unexpectedly* (as it should seem), may have had its influence in the continued protection of Jacob from Esau's anger, the latter, even in the first burst of his passion, retaining that reverence for his father which determined him to put off the execution of his evil purposes against Jacob, till *he* should be no more. And this affection seems to have been felt by him to the last; for wild and wandering as was his life, the sword or the bow ever in his hand, we nevertheless find him anxious to do honour to his father's grave, and assisting Jacob at the burial [Gen. 35:29.] . The filial feelings, therefore, which had stayed his hand at first were still tending to soothe him during Jacob's absence, and to propitiate him on Jacob's return; for the days of mourning for his father were still not come.

VII. JACOB AND STRANGE GODS

My next coincidence may not be thought in itself so convincing as some others, yet, as it at once furnishes an argument for the truth of Genesis and an answer to an objection, I will not pass it over. When Jacob is about to remove with his family to Beth-el, a place already consecrated in his memory by the vision of angels, and thenceforward to be distinguished by an altar to his God, he gives the following extraordinary command to his household and all that are with him: "Put away the strange gods that are among you, and be clean, and change your garments;" [Gen 35:2.] or as it might be translated with perhaps more closeness, "the gods of the stranger." Had Jacob, then, hitherto tolerated the worship of idols among his own attendants? Had he connived so long at a defection from the God of his fathers, even whilst he was befriended by Him, whilst he was living under his special protection, whilst he was in frequent communication with Him? This is hard to be believed; indeed it would have seemed incredible altogether, had it not been remembered that Rachel had Images which she stole from her father Laban, and which he at least considered as his household gods. Those images, however, might be taken by Rachel as valuables, silver or gold perhaps, a fair prize as she might think, serving to balance the portion which Laban had withheld from her, and the money which he had devoured. That she used them herself as idols does not appear, but rather the contrary—and that Jacob was perfectly unconscious of their being at all in his camp, whether as objects of worship or as objects of value, is evident from his giving Laban free leave to put to death the party on whom they should be found [Gen 36:32.]. He therefore was not an idolater himself; nor, as far as we know, did he wink at idolatry in those about him. Whence, then, this command, issued to his attendants on their approach to Beth-el, that holy ground, "to put away the strange gods that were amongst them, and to make themselves clean?"

Let us only refer to an event of a former chapter [Gen 34.], and all is plain. The sons of Jacob had been just destroying the city of the Shechemites—they had slain the males, but "all their wealth, and all their little ones, and their wives, took they captive, and spoiled all that was in the house." These captives, then, so lately added to the company of Jacob, were in all probability the strangers alluded to, and the idols in their possession the gods of the strangers, which accordingly the Patriarch required them to put away forthwith, before Beth-el was approached. Moreover, it may be observed, that the terms of the command extend to "all that were with him," which may well have respect to the recent augmentation of his numbers, by the addition of the Shechemite prisoners: and the further injunction, that not only the idols were to be put away, but that all were to be clean and change their garments, may have a like respect to the recent slaughter of that people, whereby all who were concerned in it were polluted.

Yet, surely, nothing can be more incidental than the connection between the sacking of the city and the subsequent command to put the idols of the stranger away—though nothing can be more natural and satisfactory than that connection when it is once perceived. Indeed so little solicitous is Moses to point out these two events as cause and consequence, that he has left himself open to misconstruction by the very unguarded and artless manner in which he expresses himself, and has even placed the character of Jacob, as an exclusive worshipper of the true God, unintentionally in jeopardy.

VIII. THE INDIVIDUALITY OF JACOB

In the character of Jacob I see an *individuality* which marks it to belong to real life: and this is my next argument for the veracity of the writings of Moses. The particulars we read of him are consistent with each other, and with the lot to which he was born; for this more or less models the character of every man. The lot of Jacob had not fallen upon the fairest of grounds. Life, especially the former part of it, did not run so smoothly with him as with his father Isaac—so that he might be tempted to say to Pharaoh towards the close of it naturally enough, that "the days of the years of it had been evil." The faults of his youth had been visited upon his manhood with a retributive justice not unfrequent in God's moral government of the world, where the very sin by which a man offends is made the rod by which he is corrected. Rebekah's undue partiality for her younger son, which leads her to deal cunningly for his promotion unto honour, works for her the loss of that son for the remainder of her days—his own unjust attempts at gaining the superiority over his elder brother entail upon him twenty years' slavery in a foreign land—and the arts by which he had made Esau to suffer are precisely those by which he suffers himself at the hands of Laban. Of this man, the first thing we hear is, his entertainment of Abraham's servant when he came on his errand to Rebekah. Hospitality was the virtue of his age and country; in his case, however, it seems to have been no little stimulated by the sight of "the ear-ring and the bracelets on his sister's hands," which the servant had already given her [Gen. 24:30.] —so he speedily made room for the camels. He next is presented to us as beguiling that sister's son, who had sought a shelter in his house, and whose circumstances placed him at his mercy, of fourteen years' service, when he had covenanted with him for seven only—endeavouring to retain his labour when he would not pay him his labour's worth—himself devouring the portion which he should have given to his daughters, counting them but as strangers [Gen. 31:15.] . Compelled at length to pay Jacob wages, he changes them ten times, and in the spirit of a crafty griping worldling makes him account for whatever of the flock was torn of beasts or stolen, whether by day or night. When Jacob flies from this iniquitous service with his family and cattle, Laban still pursues and persecutes him, intending, if his intentions had not been overruled by a mightier hand, to send him away empty, even after he had been making, for so long a period, so usurious a profit of him.

I think it was to be expected that one who had been disciplined in such a school as this, and for such a season, would not come out of it without bearing about him its marks; and that oppressed first by the just fury of his brother, which put his life in hazard, and drove him into exile, and then still more by the continued tyranny of a father-in-law, such as we have seen, Jacob should have learned, like maltreated animals, to have the *fear of man habitually before his eyes*. Now that it was so is evident from all the latter part of his history.

He is afraid that Laban will not let him go, and therefore takes the *precaution* to steal from him unawares, when he is gone to a distance to shear his sheep. He approaches the borders of Edom, but here the ancient dread of his brother revives, and he takes the *precaution* to propitiate him or to escape him by measures which breathe the spirit of the man in a singular manner. He sends him a message—it is from "Jacob thy servant" to "Esau my lord." Esau advances, and he at once fears the worst. Then does he divide his people and substance into two bands, that if the one be smitten, the other may escape—he provides a present of many cattle for his brother—he commands his servants to put a space between each drove, apparently to add effect to the splendour of his present—he charges them to deliver severally their own portion, with the tidings that he was behind who sent it—he appoints their places to the women and children with the same prudential considerations that mark his whole conduct; first the handmaids and their children; then Leah and her children; and in the hindermost and least-exposed place, his favourite Rachel and Joseph. Such are his *precautions*. They are all, however, needless—Esau owes him no wrong—he even proposes to escort him home in peace, or to leave him a guard out of the four hundred men that were with him. But Jacob evades both proposals; *apprehending*, most likely, more danger from his friends than from his foes; and dismisses his brother with a word about "following my lord to Seir;" an intention which, as far as we know, he was in more haste to express than accomplish. All this ended, the honour of his house is violated by Shechem, a son of a prince of that country. Even this insult does not throw him off his guard. He heard it, *"but he held his peace"* till his sons, who were with the cattle in the field, should come home. They soon proceed to take summary vengeance on the Shechemites. The *fear* of man, however, which had restrained the wrath of Jacob at the first, besets him still, and he now says to his sons—"Ye have troubled me to make me to stink among the inhabitants of the land; and I being few in number, they shall gather themselves together against me and slay me; and I shall be destroyed, I and my house." [Gen. 34:30.] Jacob would have been better pleased with more compromise and less cruelty—he was not prepared to give utterance to that feeling of turbulent indignation, reckless of all consequences, which spake in the words of Simeon and Levi, "Shall he deal with our sister as with an harlot?" Here again, however, his fears proved groundless. Many years now pass away, but when we meet him once more he is still the same—the same leading feature in his character continues to the last. His sons go down into Egypt for corn in the famine—they return with an injunction from Joseph to take back with them Benjamin, or else to see his face no more. This is urged upon Jacob, and the reply it extorts from him is in strict keeping with all that has gone before:—"Wherefore dealt ye so ill with me, *as to tell the man whether ye had yet a brother?*" [Gen. 43:6.] Still we see one whom suffering had rendered distrustful—who would lend many his ear, but few his tongue. The famine presses so sore that there is no alternative but to yield up his son. Still he is the same individual. Judah is in haste to be gone—he will be surety for the lad—he will bring him again, or bear the blame for ever. But Jacob gives little heed to these vapouring promises of a sanguine adviser, and, as stooping before a necessity which was too strong for him, he prudently sets himself to devise means to disarm the danger; and "if it must be so now," says he, "do this, *take of the best fruits of the land in your vessels, and carry down the man a present*, a little balm and a little honey, spices and myrrh, nuts and almonds—and take double money in your hand; and the money that was brought again in the mouth of your sacks, carry it again in your hand; peradventure it was an oversight." [Gen. 43:12.]

I cannot persuade myself that these are not marks of a *real character*—especially when I consider that this *identity* is found in incidents spread over a period of a hundred years or more—that they are mere hints, as it were, out of which we are left to construct the man; hints interrupted by a multitude of other matters; the genealogy and adventures of Esau and his Arab tribes; the household affairs of Potiphar; the dreams of Pharaoh; the polity of Egypt—that the facts thus dispersed and broken are to be brought together by ourselves, and the general induction to be drawn from them by ourselves, nothing being more remote from the mind of Moses than to present us with a portrait of Jacob; nay, that of Isaac, who happens to be less involved in the circumstances of his history, he scarcely gives us a single feature. Surely, with all this before us, it is impossible to entertain the idea for a moment of any *studied* uniformity. Yet an uniformity there is; *casual*, therefore, on the part of Moses, who was thinking nothing about it; but *complete*, because, without thinking about it, he was by some means or other drawing from the life.

And now am I thought to disparage the character of this holy man of old? God forbid! I think that in the incidents I have named his conduct may be excused, if not justified. But were it otherwise, I am not aware that any of the Patriarchs has been set up, or can be set up, as a genuine pattern of *Christian* morals. They saw the Promise, (and the more questionable parts of Jacob's conduct are to be accounted for by his impatience to obtain the Promise, and by his consequently using unlawful means to obtain it,) but "they s aw it afar off"—"they beheld it, but not nigh." They lived under a code of laws that were not absolutely good, perhaps not so good as the Levitical; for as this was but a preparation for the more perfect Law of Christ, so possibly was the Patriarchal but a preparation for the more perfect Law of Moses. Indeed I have already observed, that many scattered hints may be gathered from this latter Law, which show that it was but the Law under which the Patriarchs had lived reconstructed, augmented, and improved; and I apprehend that such a scheme of progressive advancement, first the dawn, then the day, then the perfect day, is analogous to God's dealings in general. But the broad light in which the Fathers of Israel are to be viewed is this, that they were exclusive worshippers of the One True Everlasting God, in the world of idolaters—that they were living depositaries of the great doctrine of the Unity of the Godhead, when the nations around were resorting to every green tree—that they were "faithful found among the faithless." And so incalculably important was the preservation of this Great Article of the Creed of man, at a time when it rested in the keeping of so few, that the language of the Almighty in the Law seems ever to have a respect unto it: fury, anger, indignation, jealousy, hatred, being expressions rarely, if ever, attributed to him, except in reference to idolatry; and, on the other hand, enemies of God, adversaries of God, haters of God, being there—chiefly and above all, idolaters. But in this sense God was emphatically the *God* of Abraham, the *God* of Isaac, and the *God* of Jacob, none of them, not even the last (for the only passage which savours of the contrary admits, as we have seen, of easy explanation), having ever forfeited their claim to this high and glorious title; however, such title may not be thought to imply that their moral characters and conduct were faultless, and worthy of all acceptation.

IX. JOSEPH TAKEN TO EGYPT

The marks of coincidence without design, which I have brought forward to prove the truth of the Books of Moses, as successively presenting themselves in the history of Abraham, of Isaac, and of Jacob, I shall now follow up by others in the history of Joseph.

By the ill-concealed partiality of his father, and his own incaution in declaring his dreams of future greatness, Joseph had incurred the hatred of his brethren. They were feeding the flock near Shechem, Jacob desires to satisfy himself of their welfare, and sends Joseph to inquire of them and to bring him word again. Meanwhile they had driven further a-field to Dothan, and Joseph, informed of this by a man whom he found wandering in the country, followed them thither. They beheld him when he was yet afar off; his dress was remarkable [Gen. 37:3.] , and the eye of the shepherd in the plain country of the East, like that of the mariner now, was no doubt practised and keen. They take their counsel together against him. They conclude, however, not to stain their hands in the blood of their brother, but to cast him into an empty pit, which, in those countries, where the inhabitants were constantly engaged in a fruitless search for water, was a very likely place to be on the spot. There he was to be left to die, or, as Reuben intended, to remain till he could rid him out of their hands. Nothing can be more artless than this story. Nothing can bear more indisputable signs of truth than its details. But the circumstance, on which I now rest, is another that is mentioned. The brothers having achieved their evil purpose, sat down to eat bread—possibly some household present which Jacob had sent them, and Joseph had just conveyed, such as on a somewhat similar occasion, in after-times, Jesse sent and David conveyed to his elder brethren in the camp—though on this, as on a thousand touches of truth of the like kind, the reader of Moses is left to make his own speculations. And now "they lifted up their eyes and looked, and behold a company of Ishmaelites came from Gilead with their camels, *bearing spicery and balm and myrrh, going to carry it down to Egypt."* [Gen. 37:25.] Now this, though by no means an obvious incident to have suggested itself, does seem to me a very natural one to have occurred; and, what is more, is an incident which tallies remarkably well with what we read elsewhere, in a passage, however, having no reference whatever to the one in question. For have we not reason to know, that at this very early period in the history of the world, this first of caravans upon record was charged with a cargo for Egypt singularly adapted to the wants of the Egyptians at that time? Expunge the 2nd and 3rd verses of the 50th chapter of Genesis, and the symptoms of veracity in the narrative which I here detect, or think I detect, would never have been discoverable. But in those verses I am told that "Joseph commanded the Physicians to *embalm* his father—and the Physicians *embalmed* Israel—and forty days were fulfilled to him; for so are fulfilled the days of those which are *embalmed*, and the *Egyptians* mourned threescore and ten days." I conclude, therefore, from this, that in these very ancient times it was the practice of the Egyptians (for Joseph was here doing that which was the custom of the country where he lived) to embalm their dead; and we know from the case of our Lord that an hundred pounds weight of myrrh and aloes was not more than enough for a single body [John 19:39.] . Hence, then, the camelloads of spices which the Ishmaelites were bringing from Gilead, would naturally enough find an ample market in Egypt. Now, is it easy to come to any other conclusion when *trifles* of this kind drop out, fitted one to another like the corresponding parts of a cloven tally, than that both are true?—that the historian, however he obtained his intelligence, is speaking of particulars which fell within his own knowledge, and is speaking of them faithfully? Surely nothing can be more incidental than the mention of the *lading* of these camels of the Ishmaelites; it has nothing to do with the main fact, which is merely this, that the party, whoever they were, and whatever they were bent upon, were ready to buy Joseph, and that his brethren were ready to sell him. On the other hand no one can suspect, that when Moses relates Joseph to have caused his father's body to be *embalmed*, he had an eye to corroborating his account of the adventure which he had already told concerning the Ishmaelitish merchants, who might thus seem occupied in a traffic that was appropriate. I think that this single coincidence would induce an unprejudiced person to believe, that the *ordinary* parts of this story are matters of fact fully known to the historian, and accurately reported by him. Yet it is an integral portion of this same story, uttered by the same historian, that Joseph had visions of his future destinies, which were strictly fulfilled—that the whole proceeding with regard to him had been under God's controlling influence from beginning to end—that though his brethren "thought evil against him, God meant it unto good," to bring to pass, as he did at a future day, "to save much people alive." [Gen. 1:20.]

X. EGYPT AND CORN

Nor is this all with regard to Egypt wherein is seen the image and superscription of truth. An argument for the Veracity of the New Testament has been found in the harmony which pervades the very many incidental notices of the condition of Judea at the period when the New Testament professes to have been written. A similar agreement without design may be remarked in the occasional glimpses of Egypt which open upon us in the course of the Mosaic History. For instance, I perceive in each and all of the following incidents, indirect indications of this one fact, that *Egypt was already a great corn country*, though I do not believe that such a fact is *directly* asserted in any passage in the whole Pentateuch. Thus, when Abram found a famine in the land of Canaan, "he *went down into Egypt* to sojourn there." [Gen. 12:10.] There was a second famine in a part of Canaan, in the days of Isaac: he, however, on this occasion went to Gerar, which was in the country of the Philistines, but it appears as though this was only to have been a stage in a journey which he was projecting into Egypt; for we read, that "the Lord appeared unto him and said, *Go not down into Egypt;* dwell in the land which I shall tell thee of." [Gen. 26:2.] There is a third famine in Canaan in the time of Jacob, and then "all countries *came unto Egypt* to buy corn, because the famine was so sore in all lands." [Gen. 41:57.] Again, I read of Pharaoh being wroth with two of his *officers*—they are spoken of as persons of some distinction in the court of the Egyptian King—and who were they? One was the chief of the Butlers, but the other was the chief of the *Bakers* [Gen. 40:1.] . Still I see in this an indication of Egypt being a corn country; of bread being there literally the staff of life, and the manufacturing and dispensing of it an employment of considerable trust and consequence. So again I find that, in the fabric of the bricks in Egypt, *straw* was a very essential element; and so abundant does the corn crop seem to have been—so widely was it spread over the face of the country, that the task-masters of the Israelites could exact the usual tale of the bricks, though the people had to gather the *stubble* for themselves to supply the place of the straw, which was withheld [Exod. 5:7.] Still I perceive in this an intimation of the agricultural fertility of Egypt,—there could not have been the stubble-land here implied unless corn had been the staple crop of the country. Then when Moses threatens to plague the Egyptians with a Plague of Frogs, what are the places which at once present themselves as those which are likely to be defiled by their presence? "The river shall bring forth frogs abundantly, which shall go up and come into thine house, and into thy bed-chamber, and upon thy bed, and into the house of thy servants, and upon thy people, and into thine *ovens*, and into thy *kneading-troughs*." [Exod. 8:3.] And of these kneading-troughs we again read, as utensils possessed by all, and without which they could not think even of taking a journey; for on the delivery of the Israelites from Egypt, we find that "they took their dough before it was leavened, their *kneading-troughs* being bound up in their clothes upon their shoulders." [Exod. 12:34.]

Now it may be said that we all know Egypt to have been a great corn country—that the thing admits of no doubt, and never did—I allow it to be so; and if such a fact had been asserted in the writings of Moses as a broad fact, I should have taken no notice of it, for it would then have afforded no ground for an argument like this; in such a case, Moses might have come at the knowledge as we ourselves may have done, by having visited the country himself, or by having received a report of it from others who had visited it, and so might have incorporated this amongst other incidents in his history; but I do not observe it asserted by him in round terms; it is not indeed asserted by him at all—it is *intimated*—intimated when he is manifestly not thinking about it, when his mind and his pen are quite intent upon other matters; intimated very often, very indirectly, in very various ways. The fact itself of Egypt being a great corn country was, no doubt, perfectly well known to Dr. Johnson, but though so much of the scene of Rasselas is laid in Egypt, I will venture to say, that there are in it no hints of the nature I am describing; such, I mean, as would serve to convince us that the author was relating a series of events which had happened under his own eye, and that the places with which he combines them were not ideal, but those wherein they actually came to pass. Nay, more; when anything of this kind is attempted in fiction, how sure is it to fail? Witness the *Phileleutherus Lipsiensis* of Dr. Bentley, which it is impossible to read without speedily detecting, from internal evidence, that the author of it is no man of Leipsic; even his very attempts to make himself appear so, betraying him.

Surely, then, it is very satisfactory to discover concurrence thus uniform, thus uncontrived, in particulars falling out at intervals in the course of an artless narrative which is not afraid to proclaim the Almighty as manifesting himself by signal miracles, and which connects those miracles, too, in the closest union with the subordinate matters of which we have thus been able to ascertain the probable truth and accuracy.

XI. JOSEPH AND PHARAOH

Before we dismiss this question of the Corn in Egypt, we may remark another trifling instance or two of consistency without design, declaring themselves in this part of the narrative, and tending to strengthen our belief in it. Joseph, it seems [Gen. 41:34.] , advised Pharaoh before the famine began, to appoint officers over the land, that should "take up the fifth part of the land of Egypt in the seven plenteous years." After this we have several chapters occupied with the details of the history of Jacob and his sons—the journey of the latter to Egypt—their return to their father— the repetition of their journey—the discovery of Joseph—the migration of the Patriarch with all his family, of whom the individuals are named after their respective heads—the introduction of Jacob to Pharaoh, and his final settlement in the land of Goshen. Then the affair of the famine is again touched upon in a few verses, and a permanent regulation of property in Egypt is recorded as the accidental result of that famine. For the people who had sold both themselves and their lands to Pharaoh for corn to preserve life, are now permitted to redeem both on the payment of a fifth of the produce to the King *for ever*. "And Joseph made it a *law* over the land of Egypt unto this day, that Pharaoh should have the *fifth* part." [Gen. 47:26.] Now this was, as we had been told in a former chapter, precisely the proportion which Joseph had "taken up" before the famine began. It was *then* an arrangement entered into with the proprietors of the soil prospectively, as likely to ensure the subsistence of the people; the experiment was found to answer, and the opportunity of perpetuating it having occurred, the arrangement was *now* made lasting and compulsory. Magazines of corn were henceforth to be established, which should at all times be ready to meet an accidental failure of the harvest. Can anything be more natural than this? anything more common than for great civil and political changes to spring out of provisions which chanced to be made to meet some temporary emergency? Has not our own constitution, and have not the constitutions of most other countries, ancient and modern, grown out of occasion—out of the impulse of the day?

Further still. Though Joseph possessed himself on his royal master's account of all the land of Egypt besides, and disposed of the people throughout the country just as he pleased [Gen. 47:22.] , "*he did not buy the land of the priests*, for the priests had a portion assigned them of Pharaoh, and did eat their portion which Pharaoh gave them, wherefore they sold not their lands." The *priests* then, we see, were greatly favoured in the arrangements made at this period of national distress. Now does not this accord with what we had been told on a former occasion,—that Pharaoh being desirous to do Joseph honour, causing him to ride in the second chariot that he had, and crying before him, Bow the knee, and making him ruler over all the land of Egypt [Gen. 41:43.] , added yet this as the final proof of his high regard, that "he gave him to wife Asenath, the daughter of Potipherah, *Priest* of On?" [Gen. 41:45.] When, therefore, the priests were thus held in esteem by Pharaoh, and when the minister of Pharaoh, under whose immediate directions all the regulations of the polity of Egypt were at that time conducted, had the daughter of one of them for his wife, is it not the most natural thing in the world to have happened, that their lands should be spared?

XII. JOSEPH'S AFFECTION FOR HIS FATHER

I Have already found an argument for the veracity of Moses in the *identity* of Jacob's character: I now find another in the identity of that of *Joseph*. There is one quality (as it has been often observed, though with a different view from mine,) which runs like a thread through his whole history,—*his affection for his father*. Israel loved him, we read, more than all his children—he was the child of his age—his mother died whilst he was yet young, and a double care of him consequently devolved upon his surviving parent. He made him a coat of many colours—he kept him at home when his other sons were sent to feed the flocks. When the bloody garment was brought in, Jacob in his affection for him, (that same affection which, on a subsequent occasion, when it was told him that after all Joseph was alive, made him as slow to believe the good tidings as he was now quick to apprehend the sad,) in this his affection for him, I say, Jacob at once concluded the worst, and "he rent his clothes and put sackcloth upon his loins, and mourned for his son many days, and all his daughters rose up to comfort him; but he refused to be comforted, and he said, For I will go down into the grave of my son mourning."

Now what were the feelings in Joseph which responded to these? When the sons of Jacob went down to Egypt, and Joseph knew them though they knew not him, for they (it may be remarked, and this again is not like fiction,) were of an age not to be greatly changed by the lapse of years, and were still sustaining the character in which Joseph had always seen them, whilst he himself had meanwhile grown out of the stripling into the man, and from a shepherd-boy was become the ruler of a kingdom—when his brethren thus came before him, his question was, "Is your *father* yet alive?" [Gen. 43:7.] They went down a second time, and again the question was, "Is your *father* well, the *old man* of whom ye spake, is he yet alive?" More he could not venture to ask, whilst he was yet in his disguise. By a stratagem he now detains Benjamin, leaving the others, if they would, to go their way. But Judah came near unto him, and entreated him for his brother, telling him how that he had been "surety to his *father*" to bring him back, how that "his *father* was an old man," and that this was the "child of his old age, and that he loved him,"—how it would come to pass that if he should not see the lad with him he would die, and his grey hairs be brought with sorrow to the grave; for "how shall I go to my *father*, and the lad be not with me?—lest, peradventure, I see the evil that shall come on my *father*." Here, without knowing it, he had struck the string that was the tenderest of all. Joseph's firmness forsook him at this repeated mention of his *father*, and in terms so touching—he could not refrain himself any longer, and causing every man to go out, he made himself known to his brethren. Then, even in the paroxysm which came on him, (for he wept aloud so that the Egyptians heard,) still his first words, uttered from the fulness of his heart, were, "Doth *my father* yet live?" He now bids them hasten and bring the old man down, bearing to him tokens of his love and tidings of his glory. He goes to meet him—he presents himself unto him, and falls on his neck and weeps on his neck a good while—he provides for him and his household out of the fat of the land—he sets him before Pharoah. By and by he hears that he is sick, and hastens to visit him—he receives his blessing—watches his death-bed—embalms his body—mourns for him threescore and ten days—and then carries him (as he had desired) into Canaan to bury him, taking with him as an escort to do him honour "all the elders of Egypt, and all the servants of Pharoah, and all his house, and the house of his brethren, chariots and horsemen, a very great company." How natural was it now for his brethren to think that the tie by which alone they could imagine Joseph to be held to them was dissolved, that any respect he might have felt or feigned for them, must have been buried in the Cave of Machpelah, and that he would now requite to them the evil they had done! "And they sent a message unto Joseph, saying, Thy *father* did command before he died, saying, So shall ye say unto Joseph, Forgive, I pray thee now, the trespass of thy brethren and their sin,—for they did unto thee evil." And then they add of themselves, as if well aware of the surest road to their brother's heart, "Forgive, we pray thee, the trespass of the servants of the God of *thy father*." In everything the *father's* name is still put foremost: it is his memory which they count upon as their shield and buckler. Moreover it may be added, that though all intercourse had ceased for so many years between Joseph and his family, still the lasting affection he bore a parent is manifested in the name which he gave to his son born to him only two years before the famine, even *Manasseh* or *forgetting*, for God, said he, "hath made me forget all my toil and all my father's house;" [Gen. 41:51.] as though 'instead of his father he must have children' to fill up the void in his heart which a parent's loss had created.

It is not the singular beauty of these scenes, or the moral lesson they teach, excellent as it is, with which I am now concerned, but simply the perfect, artless *consistency* which prevails through them all. It is not the constancy with which the son's strong affection for his father had lived through an interval of twenty years' absence, and, what is more, through the temptation of sudden promotion to the highest estate—it is not the noble-minded frankness with which he still acknowledges his kindred, and makes a way for them, "shepherds" as they were, to the throne of Pharaoh himself—it is not the simplicity and singleness of heart, which allow him to give all the first-born of Egypt, men over whom he bore absolute rule, an opportunity of observing his own comparatively humble origin, by leading them in attendance upon his father's corpse, to the valleys of Canaan and the modest cradle of his race—it is not, in a word, the grace, but the *identity* of Joseph's character, the light in which it is exhibited by himself, and the light in which it is regarded by his brethren, to which I now point as stamping it with marks of reality not to be gainsaid.

XIII. AMRAM AND JOCHEBED

A coincidence now presents itself in the history of Jacob's family, very similar to that noticed in No. 3.

Levi had three sons, one of whom was Kohath [Exod. 6:16. 18. 20.] . Kohath had four sons, one of whom was Amram, the father of Moses.

Amram took to wife Jochebed, his father's sister; and she became the mother of Moses.

Thus Amram, the *grandson* of Levi, was married to Jochebed, the *daughter* of Levi. This would seem to be improbable from disparity of age; the parties not being of the same generation.

But let us now turn to Numbers [Num. 26:59.] , and we there find, "And the name of Amram's wife was Jochebed, the daughter of Levi, whom her mother *bare to Levi in Egypt."*

From this we may conclude, that Jochebed was born to Levi long after his other children; that Kohath, her brother, who was born in Canaan, was much older than herself; and this the rather, forasmuch as Levi's sons born in Canaan were probably of a considerable age when they went to Egypt, since Jacob was then a hundred and thirty years old [Gen. 47:28.] , and Levi was one of his elder sons, his third [Gen. 29:34.] ; a child, therefore, most likely of Jacob's youth; Joseph being actually distinguished from his elder brethren by being described as the son of Jacob's old age [Gen. 37:3.] It would appear, therefore, to be almost certain that the difference of age between Kohath and Jochebed, his sister, must have amounted to a generation; and accordingly, that Amram of the second descent would be about coeval with Jochebed of the first. Is it possible to suppose that the short incidental notice of Jochebed being born in Egypt was introduced for the purpose of meeting the objection which might suggest itself with respect to the disparity of years of the parties in this marriage—an objection altogether of our own starting, for there is no allusion to it in the history?

XIV. NADAB AND ABIHU

I will now follow the Israelites out of Egypt into the wilderness, on their return to the land from which their fathers had wandered, and which they, or at least their children, were destined to enjoy.

In the tenth chapter of Leviticus we are told that "Nadab and Abihu, the sons of Aaron, took either of them his censer and put fire therein, and put incense thereon, and offered strange fire unto the Lord, which he commanded them not. And there went out fire from the Lord and devoured them, and they died before the Lord." Now it is natural to ask, how came Nadab and Abihu to be guilty of this careless affront to God, lighting their censers probably from their own hearths, and not from the hallowed fire of the altar, as they were commanded to do? Possibly we cannot guess how it happened—it may be one of those many matters which are of no particular importance to be known, and concerning which we are accordingly left in the dark. Yet, when I read shortly afterwards the following instructions given to Aaron, I am led to suspect that they had their origin in some recent abuse which called for them, though no such origin is expressly assigned to them. I cannot help imagining, that the offence of Nadab and Abihu was at the bottom of the statute. "Do not *drink wine nor strong drink*, thou nor thy sons with thee, when ye go into the Tabernacle of the congregation, *lest ye die*—it shall be a statute for ever throughout your generations: and that ye may put difference between holy and unholy, and between clean and unclean, and that ye may teach the children of Israel all the statutes which the Lord hath spoken unto them by the hands of Moses." Thus far at least is clear, that a grievous and thoughtless insult is offered to God by two of his *Priests*, for which they are cut off—that without any *direct* allusion to their case, but still very shortly after it had happened, a law is issued forbidding the *Priests* the use of wine when about to *minister*. I conclude, therefore, that there *was* a relation (though it is not asserted) between the specific offence and the general law; the more so, because the sin against which that law is directed is just of a kind to have produced the rash and inconsiderate act of which Aaron's sons were guilty. If, therefore, this incidental mention of such a law at such a moment, a moment so likely to suggest the enactment of it, be thought enough to establish the law as a matter of fact, then have we once more ground to stand upon; for the enactment of the law is coupled with the sin of Aaron's sons; their sin with their punishment; their punishment with a miracle. Nor, it may be added, does the unreserved and faithful record of such a death, suffered for such an offence, afford an inconsiderable argument in favour of the candour and honesty of Moses, who is no respecter of persons, it seems, but when God's glory is concerned, and the welfare of the people entrusted to him, does not scruple to be the chronicler of the disgrace and destruction even of the children of his own brother.

XV. MISHAEL, ELIZAPHAN, NADAB, AND ABIHU

Another coincidence suggests itself, arising out of this same portion of history, whether, however, founded in fact or in fancy, be my readers the judges. From the 9th chapter of Numbers, v. 15, we learn that the Tabernacle was erected in the wilderness preparatory to the celebration of the first Passover kept by the Israelites after their escape from Egypt. From the 40th chapter of Exodus we find, that it was reared on the first day of the first month (v. 2), or thirteen days before the Passover [Lev. 23:5.] , and that at the same time Aaron and his sons were consecrated to minister in it (v. 13). In the 8th and 9th chapters of Leviticus are given the particulars of their consecration (8th, 6, 12, 30), and the ceremony is said to have occupied seven days (v. 33), during which they were not to leave the Tabernacle day or night. On the eighth day they offered up sin-offerings for themselves and for the people. It was on this same day, as we read in the 10th chapter [See ch. 9:8. 12; 10:19.] , that Nadab and Abihu were cut off because of the strange fire which they offered, and their dead bodies were disposed of as follows:—"Moses called Mishael and Elizaphan the sons of Uzziel, the uncle of Aaron, and said unto them, Come near, carry your brethren from before the sanctuary out of the camp. So they went near and carried them in their coats out of the camp." (10:4.) All this happened on the eighth day of the first month, or just six days before the Passover.

Now in the 9th chapter of the Book of Numbers, which speaks of this identical Passover (v. 1), as will be seen by a reference to the first verse of that chapter (indeed there is no *mention* of more than this one Passover having been kept in the whole march [See also Josh. 5:9, 10.]), in this 9th chapter I am told of the following incidental difficulty:—that "there were *certain men* who were defiled by the *dead body* of a man, that they could not keep the Passover on that day—and they came before Moses and before Aaron on that day—and those men said unto him, We are defiled by the *dead body* of a man, wherefore are we kept back that we may not offer an offering to the Lord in his appointed season among the children of Israel." (v. 6, 7.) The case is spoken of as a solitary one.

Now it may be observed, by way of limiting the question, that the number of Israelites who paid a tax to the Tabernacle a short time, and only a short time, *before* its erection, was 603,550, being all the males above twenty years of age, the *Levites excepted* [Exod. 38:26.] —at least this exception is all but certain, that tribe being the tellers, being already consecrated, and set apart from the other tribes, and it not being usual to take the sum of them among the children of Israel [See Num. 1:47. 49, and 26:62.] . Moreover, the number is likely, in this instance, to be correct, because it tallies with the number of talents to which the poll-tax amounted at half a shekel a head. But shortly *after* the Tabernacle had been set up (for it was at the beginning of the second month of the second year), the number of the people was again taken according to the families and tribes [Num. 1:46.] , and still it is just the same as before, 603,550 men. In this short interval, therefore (which is that in which we are now interested), it should seem that no man had died of the males who were above twenty, not being Levites—for of these no account seems to have been taken in either census—indeed in the latter census they are expressly excepted. The dead body, therefore, by which these "certain men" were defiled, could not have belonged to this large class of the Israelites. But of a case of death, and of defilement in consequence, which had happened only six days before the Passover, amongst the *Levites*, we had been told (as we have seen) in the 9th chapter of Leviticus. My conclusion, therefore, is that these "certain men," who were defiled, were no others than Mishael and Elizaphan, who had carried out the *dead bodies* of Nadab and Abihu. Neither can anything be more likely than that, with the lively impression on their minds of God's wrath so recently testified against those who should presume to approach him unhallowed, they should refer their case to Moses, and run no risk.

I state the conclusion and the grounds of it. To those who require stronger proof, I can only say, I have none to give; but if the coincidence be thought well founded, then surely a more striking example of consistency without design cannot well be conceived. Indeed, after it had been suggested to me by a hint to this effect, thrown out by Dr. Shuckford, unaccompanied by any exposition of the arguments which might be urged in support of it, I had put it aside as one of those gratuitous conjectures in which that learned Author may perhaps be thought sometimes to indulge—till, by searching more accurately through several detached parts of several detached chapters in Exodus, Leviticus, and Numbers, I was able to collect the evidence I have produced; whether satisfactory or not—be my readers, as I have said, the judges. For myself, I confess, that though it is not demonstrative, it is very persuasive.

XVI. THEN CAME AMALEK

"All the congregation of the children of Israel," we read [Exod. 17:1.] , "journeyed from the wilderness of Sin, after their journeys according to the commandment of the Lord, and pitched in *Rephidim*, and *there was no water for the people to drink*."—"And the people thirsted there for water; and the people murmured against Moses, and said, Wherefore is this, that thou hast brought us up out of Egypt to kill us and our children and our cattle with thirst?" (v. 3.) Moses upon this entreats the Lord for Israel; and the narrative proceeds in the words of the Almighty—"Behold, I will stand before thee there upon the rock in Horeb, and thou shalt smite the rock, and there shall come water out of it, that my people may drink. And Moses did so in the sight of the elders of Israel. And he called the name of the place Massah, and Meribah, because of the chiding of the children of Israel, and because they tempted the Lord, saying, Is the Lord among us, or not?" "*Then came Amalek*," the narrative continues, "*and fought with Israel in Rephidim*."

Now this last incident is mentioned, as must be perceived at once, without any other reference to what had gone before than a reference of *date*. It was "*then*" that Amalek came. It is the beginning of another adventure which befel the Israelites, and which Moses now goes on to relate. Accordingly, in many copies of our English version, a mark is here introduced indicating the commencement of a fresh paragraph. Yet I cannot but suspect, that there is a coincidence in this case between the production of the water, in an arid wilderness, and the attack of the Amalekites—that though no hint whatever to this effect is dropped, there is nevertheless the relation between them of cause and consequence. For what, in those times and those countries, was so common a bone of contention as the possession of a well? Thus we read of Abraham reproving Abimelech "because of a *well of water*, which Abimelech's servants had *violently taken* away." [Gen. 21:25.] And again we are told, that "Isaac's servants digged in a valley and found there a well of *springing water*—and the herdsmen of Gerar did strive with Isaac's herdsmen, saying, The water is ours, and he called the name of the well Esek, because they *strove* with him. And they digged *another well*, and *strove* for that also; and he called the name of it Sitnah. And he removed from thence, and digged *another well*, and for that they strove not; and he called the name of it Rehoboth; and he said, For now the Lord hath made room for us, and we shall be fruitful in the land." [Gen. 26:22.] In like manner when the daughters of the Priest of Midian "came and drew water, and filled the troughs to water their father's flock, the shepherds," we find, "*came and drove them away*: but Moses stood up and *helped* them, and watered their flock." [Exod. 2:17.] And again, when Moses sent messengers to the King of Edom with proposals that he might be permitted to lead the people of Israel through his territory, the subject of *water* enters very largely into the terms: "Let me pass, I pray thee, through thy country: we will not pass through the fields and through the vineyards, neither will we drink of the *water of the wells*: we will go by the king's highway—we will not turn to the right hand nor to the left, until we have passed thy borders. And Edom said unto him, Thou shalt not pass by me lest I come out against thee with the sword. And the children of Israel said unto him, We will go by the highway: and if I and my cattle *drink of thy water, then I will pay for it*." [Num. 20:17.] Again, on a subsequent occasion, Moses sent messengers to Sihon, king of the Amorites, with the same stipulations:—"Let me pass through thy land: we will not turn into the fields or into the vineyards; we will not *drink of the waters of the well*, but we will go along by the king's highway, until we be past thy borders." [Num. 21:22.] And when Moses in the Book of Deuteronomy recapitulates some of the Lord's commands, one of them is, as touching the children of Esau, "Meddle not with them; for I will not give you their land, no, not so much as a foot breadth, because I have given Mount Seir unto Esau for a possession. Ye shall buy meat of them for money that ye may eat, and ye shall also buy *water of them for money that ye may drink*." [Deut. 2:6.] And at a later date we find the well still associated with scenes of strife—"They that are delivered *from the noise of archers in the places of drawing water*, there shall they rehearse the righteous acts of the Lord." [Judges 5:11.] Indeed the *well* is quite a feature in the narrative of Moses, brief as that narrative is. It unobtrusively but constantly reminds us of our scene lying ever in the East— just as the Forum could not fail to be perpetually mixing itself up with the details of any history of Rome which was not spurious. The *well* is the spring of life. It is the place of meeting for the citizens in the cool of the day—the place of resort for the shepherds and herdsmen; it is here that we may witness acts of courtesy or of stratagem—acts of religion—acts of civil compact—acts commemorative of things past; it is here that the journey ends—it is by this that the next is regulated; hither the fugitive and the outcast repair—here the weary pilgrim rests himself; the lack of it is the curse of a kingdom, and the prospect of it in abundance the blessing which helps forward the steps of the stranger when he seeks another country. It enters as an element into the language itself of Holy Writ, and the simile, the illustration, the metaphor, are still telling forth the great Eastern apophthegm, that of "all things water is the first." Of such value was the *well*—so fruitful a source of contention in those parched and thirsty lands was the possession of a *well*.

Now, applying these passages to the question before us, I think it will be seen, that the sudden gushing of the water from the rock (which was the sudden discovery of an invaluable treasure), and the subsequent onset of the Amalekites at the very same place—for both occurrences are said to have happened at *Rephidim*, though given as perfectly distinct and independent matters, do coincide very remarkably with one another; and yet so undesigned is the coincidence (if indeed coincidence it is after all), that it *might* not suggest itself even to readers of the Pentateuch whose lot is cast in a torrid clime, and to whom the value of a draught of cold water is therefore well known; still less to those who live in a land of brooks, like our own, a land of fountains and depths that spring out of the valleys and hills, and who may drink of them freely, without cost and without quarrel.

If then it be admitted, that the issue of the torrent from the rock synchronizes very singularly with the aggression of Amalek, yet that the narrative of the two events does not hint at any connection whatever between them, I think that all suspicion of *contrivance* is laid to sleep, and that whatever force is due to the argument of consistency without contrivance, as a test, and as a testimony of truth, obtains here. Yet here, as in so many other instances already adduced, the stamp of truth, such as it is, is found where a miracle is intimately concerned; for if the coincidence in question be thought enough to satisfy us that Moses was relating an indisputable matter of fact when he said that the Israelites received a supply of water at Rephidim, it adds to our confidence that he is relating an indisputable matter of fact, too, when he says in the same breath, that it was a *miraculous* supply: where we can prove that there is truth in a story, so far as a scrutiny of our own, which was not contemplated by the party whose words we are trying, enables us to go, it is only fair to infer, in the absence of all testimony to the contrary, that there is truth also in such parts of the same story as our scrutiny cannot attain unto. And indeed it seems to me, that the sin of Amalek on this occasion, a sin which was so offensive in God's sight as to be treasured up in judgment against that race, causing Him eventually to destroy them utterly, derived its heinousness from this very thing, that the Amalekites were here endeavouring to dispossess the Israelites of a vital blessing which God had sent to them by *miracle*, and which He could not so send without making it manifest, even to the Amalekites themselves, that the children of Israel were under his special care—that in fighting therefore against Israel, they were fighting against God. And such, I persuade myself, is the true force of an expression in Deuteronomy used in reference to this very incident—for Amalek is there said to "have smitten them when they were weary, and to *have feared not God*;" [Deut. 25:18.] that is, to have done it in defiance of a miracle, which ought to have impressed them with a fear of God, indicating, as of course it did, that God willed not the destruction of this people.

XVII. THE MONTH ABIB AND THE PASSOVER

Amongst the institutions established or confirmed by the Almighty whilst the Israelites were on their march, for their observance when they should have taken possession of the land of Canaan, this was one— "Three times thou shalt keep a feast unto me in the year. Thou shalt keep the Feast of Unleavened Bread—thou shalt eat unleavened bread seven days, as I commanded thee, in the time appointed of the month Abib; for in it thou camest out from Egypt; and none shall appear before me empty:—and the Feast of Harvest, the first-fruits of thy labours, which thou hast sown in thy field:—and the Feast of In-gathering, which is in the end of the year, when thou hast gathered in thy labours out of the field." [Exod. 23:14.]

Such then were the three great annual feasts. The first, in the month Abib, which was the Passover. The second, which was the Feast of Weeks. The third, the Feast of In-gathering, when all the fruits, wine, and oil, as well as corn, had been collected and laid up. The season of the year at which the first of these occurred is all that I am anxious to settle, as bearing upon a coincidence which I shall mention by and by. Now this is determined with sufficient accuracy for my purpose, by the second of the three being the Feast of *Harvest*, and the fact that the interval between the first and second was just seven weeks [Lev. 23:14.] : "And ye shall count unto you from the morrow after the Sabbath" (this was the Sabbath of the *Passover*), "from the day that ye brought the *sheaf* of the wave-offering; seven Sabbaths shall be complete. Even unto the morrow after the seventh Sabbath shall ye number fifty days, and ye shall offer a new meat-offering unto the Lord. Ye shall bring out of your habitations two wave-*loaves*, of two tenth-deals, they shall be of fine flour, they shall be baken with leaven. They are the first-fruits unto the Lord."

At the Feast of Weeks, therefore, the corn was ripe and just gathered, for then were the first-fruits to be offered in the *loaves* made out of the new corn. If then the *wheat* was in this state at the second great festival, it must have been very far from ripe at the Passover, which was seven weeks earlier; and the wave-*sheaf*, which, as we have seen, was to be offered at the Pass-over, must have been of some grain which came in before wheat—it was in fact *barley* [See Ruth 2:23.] . Now does not this agree in a remarkable, but most incidental manner, with a circumstance mentioned in the description of the Plague of the Hail? The hail, it is true, was sent some little time previous to the destruction of the firstborn, or the date of the Passover, for the Plague of Locusts and the Plague of Darkness intervened, but it was evidently only a little time; for Moses being *eighty* years old when he went before Pharoah [Exod. 7:7.] , and having walked *forty* years in the wilderness [Joshua 5:6.] , and being only a *hundred and twenty* years old when he died [Deut. 34:7.] , it is plain that he could have lost very little time by the delay of the plagues in Egypt, the period of his life being filled up without any allowance for such delay. I mention this, because it will be seen that the argument requires the time of the hail and that of the death of the firstborn (or in other words the Passover) to be nearly the same. Now the state of the crops in *Egypt* at the period of the hail we happen to know—was it then such as we might have reason to expect from the state of the crops of *Judea* at or near the same season?—

i. e. the *barley* ripe, the *wheat* not ripe by several weeks?

It is well, inasmuch as it involves a point of evidence, that one of the Plagues proved to be that of Hail—for it is the only one of them of a nature to give us a clue to the time of year when they came to pass, and this it does in the most casual manner imaginable, for the mention of the hail draws from the historian who records it the remark, that "the flax and the *barley* were smitten, for the barley was in *the ear* and the flax was bolled; but the *wheat* and the rye were not smitten, for they were not grown up" (or rather perhaps, were not out of sheath [Exod 9:32.]). Now this is precisely such a degree of forwardness as we should have respectively assigned to the barley and wheat—deducing our conclusion from the simple circumstance that the seasons in Egypt do not greatly differ from those of Judea, and that in the latter country wheat was ripe and just gathered at the Feast of Weeks, barley just fit for putting the sickle into fifty days sooner, or at the Passover, which nearly answered to the time of the hail. Yet so far from obvious is this point of harmony, that nothing is more easy than to mistake it; nay, nothing more likely than that we should even at first suspect Moses himself to have been out in his reckoning, and thus to find a knot instead of an argument. For on reading the following passage [Deut. 16:9.] , where the rule is given for determining the second feast, we might on the instant most naturally suppose that the great *wheat*-harvest of Judea was in the month Abib, at the Passover—"Seven weeks shalt thou number unto thee, begin to number the seven weeks from such time as thou beginnest to put the *sickle to the corn*." Now this "putting the sickle to the corn" is at once perceived to be at the Passover, when the wave-sheaf was offered, the ceremony from which we see the Feast of Weeks was measured and fixed. Yet had the great *wheat*-harvest been here actually meant, it would have been impossible to reconcile Moses with himself; for he would then have been representing the wheat to be ripe in Judea at a season when, as we had elsewhere gathered from him, it was not grown up or out of the sheath in Egypt. But if the sickle was to be put into some grain much earlier than wheat, such as barley, and if the barley-harvest is here alluded to as falling in with the Passover, and not the wheat-harvest, then all is clear, intelligible, and free from difficulty.

In a word then, my argument is this—that at the Passover the *barley* in Judea was ripe, but that the *wheat* was not, seven weeks having yet to elapse before the first-fruits of the loaves could be offered. This I collect from the history of the Great Jewish Festivals. Again, that at the Plague of Hail (which corresponds with the time of the Passover to a few days), the *barley* in Egypt was smitten, being in the ear, but that the *wheat* was not smitten, not being yet bolled. This I collect from the history of the Great

Egyptian Plagues. The two statements on being compared together, agree together.

I cannot but consider this as very far from an unimportant coincidence, tending, as it does, to give us confidence in the good faith of the historian, even at a moment when he is telling of the Miracles of Egypt, "the wondrous works that were done in the land of Ham." For, supported by this circumstantial evidence, which, as far as it goes, cannot lie, I feel that I have very strong reason for believing that a hail-storm there actually was, as Moses asserts; that the season of the year to which he assigns it was the season when it did in fact happen; that the crops were really in the state in which he represents them to have been—more I cannot *prove*— for further my test will not reach: it is not in the nature of miracles to admit of its immediate application to themselves. But when I see the *ordinary* circumstances which attend upon them, and which are most closely combined with them, yielding internal evidence of truth, I am apt to think that these in a great measure vouch for the truth of the rest. Indeed, in all common cases, even in judicial cases of life and death, the corroboration of the evidence of an unimpeached witness in one or two particulars is enough to decide a jury that it is worthy of credit in every other particular—that it may be safely acted upon in the most awful and responsible of all human decisions.

XVIII. TWO UNEQUAL OFFERINGS

The argument which I have next to produce has been urged by Dr. Graves [On the Pentateuch, Vol. i. p. 111.] , though others had noticed it before him [See Dr. Patrick on Num. 7:7, 8.] ; I shall not, however, scruple to introduce it here in its order, connected as it is with several more arguments, all relating to the economy of the camp. The incident on which it turns is trifling in itself, but nothing can be more characteristic of truth. On the day when Moses set up the Tabernacle and anointed and sanctified it, the princes of the tribes made an offering, consisting of six waggons and twelve oxen. These are accordingly assigned to the service of the Tabernacle: "And Moses gave them unto the Levites; *Two waggons and four oxen* he gave unto the sons of Gershon according to their service, and *four waggons and eight oxen* he gave unto the sons of Merari according to their service." [Num. 7:7, 8.] Now whence this unequal division? Why twice as many waggons and oxen to Merari as to Gershon? No reason is expressly avowed. Yet if I turn to a former chapter, separated however from the one which has supplied this quotation, by sundry and divers details of other matters, I am able to make out a very good reason for myself. For there, amongst the instructions given to the families of the Levites, as to the shares they had severally to take in removing the Tabernacle from place to place, I find that the sons of Gershon had to bear "the curtains," and the "Tabernacle" itself (*i. e.*, the linen of which it was made), and "its covering, and the covering of badgers' skins that was above upon it, and the hanging for the door," and "the hangings of the court, and the hanging for the door of the gate of the court," and "their cords, and all the instruments of their service;" [Num. 4:25.] in a word, all the *lighter* part of the furniture of the Tabernacle. But the sons of Merari had to bear "the boards of the Tabernacle, and the bars thereof, and the pillars thereof, and the sockets thereof, and the pillars of the court round about, and their sockets, and their pins, and their cords, with all their instruments;" [Num. 4:32.] in short, all the cumbrous and *heavy* part of the materials of which the frame-work of the Tabernacle was constructed. And hence it is easy to see why more oxen and waggons were assigned to the one family than to the other. Is chance at the bottom of all this? or cunning contrivance? or truth and only truth?

XIX. THE MARCHING ORDERS OF ISRAEL

In the tenth chapter of the Book of Numbers we have a particular account of the order of march which was observed in the Camp of Israel on one remarkable occasion, *viz.*, when they broke up from Sinai. "In the first place went the standard of the camp of *Judah* according to their armies" (v. 14). Does this precedence of Judah agree with any former account of the disposition of the armies of Israel? In the second chapter of the same book I read, "on the *East* side toward the rising of the sun shall they of the standard of the camp of *Judah* pitch throughout their armies" (v. 3). All that is to be gathered from this passage is, that Judah pitched *East* of the Tabernacle. I now turn to the tenth chapter (v. 5), and I there find amongst the orders given for the signals, "when ye blow an alarm (*i. e.*, the *first* alarm, for the others are mentioned successively in their turn), then the camps that lie on the *East* parts shall go forward." But from the last passage it appears that *Judah* lay on the *East* parts, therefore when the first alarm was blown, *Judah* should be the tribe to move. Thus it is implied from two passages brought together from two chapters, separated by the intervention of eight others relating to things indifferent, that Judah was to lead in any march. Now we see in the account of a specific movement of the camp from Sinai, with which I introduced these remarks, that on that occasion Judah did in fact lead. This, then, is as it should be. The *three* passages agree together as three concurring witnesses—in the mouth of these is the word established. Yet there is some little intricacy in the details—enough at least to leave room for an inadvertent slip in the arrangements, whereby a fiction would have run a risk of being self-detected.

Pursue we this inquiry a little further; for the next article of it is perhaps rather more open to a blunder of this description than the last. It may be thought that the leading tribe, the van-guard of Israel, was an object too conspicuous to be overlooked or misplaced. In the 18th verse of the same chapter of Numbers, it is said, that after the first division was gone, and the Tabernacle, "the standard of the camp of *Reuben* set forward according to their armies."—The camp of Reuben, therefore, was that which moved *second* on this occasion. Does this accord with the position it was else-where said to have occupied? It is obvious that a mistake might here most readily have crept in; and that if the writer had not been guided by a real knowledge of the facts which he was pretending to describe, it is more than probable he would have betrayed him-self. Turn we then to the second chapter (v. 10), where the order of the tribes in their tents is given, and we there find that "on the *south* side was to be the standard of the camp of *Reuben*, according to their armies." Again, let us turn to the 10th chapter (v. 6), where the directions for the signals are given, and we are there told, "When ye blow the alarm the *second* time, then the camps on the *south* side shall take their journey;"—but the passage last quoted (which is far removed from this) informs us that *Reuben* was on the *south* side of the Tabernacle; the camp of *Reuben* therefore it was, which was appointed to move when the alarm was blown the *second* time. Accordingly we see in the description of the actual breaking up from Sinai, with which I set out, that the camp of *Reuben* was in fact the *second* to move. The same argu-ment may be followed up, and the same satisfactory conclusions obtained in the other two camps of Ephraim and Dan; though here recourse must be had to the Septuagint, of which the text is more full in these two latter instances than the Hebrew text of our own version, and more full precisely upon those points which are wanted in evidence [Septuagint, Num. 10:6.] . On such a trifle does the practicability of establishing an argument of coin-cidence turn; and so perpetually, no doubt (were we but aware of it), are we prevented from doing justice to the veracity of the writings of Moses, by the lack of more abundant details.

In all this, it appears to me, that without any care or circumspection of the historian, as to how he should make the several parts of his tale agree together—without any display on the one hand, or mock concealment on the other, of a harmony to be found in those several parts—and in the meantime, with ample scope for the admission of unguarded mistakes, by which a mere impostor would soon stand convicted, the whole is at unity with itself, and the internal evidence resulting from it clear, precise, and above suspicion.

XX. THE ARRANGEMENT OF THE ISRAELITE'S CAMP IN THE WILDERNESS

1. The arrangements of the camp provide us with another coincidence, no less satisfactory than the last—for it may be here remarked, that in proportion as the history of Moses descends to particulars (which it does in the camp), in that proportion is it fertile in the arguments of which I am at present in search. It is in general the extreme brevity of the history, and nothing else, that baffles us in our inquiries; often affording (as it does) a hint which we cannot pursue for want of details, and exhibiting a glimpse of some corroborative fact which it is vexatious to be so near grasping, and still to be compelled to relinquish it.

In the sixteenth chapter of the Book of Numbers we read, "Now Korah the son of Izhar, the son of *Kohath*, the son of *Levi*, and Dathan, and Abiram, the sons of Eliab, and On, the son of Peleth, sons of *Reuben*, took men: and they rose up before Moses, with certain of the children of Israel, two hundred and fifty princes of the assembly, famous in the congregation, men of renown: and they gathered themselves together against Moses and against Aaron, and said unto them, Ye take too much upon you, seeing all the congregation are holy, every one of them, and the Lord is among them: wherefore then lift ye up yourselves above the congregation of the Lord?" [Num. 16:1.] Such is the history of the conspiracy got up against the authority of the leaders of Israel. The principal parties engaged in it, we see, were Korah of the family of *Kohath*, and Dathan, Abiram, and On, of the family of *Reuben*. Now it is a very curious circumstance, that some thirteen chapters before this—chapters occupied with matters of quite another character—it is mentioned incidentally that "the families of the sons of *Kohath* were to pitch on the side of the Tabernacle *southward*." [Num. 3:29.] And in another chapter yet further back, and as independent of the latter as the latter was of the first, we read no less incidentally, "on the *south* side (of the Tabernacle) shall be the standard of the camp of *Reuben*, according to their armies." [Num. 2:10.] The family of *Kohath*, therefore, and the family of *Reuben*, both pitched on the same side of the Tabernacle—*they were neighbours, and were therefore conveniently situated for taking secret counsel together.* Surely this singular coincidence comes of truth—not of accident, not of design;—not of accident, for how great is the improbability that such a peculiar propriety between the relative situations of the parties in the conspiracy should have been the mere result of chance; when three sides of the Tabernacle were occupied by the families of the Levites, and all four sides by the families of the tribes, and when combinations (arithmetically speaking) to so great an extent might have been formed between these in their several members, without the one in question being of the number. It does not come of design, for the agreement is not obvious enough to suit a designer's purpose—it might most easily escape notice:—it is indeed only to be detected by the juxtaposition of several unconnected passages falling out at long intervals. Then, again, had no such coincidence been found at all; had the conspirators been represented as drawn together from more distant parts of the camp, from such parts as afforded no peculiar facilities for leaguing together, no *objection* whatever would have lain against the accuracy of the narrative on that account. The argument, indeed, *for* its veracity would then have been lost, but that would have been all; no suspicion whatever *against* its veracity would have been thereby incurred.

2. But there is yet another feature of truth in this same most remarkable portion of Mosaic history; and this has been enlarged upon by Dr. Graves [On the Pentateuch, Vol. i. p. 155.] . I shall not, however, scruple to touch upon it here, both because I do not take quite the same view of it throughout, and because this incident combines with the one I have just brought forward, and thus acquires a value beyond its own, from being a *second of its kind* arising out of one and the same event—the united value of two incidental marks of truth being more than the sum of their separate values. Indeed, these two instances of consistency without design, *taken together*, hedge in the main transaction on the right hand and on the left, so as almost to close up every avenue through which suspicion could insinuate the rejection of it.

On a common perusal of the whole history of this rebellion, in the 16th chapter of Numbers, the impression left would be, that, in the punishment of Korah, Dathan, and Abiram, there was no distinction or difference; that their tents and all the men that appertained unto Korah, and all their goods, were destroyed alike. Nevertheless, ten chapters after, when the number of the children of Israel is taken, and when, in the course of the numbering, the names of Dathan and Abiram occur, there is added the following incidental memorandum—"This is that Dathan and Abiram who were famous in the congregation, who strove against Moses and against Aaron, in the company of Korah, when they strove against the Lord." Then the death which they died is mentioned, and last of all it is said, "*Notwithstanding the children of Korah died not.*" [Num. 26:11.] This, at first sight, undoubtedly looks like a contradiction of what had gone before. Again, then, let us turn back to the 16th chapter, and see whether we have read it right. Now, though upon a second perusal I still find *no express assertion* that there was any difference in the fate of these several rebellious house-holds, I think upon a close inspection I do find (what answers my purpose better) some difference *implied*. For, in verse 27, we are told, "So they gat up from the Tabernacle of Korah, Dathan, and Abiram, on every side;"—*i. e.* from a Tabernacle which these men in their political rebellion and religious dissent (for they went together) had set up in common for themselves and their adherents, in opposition to the great Tabernacle of the congregation. "And Dathan and Abiram," it is added, "came out and stood in the door of their tents; and their wives, and their sons, and their little children." Here we perceive that mention is made of the sons of Dathan and the sons of Abiram, but not of the sons of *Korah*. So that the victims of the catastrophe about to happen, it should seem from this account too, were indeed the sons of Dathan and the sons of Abiram, but not (in all appearance) the sons of *Korah*. Neither is this difference difficult to account for. The Levites pitching nearer to the Tabernacle than the other tribes, forming, in fact, three sides of the inner square, whilst the others formed the four sides of the outer, it would necessarily follow, that the dwelling-tent of *Korah*, a Levite, would be at some distance from the dwelling-tents of Dathan and Abiram, *Reubenites*, and, as brothers, probably contiguous; at such a distance, at least, as might serve to secure it from being involved in the destruction which overwhelmed the others; for, that the desolation was very limited in extent, seems a fact conveyed by the terms of the warning—"Depart from the tents of these wicked men" (*i. e.* the tabernacle which the three leaders had reared in common, and the two dwelling-tents of Dathan and Abiram) [See chap. 16: ver. 27. An attention to this verse shows these to have been the tents meant.] , as if the danger was confined to the vicinity of those tents.

In this single event, then, the rebellion of Korah, Dathan, and Abiram, I discover two instances of coincidence without design, each independent of the other—the one, in the conspiracy being laid amongst parties whom I know, from information elsewhere given, to have dwelt on the same side of the Tabernacle, and therefore to have been conveniently situated for such a plot—the other, in the different lots of the families of the conspirators, a difference of which there is just hint enough in the direct history of it, to be brought out by a casual assertion to that effect in a subsequent casual allusion to the conspiracy, and only just hint enough for this—a difference, too, which accords very remarkably with the relative situations of those several families in their respective tents.

But if the existence of a conspiracy be by this means established, above all dispute, as a matter of fact—if the death of some of the families of the conspirators, and the escape of others, be also by the same means established, above all dispute, as another matter of fact—if the testimony of Moses, after having been submitted to a test which he could never have contemplated or been provided against, turn out in these particulars at least to be worthy of credit—to what are we led on? Is not the historian still the same? is he not still treating of the same incident, when he informs us that the punishment of this rebellious spirit was a *miraculous* punishment? that the ground clave asunder that was under the ringleaders, and swallowed them up, and their houses, and all the men that appertained unto them, and all their goods; so that they, and all that appertained unto them, went down alive into the pit, and the earth closed upon them, and they perished from among the congregation?

XXI. THE CHILDREN OF REUBEN AND GAD

The arrangements of the camp suggest one point of coincidence more, not perhaps so remarkable as the last, yet enough so to be admitted amongst others as an indication of truth in the history.

In the 32nd chapter of Numbers (v. 1), it is said, "Now the children of *Reuben*, and the children of *Gad*, had a very great multitude of cattle; and when they saw the land of Jazer and the land of Gilead, that behold the place was a place for cattle, the children of *Gad* and the children of *Reuben* came and spake unto Moses, and to Eleazar the priest, and unto the princes of the congregation, saying, Ataroth, and Dibon, and Jazer, and Nimrah, and Heshbon, and Elealeh, and Sheban, and Nebo, and Beon, even the country which the Lord smote before the congregation of Israel, is a land for cattle, and thy servants have cattle; wherefore, said they, if we have received grace in thy sight, let this land be given unto thy servants for a possession, and bring us not over Jordan."

Here was a petition from the tribes of *Reuben* and of *Gad*, to have a portion assigned them on the east side of Jordan, rather than in the land of Canaan. But how came the request to be made conjointly by the children of *Reuben* and the children of *Gad?*—Was it a mere accident?—Was it the simple circumstance that these two tribes being richer in cattle than the rest, and seeing that the pasturage was good on the east side of Jordan, desired on that account only to establish themselves there together, and to separate from their brethren? Perhaps something more than either. For I read in the 2nd chapter of Numbers (v. 10, 14), that the camp of *Reuben* was on the south side of the tabernacle, and that the tribe of *Gad* formed a division of the camp of Reuben. It may very well be imagined, therefore, that after having shared together the perils of the long and arduous campaign through the wilderness, these two tribes, in addition to considerations about their cattle, feeling the strong bond of well-tried companionship in hardships and in arms, were very likely to act with one common council, and to have a desire still to dwell beside one another, after the toil of battle, as quiet neighbours in a peaceful country, where they were finally to set up their rest. Here again is an incident, I think, beyond the reach of the most refined impostor in the world. What vigilance, however alive to suspicion, and prepared for it—what cunning, however bent upon giving credibility to a worthless narrative, by insidiously scattering through it marks of truth which should turn up from time to time and mislead the reader, would have suggested one so very trivial, so very farfetched, as a desire of two tribes to obtain their inheritance together on the same side of a river, simply upon the recollection that such a desire would fall in very naturally with their having pitched their tents side by side in their previous march through the wilderness?

XXII. HOBAB AND THE CHILDREN OF THE KENITE

Numbers 10:29. "And Moses said unto Hobab, the son of Raguel the Midianite, Moses' father-in-law, We are journeying unto the place of which the Lord said, I will give it you: come thou with us, and we will do thee good: for the Lord hath spoken good concerning Israel.

30. "And he said unto him, I will not go; but I will depart to mine own land, and to my kindred.

31. "And he said, Leave us not, I pray thee; forasmuch as thou knowest how we are to encamp in the wilderness, and thou mayest be to us instead of eyes.

32. "And it shall be, if thou go with us, yea, it shall be, that what goodness the Lord shall do unto us, the same will we do unto thee.

33. "And they departed from the mount of the Lord," &c.

It does not appear from this passage, whether Hobab accepted or rejected Moses' invitation. Yet, on turning to Judges 1:16, we find it said quite incidentally, and in the midst of a chapter relating to various adventures of the tribe of Judah after the death of Joshua, "And *the children of the Kenite, Moses' father-in-law*, went up out of the city of palm-trees with the children of Judah into the wilderness of Judah, which lieth in the south of Arad; and they went and dwelt among the people." This casual mention of "the children of the Kenite," was evidently here suggested by the subject of Judah being that of which the history was treating, and amongst which tribe their lot happened to be cast. Thus we learn, for the first time, that Moses' invitation to his father-in-law was accepted,—that he joined himself to the Israelites, and shared their fortunes. The fact transpires in the course of the narrative some sixty or seventy years after Moses had made his proposal to Hobab, the issue of which had been hitherto uncertain, and transpires, too, not in the reappearance of Hobab himself, but in the discovery of his posterity, and the place of their settlement.

It is incredible that so very unobtrusive a coincidence as this in the narratives of two authors (for the Books of Numbers and of Judges of course are such) should have presented itself, had the whole been a forgery; or that an incomplete transaction, as occurring in the one, should have had its character fixed by its results, as those results happen to pass before us, in the other.

XXIII. THE CIRCULATION OF INTELLIGENCE IN ANCIENT TIMES

Some circumstances in the history of Balak and Balaam supply me with another argument for the veracity of the Pentateuch. But before I proceed to those which I have more immediately in my eye, I would observe, that the simple fact of a King of Moab *knowing* that a Prophet dwelt in Mesopotamia, in the mountains of the East, a country so distant from his own, in itself supplies a point of harmony favouring the truth and reality of the narrative. For I am led by it to remark this, that very many hints may be picked up in the writings of Moses, all *concurring* to establish one position, viz. that there was a *communication* amongst the scattered inhabitants of the earth in those early times, a *circulation* of intelligence, scarcely to be expected, and not easily to be accounted for. Whether the caravans of merchants, which, as we have seen, traversed the deserts of the East—whether the unsettled and vagrant habits of the descendants of Ishmael and Esau, which singularly fitted them for being the carriers of news, and with whom the great wilderness was alive—whether the pastoral life of the Patriarchs, and of those who more immediately sprang from them, which led them to constant changes of place in search of herbage—whether the frequent petty wars which were waged amongst lawless neighbours—whether the necessary separation of families, the parent hive casting its little colony forth to settle on some distant land, and the consequent interest and curiosity which either branch would feel for the fortunes of the other—whether these were the circumstances that encouraged and maintained an intercourse among mankind in spite of the numberless obstacles which must then have opposed it, and which we might have imagined would have intercepted it altogether; or whether any other channels of intelligence were open of which we are in ignorance, sure it is, that such intercourse seems to have existed to a very considerable extent. Thus Abraham had a servant, Eliezer, whose ancestors were of Damascus [Gen. 15:2, 3.] , Thus, far as Abraham was removed from the branch of his family which remained in Mesopotamia, "it came to pass that it *was told him*, saying, Behold, Milcah, she hath also born children unto thy brother Nahor;" and their names are then added [Gen. 22:20.] . In like manner Isaac and Rebekah appear in their turn to have known that Laban had marriageable daughters [Gen. 28:2.] ;—and Jacob, when he came back to Canaan after his long sojourn in Haran, seems to have known that Esau was alive and prosperous, and that he lived at Seir, whither he sent a message to him [Gen. 32:3.] ;—and Deborah, Rebekah's nurse, who went with her to Canaan on her marriage, is found many years afterwards in the family of Jacob, for she dies in his camp as he was returning from Haran [Gen. 35:8.] , and therefore must have been sent back again meanwhile, for some purpose or other, from Canaan to Haran;—and at Elim, in the desert, the Israelites discover *twelve* wells of water and *threescore* and *ten* palms, the numbers, no doubt, not accidental, but indicating that some persons had frequented this secluded spot acquainted with the sons and grandsons of Jacob [Exod. 15:27.] ;—and Jethro, the father-in-law of Moses, is said "to *have heard* of all that God had done for Moses and for Israel his people." [Exod. 18:1.] And when Moses, on his march, sends a message to Edom, it is worded, "*thou knowest* all the travail that hath befallen us—how our fathers went down into Egypt, and we have dwelt in Egypt a long time;" [Num. 20:15.] together with many more particulars, all of which Moses reckons matters of notoriety to the inhabitants of the desert. And on another occasion he speaks of "their *having heard* that the Lord was among his people, that he was seen by them face to face, that his cloud stood over them, and that he went before them by day-time in a pillar of cloud, and in a pillar of fire by night." [Num. 14:14.] And this may, in fact, account for the vestiges of so many laws which we meet with throughout the East, even in this very early period, as held in common—and the many just notions of the Deity, mixed up, indeed, with much alloy, which so many nations possessed in common—and the rites and customs, whether civil or sacred, to which in so many points they conformed in common. Now all these unconnected matters hint at this *one circumstance*, that intelligence travelled through the tribes of the Desert more freely and rapidly than might have been thought, and the *consistency* with which the writings of Moses *imply* such a fact (for they neither affirm it, nor trouble themselves about explaining it) is a feature of truth in those writings.

XIV. THE ELDERS OF MOAB AND OF MIDIAN

Through some or other of the channels of information enumerated in the last paragraph, Balak, King of Moab, is aware of the existence of a Prophet at Pethor, and sends for him. It is not unlikely, indeed, that the Moabites, who were the children of *Lot*, should have still maintained a communication with the original stock of all which continued to dwell in Aram or Mesopotamia. Neither is it unlikely that Pethor, which was in that country [Num. 23:7.] , the country whence Abraham emigrated, and where Nahor and that branch of Terah's family remained, should possess a Prophet of the true God. Nor is it unlikely again, that, living in the midst of idolaters, Balaam should in a degree partake of the infection, as Laban had done before him in the same country; and that whilst he acknowledged the Lord for his God, and offered his victims by *sevens* (as some patriarchal tradition perhaps directed him [See Job 42:8.]), he should have had recourse to enchantments also—mixing the profane and sacred, as Laban did the worship of his images with the worship of his Maker. All this is in character. Now it was not Balak *alone* who sent the embassy to Balaam. He was but King of the Moabites, and had nothing to do with Midian. With the elders of Midian, however, he consulted, they being as much interested as himself in putting a stop to the triumphant march of Israel. Accordingly we find that the mission to the Prophet came from the two people conjointly;—"the elders of Moab and the *elders of Midian* departed, with the rewards of divination in their hand." [Num. 22:7.] In the remainder of this interview, and in the one which succeeded it, all mention of *Midian* is dropped, and the "princes of Balak," and the servants of Balak," are the titles given to the messengers. And when Balaam at length consents to accept their invitation, it is to Moab, the kingdom of Balak, that he comes, and he is received by the King at one of his own border-cities near the river of Arnon. Then follows the Prophet's fruitless struggle to curse the people whom God had blessed, and the consequent disappointment of the King, who bids him "flee to his place, the Lord having kept him back from honour;" "and Balaam rose up," the history concludes, "and *went and returned to his place*, and Balak also went his way." [Num. 24:25.] So they parted in mutual dissatisfaction.

Hitherto, then, although the elders of *Midian* were concerned in inviting the Prophet from Mesopotamia, it does not appear that they had any intercourse whatever with him on their own account—Balak and the Moabites had engrossed all his attention. The subject is now discontinued: Balaam disappears, gone, as we may suppose, to his own country again, to Pethor, in Mesopotamia, for he had expressly said on parting, "Behold, I go unto *my people*." [Num. 24:14.] Meanwhile the historian pursues his onward course, and details, through several long chapters, the abandoned profligacy of the Israelites, the numbering of them according to their families, the method by which their portions were to be assigned in the land of promise, the laws of inheritance, the choice and appointment of a successor, a series of offerings and festivals of various kinds, more or less important, the nature and obligation of vows, and the different complexion they assumed under different circumstances enumerated, and then (as it often happens in the history of Moses, where a battle or a rebellion perhaps interrupts a catalogue of rites and ceremonies)—then, I say, comes an account of an attack made upon the *Midianites* in revenge for their having seduced the people of Israel by the wiles of their women. So "they slew the kings of Midian, beside the rest of them that were slain, viz. Evi, and Rekem, and Zur, and Hur, and Reba, five kings of Midian;" and lastly, there is added, what we might not perhaps have been prepared for, "*Balaam also, the son of Beor, they slew with the sword*." [Num. 31:8.]

It seems then, but how incidentally, that the Prophet did not, after all, return to Mesopotamia, as we had supposed. Now this coincides in a very satisfactory manner with the circumstances under which, we have seen, Balaam was invited from Pethor. For the deputation, which then waited on him, did not consist of Moabites exclusively, but of *Midianites* also. When dismissed, therefore, in disgust by the Moabites, he would not return to Mesopotamia until he had paid his visit to the *Midianites*, who were equally concerned in bringing him where he was. Had the details of his achievements in Midian been given, as those in Moab are given, they might have been as numerous, as important, and as interesting. One thing only, however, we are told, that by the counsel which he suggested during this visit concerning the matter of Peor, and which he probably thought was the most likely counsel to alienate the Israelites from God, and to make Him curse instead of blessing them, he caused the children of Israel to commit the trespass he anticipated, and to fall into the trap which he had provided for them. Unhappily for him, however, his stay amongst the Midianites was unseasonably protracted, and Moses coming upon them, as we have seen, by command of God, slew them and him together. The undesigned coincidence lies in the Elders of Moab and the Elders of *Midian* going to Balaam; in *Midian* being then mentioned no more, till Balaam, having been sent away from Moab, apparently that he might go home, is subsequently found a corpse amongst the slaughtered *Midianites*.

XXV. ZIMRI, ONE OF 24,000 WHO DIED IN THE PLAGUE

In the consequences which followed from this evil counsel of Balaam, I fancy I discover another instance of coincidence without design. It is this.—As a punishment for the sin of the Israelites in partaking of the worship of Baal-Peor, God is said to have sent a Plague upon them. Who were the leaders in this defection from the Almighty, and in this shameless adoption of the abomination of the Moabites, is not disclosed—nor indeed whether any one tribe were more guilty before God than the rest—only it is said that the number of "those who died in the Plague was twenty and four thousand." [Num. 25:9.] I read, however, that the name of a certain Israelite that was slain on that occasion (who in the general humiliation and mourning defied, as it were, the vengeance of the Most High, and determined, at all hazards to continue in the lusts to which the idolatry had led), I read, I say, that "the name of this Israelite that was slain, even that was slain with the Midianitish woman, was Zimri, the son of Salu, a prince of a chief house among the *Simeonites*." [Num. 25:14.] And very great importance is attached to this act of summary punishment—as though this one offender, a *prince* of a *chief* house of his tribe, was a representative of the offence of many—for on Phinehas, in his holy indignation, putting him to instant death, the Plague ceased. "*So* the plague was stayed from the children of Israel." [Num. 25:8.]

Shortly after this a census of the people is taken. All the tribes are numbered, and a separate account is given of each. Now in this I observe the following particular—that, although on comparing this census with the one which had been made nearly forty years before at Sinai, it appears that the majority of the tribes had meanwhile increased in numbers, and none of them very materially diminished [Comp. Num. 1. and 26.] , the tribe of *Simeon* had lost almost two-thirds of its whole body, being reduced from "*fifty-nine* thousand and three hundred," [Num. 1:23.] to "*twenty-two* thousand and two hundred." [Num. 26:14.] No reason is assigned for this extraordinary depopulation of this one tribe—no hint whatever is given as to its eminence in suffering above its fellows. Nor can I pretend to say that we can detect the reason with any certainty of being right, though the fact speaks for itself that the tribe of Simeon must have experienced disaster beyond the rest. Yet it does seem very natural to think, that, in the recent Plague, the tribe to which *Zimri* belonged, who is mentioned as a leading person in it with great emphasis, *was the tribe upon which the chief fury of the scourge fell—as having been that which had been the chief transgressors in the idolatry.*

Moreover, that such was the case, I am further inclined to believe from another circumstance. One of the last great acts which Moses was commissioned to perform before his death, has a reference to this very affair of Baal-Peor. "Avenge the children of Israel," says God to him, "of the *Midianites;* afterward thou shalt be gathered unto thy people." [Num. 31:2.] Moses did so: but before he actually was gathered to his people, and while the recent extermination of this guilty nation must have been fresh in his mind, he proceeds to pronounce a parting blessing on the tribes. Now it is singular, and except upon some such supposition as this I am maintaining, unaccountable, that whilst he deals out the bounties of earth and heaven with a prodigal hand upon all the others, the tribe of *Simeon he passes over in silence*, and none but the tribe of *Simeon*—for this he has no blessing [Deut. 33:6. It is nothing but fair to state that the reading of the Codex Alexandr. is "Let Reuben live and not die, and let *Simeon* be many in number." This reading, however, the Codex Vaticanus, the rival MS. of the Alexandrine, and at least its equal in authority, does not recognise; neither is it found in the Hebrew text, nor in any of the various readings of that text as given by Dr. Kennicott—nor in the Samaritan—nor in the early Versions. It is difficult to believe that the name of Simeon should have been omitted, in so many instances, by mistake; whilst it is easy to suppose that it might have been introduced in some one instance by design, the transcriber not being aware of any cause for the exclusion of this one tribe, and saying, "Peradventure, it is an oversight." Moreover, the blessing of Reuben thus curtailed, "Let Reuben live, and not die," seems tame, and unworthy the party and the occasion.] —an omission which should seem to have some meaning, and which does in fact, as I apprehend, point to this same matter of Baal-Peor. For if that was pre-eminently the offending tribe, nothing could be more likely than that Moses, fresh, as I have said, from the destruction of the Midianites for their sin, should remember their principal partners in it too, and should think it hard measure to slay the one and forthwith bless the other. Nor can I help remarking, in further support of this conjecture, that the little consideration paid to this tribe by their brethren shortly afterwards, in the allotment of the portions of the Holy Land, implies it to have been in disgrace—their inheritance being only the remnant of that assigned to the children of Judah, which was too much for them [Josh. 19:9.] ; and so inadequate to their wants did it prove, that in aftertimes they sent forth a colony even to Mount Seir.

Admitting, then, the fact to be as I have supposed, it supports (as in so many other cases already mentioned) the credibility of a miracle. For the name of the audacious offender points incidentally to the offending tribe—the extraordinary diminution of that tribe points to some extraordinary cause of the diminution—the pestilence presents itself as a *probable* cause—and if the *real* cause, then it becomes the judicial punishment of a transgression, a miracle wrought by God (as Moses would have it), in token that his wrath was kindled against Israel.

XXVI. SUMMARY OF THE VERACITY OF THE BOOKS OF MOSES

So much for the Books of Moses; not that I believe the subject exhausted, for I doubt not that many examples of coincidence without design in the writings of Moses have escaped me, which others may detect, as one eye will often see what another has overlooked. Still I cannot account for the number and nature of those which I have been able to produce, on any other principle than the veracity of the narrative which presents them;—accident could not have touched upon truth so often— design could not have touched upon it so artlessly; the less so, because these coincidences do not discover themselves in certain detached and isolated passages, but break out from time to time as the history proceeds, running witnesses (as it were) to the accuracy not of one solitary detail, but of a series of details, extending through the lives and actions of many different individuals, relating to many different events, and dating at many different points of time. For, I have travelled through the writings of Moses, beginning from the history of Abraham, when a sojourner in the land of Canaan, and ending with a transaction which happened on the borders of that land, when the descendants of Abraham, now numerous as the stars in heaven, were about to enter and take possession. I have found, in the progress of this chequered series of events, the marks of truth never deserting us—I have found (to recapitulate as briefly as possible) *consistency without design* in the many hints of a Patriarchal Church incidentally scattered through the Book of Genesis taken as a *whole*—I have found it in *particular* instances; in the impassioned terms wherein the Father of the Faithful intercedes for a devoted city, of which his *brother's son* was an inhabitant—in the circumstance of his own son receiving in marriage the *grand-daughter* of his brother, a singular confirmation that he was the child of his parent's old age, the miraculous offspring of a sterile bed—I have found it in the several oblique intimations of the imbecility and insignificance of *Bethuel* —in the concurrence of Isaac's meditation in the field, with the fact of his mother's recent *death*—and in the desire of that Patriarch on a subsequent occasion to impart the blessing, as compared with what seem to be symptoms of a present and serious *sickness*—I have found it in the singular command of Jacob to his followers, to put away their idols, as compared with the sacking of an *idolatrous city*, and the capture of its idolatrous inhabitants shortly before—I have found it in the *identity* of the character of Jacob, a character offered to us in many aspects and at many distant intervals, but still ever the same—I have found it in the *lading* of the camels of the Ishmaelitish merchants, as compared with the mode of sepulture amongst the Egyptians—in the allusions to the *corn crop* of Egypt, thrown out in such a variety of ways, and so inadvertently in all, as compared one with another—I have found it in the proportion of that crop *permanently* assigned to Pharaoh, as compared with that which was taken up by Joseph for the famine; and in the very natural manner in which a great revolution of the state is made to arise out of a temporary emergency—I have found it in the tenderness with which the property of the *priests* was treated, as compared with the honour in which they were held by the King, and the alliance which had been formed with one of their families by the minister of the King—I have found it in the character of *Joseph*, which, however and whenever we catch a glimpse of it, is still *one:* and whether it be gathered from his own words or his own deeds, from the language of his father or from the language of his brethren, is still uniform throughout—I have found it in the marriage of Amram, the grandson of Levi, with Jochebed his daughter—I have found it in the death of Nadab and Abihu, as compared with the remarkable law which follows touching the *use of wine*—and in the removal of their corpses by the sons of Uzziel, as compared with the defilement of certain in the camp about the same time by the *dead body* of a man—I have found it in the gushing of *water* from the rock at Rephidim, as compared with the attack of the Amalekites which followed—in the state of the crops in *Judea* at the *Passover*, as compared with that of the crops in *Egypt* at the plague of *Hail*—in the proportion of *oxen and waggons* assigned to the several families of the Levites, as compared with the different services they had respectively to discharge— I have found it in the order of march observed in one *particular* case, when the Israelites broke up from Mount Sinai, as compared with the *general* directions given in other places for pitching the tents and sounding the alarms—I have found it in the peculiar propriety of the *grouping* of the conspirators against Moses and Aaron, as compared with their relative situations in the camp—consisting, as they do, of such a family of the Levites and such a tribe of the Israelites as dwelt on the same side of the Tabernacle, and therefore had especial facilities for clandestine inter-course—I have found it in an *inference* from the direct narrative, that the families of the conspirators did not perish alike, as compared with a subsequent most casual assertion, that though the households of Dathan and Abiram were destroyed, the *children of Korah died not*—I have found it in the desire expressed conjointly by the Tribe of Reuben and the Tribe of Gad to have lands allotted them together on the east side of Jordan, as compared with their *contiguous* position in the camp during their long and trying march through the wilderness—I have found it in the unifor-mity with which Moses implies a free *communication* to have subsisted amongst the scattered inhabitants of the East—in the unexpected discov-ery of Balaam amongst the dead of the *Midianites*, though he had departed from Moab apparently to return to his own country, as compared with the *united* embassy that was sent to invite him—and, finally, I have found it in the extraordinary diminution of the Tribe of *Simeon*, as compared with the occasion of the death of Zimri, a chief of that tribe, the only individual whom Moses thinks it necessary to name, and the victim by which the Plague is appeased.

These indications of truth in the Mosaic writings (to which, as I have said, others of the same kind might doubtless be added) may be some-times more, sometimes less strong; still they must be acknowledged, I think, on a general review, and when taken in the aggregate, to amount to evidence of great cumulative weight—evidence the more valuable in the present instance, because the extreme antiquity of the documents precludes any arising out of contemporary history. But though the argu-ment of coincidence without design is the only one with which I proposed to deal, I may be allowed, in closing my remarks on the Books of Moses, to make brief mention of a few other points in favour of their veracity, which have naturally presented themselves to my mind whilst I have been engaged in investigating that argument—several of these also bespeaking *undesignedness* in the narrative more or less, and so far allied to my main proposition.—For example—

1. There is a *minuteness* in the details of the Mosaic writings, which argues their truth; for it often argues the eye-witness, as in the adventures of the wilderness; and often seems intended to supply directions to the artificer, as in the construction of the Tabernacle.

2. There are *touches of nature* in the narrative which argue its truth, for

it is not easy to regard them otherwise than as strokes from the life—as where "the *mixed* multitude," whether half-casts or Egyptians, are the first to sigh for the cucumbers and melons of Egypt, and to spread discontent through the camp [Num. 11:4.] —as, the miserable exculpation of himself, which Aaron attempts, with all the cowardice of conscious guilt—"I cast into the fire, and *there came out* this calf:" the fire, to be sure, being in the fault [Exod. 32:24.] .

3. There are certain little *inconveniences* represented as turning up unexpectedly, that argue truth in the story; for they are just such accidents as are characteristic of the working of a new system, an untried machinery. What is to be done with the man who is found gathering sticks on the sabbath-day [Num. 15:32.] ? (Could an impostor have devised such a trifle?) How the inheritance of the daughters of Zelophehad is to be disposed of, there being no heir-male [Num. 36:2.] . Either of them inconsiderable matters in themselves, but both giving occasion to very important laws; the one touching life, and the other property.

4. There is a *simplicity* in the manner of Moses, when telling his tale, which argues its truth—no parade of language, no pomp of circumstance even in his miracles—a modesty and dignity throughout all. Let us but compare him in any trying scene with Josephus; his description, for instance, of the passage through the Red Sea [Exod. 14: Joseph. Antiq. b. 2. c. xvi.] , of the murmuring of the Israelites and the supply of quails and manna, with the same as given by the Jewish historian, or rhetorician, we might rather say,—and the force of the observation will be felt [Exod. 16: Joseph. Antiq. b. 3. c. i.] .

5. There is a *candour* in the treatment of his subject by Moses, which argues his truth; as when he tells of his own want of eloquence, which unfitted him for a leader [Exod. 4:10.] —his own want of faith, which prevented him from entering the promised land [Num. 20:12.] —the idolatry of Aaron his brother [Exod. 32:21.] —the profaneness of Nadab and Abihu, his nephews [Levit. 10:1.] —the disaffection and punishment of Miriam, his sister [Num. 12:1.] . The relationship which Amram his father bore to Jochebed his mother, which became afterwards one of the prohibited degrees in the marriage Tables of the Levitical Law [Exod. 6:20; Levit. 18:12.] .

6. There is a *disinterestedness* in his conduct, which argues him to be a man of truth; for though he had sons, he apparently takes no measures during his life to give them offices of trust or profit; and at his death he appoints as his successor one who had no claims upon him, either of alliance, of clan-ship, or of blood.

7. There are certain *prophetical* passages in the writings of Moses, which

argue their truth; as several respecting the future Messiah; and the very sublime and literal one respecting the final fall of Jerusalem [Deut. 28.] .

8. There is a *simple key* supplied by these writings to the meaning of many ancient traditions current amongst the heathens, though greatly disguised, which is another circumstance that argues their truth—as, the golden age—the garden of the Hesperides—the fruit-tree in the midst of the garden which the dragon guarded—the destruction of mankind by a flood, all except two persons, and those righteous persons—
"*Innocuos ambos, cultores numinis ambos:*" [Ovid, Met. i. 327.]
the rainbow, "which Jupiter set in the cloud, a sign to men" [Hom. II xi. 27, 28.] —the seventh day a sacred day [Hesiod. Oper. et Di. 770. See Grot. de Verit. Rel. Christ. 1. 1. xvi.] —with many others: all conspiring to establish the reality of the facts which Moses relates, because tending to show that vestiges of the like present themselves in the traditional history of the world at large.

9. The concurrence which is found between the writings of Moses and those of the New Testament, argues their truth: the latter constantly appealing to them, being indeed but the completion of the system which the others are the first to put forth. Nor is this an illogical argument—for, though the credibility of the New Testament itself may certainly be reasoned out from the truth of the Pentateuch once established, it is still very far from depending on that circumstance exclusively, or even principally. The New Testament demands acceptance on its own merits, on merits distinct from those on which the Books of Moses rest—therefore (so far as it does so) it may fairly give its suffrage for their veracity—valeat quantum valet—and surely it is a very improbable thing, that two dispensations, separated by an interval of some fifteen hundred years, each exhibiting prophecies of its own, since fulfilled—each asserting miracles of its own, on strong evidence of its own—that two dispensations, with such individual claims to be believed, should also be found to stand in the closest relation to one another, and yet both turn out impostures after all.

10. Above all, there is a comparative *purity* in the theology and morality of the Pentateuch, which argues not only its truth, but its high original; for how else are we to account for a system like that of Moses, in such an age and amongst such a people; that the doctrine of the unity, the self-existence, the providence, the perfections of the great God of heaven and earth, should thus have blazed forth (how far more brightly than even in the vaunted schools of Athens at its most refined æra!) from the midst of a nation, of themselves ever plunging into gross and grovelling idolatry; and that principles of social duty, of benevolence, and of self-restraint, extending even to the thoughts of the heart [Exod. 20:3; Deut. 6:4; Exod.

3:14; Deut 11:14; Levit. 19:2,18; Deut. 30:6; Exod. 20:17.] should have been the produce of an age, which the very provisions of the Levitical Law itself show to have been full of savage and licentious abominations?

Such are some of the *internal* evidences for the veracity of the Books of Moses.

11. Then the situation in which the Jews actually found themselves placed, as a matter of fact, is no slight argument for the truth of the Mosaic accounts; reminded, as they were, by certain *memorials* observed from year to year, of the great events of their early history, just as they are recorded in the writings of Moses—memorials, universally recognised both in their object and in their authority. The Passover, for instance, celebrated by all—no man doubting its meaning, no man in all Israel assigning to it any other origin than one, viz. that of being a contemporary monument of a miracle displayed in favour of the people of Israel; by right of which credentials, and no other, it summoned from all quarters of the world, at great cost, and inconvenience, and danger, the dispersed Jews—none disputing the obligation to obey the summons.

12. Then the heroic *devotion* with which the Israelites continued to regard the Law, even long after they had ceased to cultivate the better part of it, even when that very Law only served to condemn its worshippers, so that they would offer themselves up by thousands, with their children and wives, as martyrs to the honour of their temple, in which no image, even of an emperor, who could scourge them with scorpions for their disobedience, should be suffered to stand, and they live [Joseph. Bell. Jud. b. 2. c. x.§ 4.] —so that rather than violate the sanctity of the Sabbath Day, the bravest men in arms would lay down their lives as tamely as sheep, and allow themselves to be burnt in the holes where they had taken refuge from their cruel and cowardly pursuers [Antiq. Jud. b. 12. c. 6. § 2.] . All this points to their Law, as having been at first promulgated under circumstances too awful to be forgotten even after the lapse of ages.

13. Then, again, the extraordinary degree of *national pride* with which the Jews boasted themselves to be God's *peculiar* people, as if no nation ever was or ever could be so nigh to Him; a feeling which the early teachers of Christianity found an insuperable obstacle to the progress of the Gospel amongst them, and which actually did effect its ultimate rejection—this may well seem to be founded upon a strong traditional sense of uncommon tokens of the Almighty's regard for them above all other nations of the earth, which they had heard with their ears, or their fathers had declared unto them, even the noble works that He had done in the old time before them.

14. Then again, the constant craving after "a sign," which beset them in

the latter days of their history, as a lively certificate of the prophet; and not after a sign only, but after such an one as they would themselves prescribe: "What sign shewest thou that we may see and believe?... *our fathers did eat manna in the desert;*" [John 6:13.] this desire, so frequently expressed, and with which they are so frequently reproached, looks like the relic of an appetite engendered in other times, when they had enjoyed the privilege of more intimate communion with God—it seems the wake, as it were, of miracles departed.

15. Lastly, the very *onerous* nature of the Law—so studiously meddling with all the occupations of life, great and small—this yoke would scarcely have been endured, without the strongest assurance on the part of those who were galled by it, of the authority by which it was imposed. For it met them with some restraint or other at every turn. Would they plough?—Then it must not be with an ox and an ass [Deut. 22:10.] . Would they sow?—Then must not the seed be mixed [Deut. 22:9.] . Would they reap?—Then must they not reap clean [Lev. 19:9.] . Would they make bread?—Then must they set apart dough enough for the consecrated loaf [Num. 15:20.] . Did they find a bird's nest?—Then must they let the old bird fly away [Deut. 22:6.] . Did they hunt?—Then they must shed the blood of their game, and cover it with dust [Lev. 17:13.] . Did they plant a fruit tree?—For three years was the fruit to be uncircumcised [Lev. 19:23.] . Did they shave their beards?—They were not to cut the corners [Lev. 19:27.] . Did they weave a garment?—Then must it be only with threads prescribed [Lev. 19:19.] . Did they build a house?—They must put rails and battlements on the roof [Deut. 22:8.] . Did they buy an estate?—At the year of Jubilee back it must go to its owner [Lev. 25:13.] . This last was in itself and alone a provision which must have made itself felt in the whole structure of the Jewish commonwealth, and have sensibly affected the character of the people; every transfer of land throughout the country having to be regulated in its price according to the remoteness or proximity of the year of release; and the desire of accumulating a species of property usually considered the most inviting of any, counteracted and thwarted at every turn. All these (and how many more of the same kind might be named!) are enactments which it must have required extraordinary influence in the Lawgiver to enjoin, and extraordinary reverence for his powers to perpetuate.

Still, after all, unbelievers may start difficulties, —this I dispute not, —difficulties too, which we may not always be able to answer, though I think we may be always able to neutralize them. It may be a part of our trial that such difficulties should exist, and be encountered, for there can be no reason why temptations should not be provided for the natural pride of our understanding, as well as for the natural lusts of our flesh; to many, indeed, they would be the more formidable of the two, perhaps to the angels who kept not their first estate they proved so. With such facts, however, before me, as these which I have submitted to my readers, I can come to no conclusion but one—that when we read the writings of Moses, we read no cunningly-devised fables, but solemn and safe records of great and marvelous events, which court examination and sustain it –records of that apparent veracity and faithfulness, that I can understand our Lord to have spoken almost without a figure, when he said, that he who believed not Moses, neither would he be persuaded though one rose from the dead.

Part II

The Veracity of the Historical Scriptures

Hitherto I have endeavoured to prove the veracity of the Mosaic writings by the instances they contain of *coincidence without design* in their several parts; and I hope and believe that I have succeeded in pointing out such coincidences as might come of truth, and could come of nothing but truth. These presented themselves in the history of the Patriarchs, from Abraham to Joseph; and in the history of the chosen race in general, from their departure out of Egypt to the day when their great Lawgiver expired on the borders of that land of Promise into which Joshua was now to lead them—a long and eventful history. I shall now resume the subject; pursue the adventures of this extraordinary people, as they are unfolded in some of the subsequent books of holy writ; and, still using the same test as before, ascertain whether these portions of Scripture do not appear to be equally trustworthy, and whilst, like the former, they assert, often without any recourse to the intervention of second causes, miracles many and mighty, they do not challenge confidence in those miracles by marks of reality, consistency, and accuracy, which the ordinary matters of fact combined with them constantly exhibit. "For this credibility of the common scripture history," says Bishop Butler, "gives some credibility to its miraculous history; especially as this is interwoven with the common, so as that they imply each other, and both together make up one revelation." (Analogy, p. 389).

I. JOSHUA CROSSING THE JORDAN

Moses then being dead, Joshua takes the command of the armies of Israel, and marches them over Jordan to the possession of the land of Canaan. It was a day and a deed much to be remembered. "It came to pass, when the people removed from their tents, to pass over Jordan, and the priests bearing the ark of the covenant before the people; and as they that bare the ark were come unto Jordan, and the feet of the priests that bare the ark were dipped in the brim of the water, (for Jordan overfloweth all his banks in the time of harvest,) that the waters which came down from above stood and rose up upon an heap very far from the city Adam, that is beside Zaretan: and those that came down toward the sea of the plain, even the salt sea, failed, and were cut off: and the people passed over right against Jericho. And the priests that bare the ark of the covenant of the Lord stood firm on dry ground in the midst of Jordan, and all the Israelites passed over on dry ground, until all the people were passed clean over Jordan." [Josh. 3:14–17.]

Such is the language of the Book of Joshua. Now in the midst of this miraculous narrative, an incident is mentioned, though very casually, which dates the season of the year when this passage of the Jordan was effected. The feet of the priests, it seems, were dipped in the brim of the water; and this is explained by the season being that of the periodical inundation of Jordan, that river overflowing his banks all the time of harvest. The *barley*-harvest is here meant, or the former harvest, as it is elsewhere called, in contradistinction to the *wheat*, or latter harvest; for in the fourth chapter (v. 19) we read, "the people came up out of Jordan on the tenth day of the *first month*," that is, four days before the Passover, which fell in with the barley-harvest; the wheat-harvest not being fully completed till Pentecost, or fifty days later in the year, when the wave-loaves of the first-fruits of the wheat were offered up [This question of the harvests is examined in greater detail in Part I. No. xvi.] . The Israelites passed the Jordan then, it appears, at the time of *barley*-harvest. But we are told in Exodus, that at the Plague of Hail, which was but a day or two before the Passover, "the *flax* and the *barley* were smitten, for the barley was in the ear and the flax was boiled, but the wheat and the rye were not smitten, for they were not grown up." [Exod. 9:31.] It should seem, there-fore, that the flax and the barley were crops which ripened about the same time in Egypt; and as the climate of Canaan did not differ materially from that of Egypt, this, no doubt, was the case in Canaan too; there also these two crops would come in at the same time. The Israelites, therefore, who crossed the Jordan, as we have seen in one passage, at the harvest, and that harvest, as we have seen in another passage, the *barley*-harvest, must, if so, have crossed it at the *flax*-harvest.

Now, in a former chapter, we are informed, that three days before Joshua ventured upon the invasion, he sent two men, spies, to view the land, even Jericho [Josh. 1:2; 2:1. 22; 3:2.] . It was a service of peril: they were received by Rahab, a woman of that city, and lodged in her house: but the entrance of these strangers at night-fall was observed: it was a moment, no doubt, of great suspicion and alarm: an enemy's army encamped on the borders. The thing was reported to the King of Jericho, and search was made for the men. Rahab, however, fearing God—for by faith she felt that the miracles wrought by Him in favour of Israel were proofs that for Israel He fought,—by faith, which, living as she did in the midst of idolaters, might well be counted to her for righteousness, and the like to which, in a somewhat similar case, was declared by our Lord enough to lead those who professed it into the kingdom of God, even before the chief priests and elders themselves [Heb. 11:31; Matt. 21:31.] —she, I say, having this faith in God, and true to those laws of hospitality which are the glory of the eastern nations, and more especially of the females of the East, even to this day, at much present risk protected her guests from their pursuers. But how! "She brought them up to the roof of her house, and hid them with the *stalks of flax*" [Josh. 2:6.] —the stalks of flax, no doubt just cut down, which she had spread upon the roof of her house to steep and to season.

Here I see truth. Yet how very minute is this incident! how very casually does it present itself to our notice! how very unimportant a matter it seems in the first instance, under what the spies were hidden! enough that, whatever it was, it answered the purpose, and saved their lives. Could the historian have contemplated for one moment the effect which a trifle about a flax-stalk might have in corroboration of his account of the passage of the Jordan? Is it possible for the most jealous examiner of human testimony to imagine that these flax-stalks were fixed upon above all things in the world for the covering of the spies, because they were known to be ripe with the barley, and the barley was known to be ripe at the Passover, and the Passover was known to be the season when the Israelites set foot in Canaan? Or rather, would he not fairly and candidly confess, that in one particular, at least, of this adventure (the only one which we have an opportunity of checking), a religious attention to truth is manifested; and that when it is said, "the feet of the Priests were dipped in the brim of the water," and when a reason is assigned for this gradual approach to the bed of a river, of which the banks were in general steep and precipitous, we are put in possession of one unquestionable fact at least, one particular upon which we may safely repose, whatever may be said of the remainder of the narrative, and that assuredly truth leads us by the hand to the very edge of the miracle, if not through the miracle itself?

II. JOSHUA AND THE CITY OF LACHISH

Josh. 10:31, 32—"And Joshua passed from Libnah, and all Israel with him, unto Lachish, and encamped against it, and fought against it. And the Lord delivered Lachish into the hand of Israel, which took it on *the second day* and smote it with the edge of the sword."

It may be remarked, that from the account here given of Joshua's campaign against the cities of Canaan, it would seem that all of them fell before him at once, except Lachish. He took Makkedah, and Libnah, and Eglon, and Hebron, and Debir; but of Lachish, and Lachish alone, it is said, that he took it on "the second day." There is no express assertion of any particular difficulty which attended the conquest of this town. That there was, however, a difficulty, greater than presented itself in the other cases we are led to infer from the incidental mention of its being taken on *the second day.*

Now, if we turn to other passages in Scripture, we shall find reason to believe that Lachish was in fact a very strong place. When Sennacherib invaded Judah he attacked "the fenced cities," and (we read) "took them;" but the sequel seems to show that on that occasion Lachish foiled him. Whilst he laid siege against it himself, [2 Chr. 32:9] he sent his servants Tartan and Rabsaris and Rabshakeh with a detachment, it should appear, to summon Jerusalem. His summons not being attended to, Rabshakeh returned, and "found the king of Assyria warring against Libnah, for he heard *that he was departed from Lachish* ;" i.e., I apprehend, that he had raised the siege. And this conclusion receives further confirmation from a passage in Jeremiah, which relates to a similar transaction at a subsequent period under Nebuchadnezzar. "Then Jeremiah the prophet spake all these words unto Zedekiah king of Judah, in Jerusalem, when the king of Babylon's army fought against Jerusalem and against all the cities of Judah *that were left*, against *Lachish*, and against Azekah; *for these defenced cities remained of the cities of Judah*;" i.e. these had strength enough to stand out, when the others had fallen.

Thus it may be argued, with the utmost probability, that the writer of the

Book of Joshua, whoever he might be, was intimately acquainted with the facts he records; and that, when in describing the assault on Lachish he tells us it was the *second day* before it succeeded, he *undesignedly* leads us to suspect that Lachish was a stronghold; and on consulting other portions of the subsequent history of the Jews, we discover that suspicion to be confirmed; and on the whole, a coincidence results very characteristic of truth and accuracy, and this in a narrative full of the miraculous.

III. ISRAEL AND THE CANAANITES

The Israelites having made this successful inroad into the land of Canaan, divided it amongst the Tribes. But the Canaanites, though panic-struck at their first approach, soon began to take heart, and the covetous policy of Israel (a policy which dictated attention to present pecuniary profits, no matter at what eventual cost to the great moral interests of the Commonwealth) had satisfied itself with making them tributaries, contrary to the command of God, that they should be driven out [Exod. 23:31.] ; and, accordingly, they were suffered, as it was promised, to become thorns in Israel's side, always vexing, often resisting, and sometimes oppressing them for many years together. Meanwhile the Tribe of Dan had its lot cast near the Amorites. It struggled to work out for itself a settlement; but its fierce and warlike neighbours drove in its outposts, and succeeded in confining it to the mountains [Judges 1:34.] . The children of Dan became straitened in their borders, and, unable to extend them at home, "they sent of their family five men from their coasts, men of valour, to spy out the land and to search it." So these five men departed, and, directing their steps northwards, to the nearest parts of the country which held out any prospect to settlers, "they came," we are told, "to Laish, and saw the people that were therein, how they dwelt careless, after *the manner of the Zidonians*, quiet and secure, and there was no magistrate in the land that might put them to shame in anything, and they were far from the *Zidonians*, and had no business with any man." [Judges 18:7.] Thus the circumstances of the place and the people were tempting to the views of the strangers. They return to their brethren, and advise an attempt upon the town. Accordingly, they march against it, take it, and, rebuilding the city, which was destroyed in the assault, change its name from Laish to Dan, and colonise it. From this it should appear that Laish, though far from Sidon, was in early times a town belonging to Sidon, and probably inhabited by Sidonians, for it was *after their manner* that the people lived.

Such is the information furnished us in the eighteenth chapter of the Book of Judges.

I now turn to the third chapter of the Book of Deuteronomy, and I there find the following passage: "We took at that time," says Moses, "out of the hand of the two kings of the Amorites the land that was on this side Jordan, from the river of Arnon unto Mount Hermon—*which Hermon the Sidonians call Sirion*, and the Amorites call it Shenir." [Deut. 3:8, 9.] But why this mention of the Sidonian name of this famous mountain? It was not near to Sidon—it does not appear to have belonged to Sidon, but to the king of Bashan [Josh. 12:4, 5.] . The reason, though not obvious, is nevertheless discoverable, and a very curious geographical coincidence it affords between the former passage in Judges and this in Deuteronomy.

For Hermon, we know, was close to Cæsarea Philippi. But Cæsarea Philippi, we are again informed, was the modern name of Paneas, the seat of Jordan's flood: and Paneas, we further learn, was the same as the still more ancient Dan or Laish ["Dan *Phœnices oppidum, quod nunc Paneas dicitur. Dan autem unus e fontibus est Jordanis.*"—Hieronym, in Quæstionibus in Genesin i.p. 382. It was also Cæsarea Philippi.—Euseb. Eccl. Hist. vii. c. xvii. 'The Hierusalem Targum, Num. 35. writes thus, "The mountain of Snow at Cæsarea (Philippi)—this was Hermon." '—Lightfoot, Vol. ii. p. 62, fol. See also Psalm 42:8.] . Now Laish, we have seen, was probably at first a settlement of the Sidonians, after whose manner the people of Laish lived. Accordingly, it appears,—but how distant and unconnected are the passages from which such a conclusion is drawn!—that although this Hermon was far from Sidon itself, still at its foot there was dwelling a Sidonian colony, a race speaking the Sidonian language; and, therefore, nothing could be more natural than that the mountain which overhung the town should have a Sidonian name, by which it was commonly known in those parts, and that this should suggest itself, as well as its Hebrew name, to Moses.

IV. SOLOMON AND HIRAM

Connected with the circumstances of this same colony of Laish is another coincidence which I have to offer, and I introduce it in this place, because it is so connected, for otherwise it anticipates a point of Jewish history, which, in the order of the books of Scripture, lies a long way before me. The construction of Solomon's Temple at Jerusalem is the event at which it dates.

In the seventh chapter of the First Book of Kings I read, "And king

Solomon sent and fetched Hiram out of Tyre. He was a widow's son of the Tribe of *Naphtali*, and his father was a man of *Tyre*, a worker in brass; and he was filled with wisdom and understanding, and cunning to work all works in brass. And he came to king Solomon, and wrought all his work." (v. 13.) But in the parallel passage in the second chapter of the Second Book of Chronicles (v. 13), where we have the answer which king Hiram returned to Solomon, when the latter desired him to "send him a man, cunning to work in gold, and in silver, and in brass;" I find it running thus:—"Now I have sent a cunning man, endued with understanding, of Huram my father's (or perhaps Huram-Abi by name), the son of a woman of the daughters of *Dan*, and his father was a man of Tyre, skilful to work in gold." It is evident, that the same individual is meant in both passages; yet there is an apparent discrepancy between them: the one in Kings asserting his mother to be a woman of the Tribe of *Naphtali;* the other, in Chronicles, asserting her to be a woman of the daughters of *Dan*. The difficulty has driven the critics to some intricate expedients, in order to resolve it. "She herself was of the Tribe of Dan," says Dr. Patrick; "but her first husband was of the Tribe of Naphtali, by whom she had this son. When she was a widow, she married a man of Tyre, who is called Hiram's father, because he bred him up, and was the husband of his mother." All this is gratuitous. The explanation only serves to show that the interpreter was aware of the knot, but not of the solution. This difficulty, however, like many others in Scripture, when once explained, helps to confirm its truth. We have seen in the last paragraph, that six hundred Danites emigrated from their own Tribe, and seized upon Laish, a city of the Sidonians. Now the Sidonians were subjects of the king of Tyre, and were the selfsame people as the Tyrians; for in the fifth chapter of the First Book of Kings, where Solomon is reported as sending to the king of *Tyre* for workmen, he is said to assign as a reason for the application, "Thou knowest that there is not among us any that can skill to hew timber like unto the *Sidonians*." (v. 6.) The Tyrians, therefore, and the Sidonians were the same nation. But Laish or Dan, we found, was near the springs of Jordan; and therefore, since the "outgoings" of the territory of Naphtali are expressly said to have been at Jordan, there is good reason to believe that Laish or Dan stood in the Tribe of Naphtali. But if so, then is the difficulty solved; for the woman was, by abode, of *Naphtali;* Laish, where she dwelt, being situated in that Tribe, as Jacob is called a Syrian, from his having lived in Syria [Deut. 26:5.] ; and by birth, she was of *Dan*, being come of that little colony of Danites, which the parent stock had sent forth in early times to settle at a distance. Meanwhile the very circumstance which interposes to reconcile the apparent disagreement, accounts no less naturally for the fact, that she had a Tyrian for her husband.

Now upon what a very trifle does this mark of truth turn! Who can suspect anything insidious here? any trap for the unwary inquisitor after internal evidence in the domestic circumstances of a master-smith, employed by Solomon to build his temple?

I am glad to have it in my power to produce this geographical coincidence, because it is rare in its kind—the geography of Canaan, owing to its extreme perplexity, scarcely furnishing its due contingent to the argument I am handling. However, that very intricacy may in itself be thought to say something to our present purpose; arising, as it in a great degree does, out of the manifold instances in which different places are called by the same name in the Holy Land. Now whilst this accident, creates a confusion, very unfavourable to determining their respective sites, and consequently stands in the way of such undesigned tokens of truth as might spring out of a more accurate knowledge of such particulars; still it accords very singularly with the circumstances under which Scripture reports the land of Canaan to have been occupied:—I mean, that it was divided amongst Twelve Tribes of one and the same nation; each, therefore, left to regulate the names within its own borders after its own pleasure; and all having many associations in common, which would often overrule them, no doubt, however unintentionally, to fix upon the same. We have only to look to our own colonies, in whatever latitude dispersed, to see the like workings of the same natural feeling familiarly exemplified in the identity of local names, which they severally present. And it may be added, that such a geographical nomenclature was the more likely to establish itself in the new settlements of the Israelites, amongst whom names of places, from the earliest times downwards, seem to have been seldom, if ever, arbitrary, but still to have carried with them some meaning, which was, or which was thought to be, significant.

V. NO ARMOUR IN ISRAEL

I have said that the Canaanites, who were spared by the Israelites after the first encounter with them, partly that they might derive from the conquered race a tribute, and partly that they might employ them in the servile offices of hewing wood and drawing water, by degrees recovered their spirit, waged war successfully against their invaders, and for many years mightily oppressed Israel. The Philistines, the most formidable of the inhabitants of Canaan, and those under whom the Israelites suffered the most severely, added policy to power. For at their bidding it came to pass (and probably the precaution was adopted by others besides the Philistines), that "there was no *smith* found throughout all the land of Israel; for the Philistines said, Lest the Hebrews make themselves swords and spears. But all the Israelites went down to the Philistines, to sharpen every man his share, and his coulter, and his axe, and his mattock." [1 Sam. 13:19.] Such is said to have been the rigorous law of the conquerors. The workers in iron were everywhere put down, lest, under pretence of making implements for the husbandman, they should forge arms for the rebel. Now that some such law was actually in force (I am not aware that direct mention is made of it except in this one passage), is a fact confirmed by a great many incidents, some of them very trifling and inconsiderable, none of them related or connected, but all of them turned by this one key.

Thus, when Ehud prepared to dispatch Eglon the King of Moab, to whom the Israelites were then subject, "he *made him*" (we are told) "a dagger, which had two edges, of a cubit length, and he did gird it under his raiment upon his *right thigh;*" [Judges 3:16.] he made it himself, it seems, expressly for the occasion, and he bound it upon his *right* thigh, instead of his left, which was the sword-side, to baffle suspicion; whilst, being left-handed, he could wield it nevertheless. Moreover it may be observed, in passing, that Ehud was a Benjamite [Judges. 3:15.] ; and that of the Benjamites, when their fighting men turned out against Israel in the affair of Gibeah, there were seven hundred choice slingers *left-handed* [Judges. 2:16.] ; and that of this discomfited army, six hundred persons escaped to the rock Rimmon, none so likely as the light-armed; and that this escape is dated by one of our most careful investigators of Scripture, Dr. Lightfoot, at thirteen years before Ehud's accession [Lightfoot's Works, i. 44–47.] . What, then, is more probable—yet I need not say how incidental is this touch of truth—than that this left-handed Ehud, a Benjamite, was one who survived of those seven hundred left-handed slingers, who were Benjamites?

Thus, again, Shamgar slays six hundred of the Philistines with an *ox-goad* [Judges 3:31.] ; doubtless having recourse to an implement so inconvenient, because it was not permitted to carry arms or to have them in possession.

Thus Samson, when he went down to Timnath with no very friendly feeling towards the Philistines, however he might feign it, nor at a moment of great political tranquillity, was still unarmed; so that when "the young lion roared against him, he *rent* him, as he would have rent a kid, and he had nothing in his hand." [Judges. 14:5, 6.] And when the same champion slew a thousand of the Philistines, it was with a jaw-bone, for he had no other choice. "Was there a shield or a spear seen among forty thousand in Israel?" [Judges 5:8.]

All these are indications, yet very oblique ones, that no smith or armourer wrought throughout all the land of Israel; for it will be perceived, on examination, that every one of these incidents occurred at times when the Israelites were under subjection.

Moreover, it was probably in consequence of this same restrictive law, that the *sling* became so popular a weapon amongst the Israelites. It does not appear that it was known, or at least used, under Moses. Whilst Israel was triumphant, it was not needed: in those happier days, her fighting-men were men that "drew the sword." In the days of her oppression they were driven to the use of more ignoble arms. The sling was readily constructed, and readily concealed. Whilst a staff or hempen-stalk grew in her fields, and a smooth stone lay in her brooks, this artillery at least was ever forthcoming. It was not a very fatal weapon, unless wielded with consummate skill. The Philistines despised it: Goliath, we may remember, scorns it as a weapon against a dog: but, by continual application to the exercise of it (for it was now their only hope), the Israelites converted a rude and rustic plaything into a formidable engine of war. That troop of Benjamites, of whom I have already spoken, had taken pains to make themselves equally expert with either hand—(every one could sling stones at an hair-breadth and not miss)—and the precision with which David directed it, would not perhaps be thought extraordinary amongst the active and practised youths of his day.

These particulars, it will be perceived, are many and divers; and though they might not of themselves have enabled us to draw them into an induction that the inhabitants of Canaan withheld from Israel the use of arms; yet, when we are put in possession of the single fact, that no smith was allowed throughout all Israel, we are at once supplied with the centre towards which they are one and all perceived to converge.

I know not how incidents of the kind here produced can be accounted for, except by the supposition that they are portions of a true and actual history; and they who may feel that there is in them some force, but who may at the same time feel that fuller evidence is wanted to compel their assent to a Scripture which makes upon them demands so large; who secretly whisper to themselves, in the temper of the incredulous Jew of old, "We would see a sign;" or of him who mocked, saying, "Let Him now come down from the cross, and we will believe"—let such calmly and dispassionately consider, that there could be no room for faith, if there were no room for doubt; that the scheme of our probation requires, perhaps as a matter of necessity, that faith should be in it a very chief ingredient; that the exercise of faith (as we may partly perceive), both the spirit which must foster it, and the spirit which must issue from it, is precisely what seems fit for moulding us into vessels for future honour; that natural religion lifts up its voice to tell us, that in this world we are undoubtedly living under the dispensation of a God, who has given us probability, and not demonstration, for the principle of our ordinary guidance; and that He may be therefore well disposed to proceed under a similar dispensation, with regard to the next world, trying thereby who is the "wise servant"—who is reasonable in his demands for evidence, for such He rejects not; and who is presumptuous, for such He still further hardens;—saying to the one with complacency and satisfaction, "Because I said unto thee, I saw thee under the fig-tree, believest thou? Thou shalt see greater things than these;" [John 1:50.] and to the other, in sorrow and rebuke, "Because thou hast seen me, thou hast believed; blessed are they that have not seen, and yet have believed." [John 20:29.]

VI. DAVID AND GOLIATH

It is most satisfactory to find, as the history of the Israelites unfolds itself, the same indications of truth and accuracy still continuing to present themselves—the same signatures (as it were) of a subscribing witness of credit, impressed on every sheet as we turn it over in its order. The glory of Israel is now brought before us: David comes upon the scene, destined to fill the most conspicuous place in the annals of his country, and furnishing, in the details of his long and eventful life, a series of arguments such as we are in search of, decisive, I think, of the reality of his story, and of the fidelity with which it is told. With these I shall be now for some time engaged.

The circumstances under which he first appears before us are such as give token at once of his intrepid character and trust in God. "And there went out a champion" (so we read in the seventeenth chapter of the First Book of Samuel), "out of the camp of the Philistines, Goliath of *Gath*, whose height was six cubits and a span." The point upon which the argument for the veracity of the history which ensues will turn is the incidental mention here made of *Gath*, as the city of Goliath, a patronymic which might have been thought of very little importance, either in its insertion or omission; here, however, it stands. Goliath of *Gath* was David's gigantic antagonist. Now let us mark the value of this casual designation of the formidable Philistine. The report of the spies whom Moses sent into

Canaan, as given in the thirteenth chapter of the Book of Numbers, was as follows:—"The land through which we have gone to search it, is a land that eateth up the inhabitants thereof; and all the people that we saw in it were men of a *great stature*. And there we saw the *giants*, the sons of *Anak*, which came of the giants. And we were in our own sight as grasshoppers, and so we were in their sight." [Num. 13:32, 33.] Moses is here a testimony unto us, that these Anakims were a race of extra-ordinary stature. This fact let us bear in mind, and now turn to the Book of Joshua. There it is recorded amongst the feats of arms of that valiant leader of Israel, whereby he achieved the conquest of Canaan, that "He cut off the *Anakims* from the mountains, from Hebron, from Debir, from Anab, and from the mountains of Judah, and from all the mountains of Israel: Joshua destroyed them utterly with their cities. There was none of the Anakims left in the land of the children of Israel, only" (observe the exception) "in Gaza, in *Gath*, and in Ashdod, there remained." [Josh. 11:21, 22.] Here, in his turn, comes in Joshua as a witness, that when he put the Anakims to the sword, he left some remaining in three cities, and in no others; and one of these three cities was *Gath*. Accordingly, when in the Book of Samuel we find Gath most incidentally named as the country of Goliath, the fact squares very singularly with those two other independent facts, brought together from two independent authorities—the Books of Moses and Joshua—the one, that the Anakims were persons of gigantic size; the other, that some of this nearly exterminated race, who survived the sword of Joshua, did actually continue to dwell at *Gath*. Thus in the mouth of three witnesses—Moses, Joshua, and Samuel, is the word established: concurring as they do, in a manner the most artless and satisfactory, to confirm one particular at least in this singular exploit of David. One particular, and that a hinge upon which the whole moves, is discovered to be matter of fact beyond all question; and therefore, in the absence of all evidence whatever to the contrary, I am disposed to believe the other particulars of the same history to be matter of fact too. Yet there are many, I will not say miraculous, but certainly most providential circumstances involved in it; circumstances arguing, and meant to argue, the invisible hand by which David fought and Goliath fell. The stripling from the sheepfold withstanding the man of war from his youth—the ruddy boy, his carriage and his cheeses left for the moment, hearing and rejoicing both to hear and accept the challenge, which struck terror into the veterans of Israel—the shepherd's bag, with five smooth stones, and no more (such assurance did he feel of speedy success), opposed to the helmet of brass, and the coat of brazen mail, and the greaves of brass, and the gorget of brass, and the shield borne before him, and the spear with the staff like a weaver's beam—the first sling of a pebble, the signal of panic and over-throw to the whole host of the Philistines—all this claims the character of more than an ordinary event, and asserts (as David declared it to do), that "The Lord saveth not with sword and spear; but that the battle is the Lord's, and that he gave it into Israel's hands." [1 Sam. 17:47.]

VII. DAVID'S PARENTS TAKEN TO MOAB

I proceed with the exploits of David: for though the coincidences them-selves are distinct, they make up a story which is almost continuous. David, we are told, had now won the hearts of all Israel. The daughters of the land sung his praises in the dance, and their words awoke the jealousy of Saul. "Saul had slain his thousands—David his ten thousands." Accordingly the King, forgetful of his obligations to the gallant deliverer of his country from the yoke of the Philistines, and regardless of the claims of the husband of his daughter, sought his life. Twice he attacked him with a javelin as he played before him in his chamber: he laid an ambuscade about his house: he pursued him with bands of armed men as he fled for his life amongst the mountains. David, however, had less fear for himself than for his kindred—for himself he could provide—his conscience was clear, his courage good, the hearts of his countrymen were with him, and God was on his side. But his name might bring evil on his house, and the safety of his *parents* was his first care. How, then, did he secure it? "And David," we read, "went thence to Mizpeh of *Moab*, and he said unto the king of *Moab*, Let my father and my mother, I pray thee, come forth, and be with you till I know what God will do for me. And he brought them before the king of Moab; and they dwelt with him all the time that David continued in the hold." [1 Sam. 22:3, 4.]

Now why should David be disposed to trust his father and mother to the protection of the Moabites above all others? Saul, it is true, had been at war with them [1 Sam. 14:47.] , whatever he might then be,—but so had he been with every people round about; with the Ammonites, with the Edomites, with the kings of Zobah. Neither did it follow that the enemies of Saul, as a matter of course, would be the friends of David. On the contrary, he was only regarded by the ancient inhabitants of the land, to whichever of the local nations they belonged, as the champion of Israel; and with such suspicion was he received amongst them, not-withstanding Saul's known enmity towards him, that before Achish, king of Gath, he was constrained to feign himself mad, and so effect his escape. And though he afterwards succeeded in removing the scruples of that prince, and obtained his confidence, and dwelt in his land, yet the princes of the Philistines, in general, continued to put no trust in him; and when it was proposed by Achish, that he, with his men, should go up with the armies of the Philistines against Israel,—and when he had actually joined,—"the princes of the Philistines said unto him, Make this fellow return, that he may go to the place which thou hast appointed him; and let him not go down with us to battle, lest in the battle he be an adversary to us: for wherewith should he reconcile himself unto his master? should it not be with the heads of these men? [1 Sam. 29:4.]

Whether, indeed, the Moabites proved themselves to be less suspicious of David than these, his other idolatrous neighbours, does not appear; nor whether their subsequent conduct warranted the trust which he was now compelled to repose in them. Tradition says, that they betrayed it, and slew his parents; and certain it is, that David, some twenty years afterwards, proceeded against them with signal severity; for "he smote Moab, and measured them with a line, casting them down to the ground; even with two lines measured he to put to death, and with one full line to keep alive." [2 Sam. 8:2.] Something, therefore, had occurred in the interval to excite his heavy displeasure against them: and if the punishment seems to have tarried too long to be consistent with so remote a cause of offence, it must be remembered that for fourteen of those years the throne of David was not established amongst the Ten Tribes; and that, amidst the domestic disorders of a new reign, leisure and opportunity for taking earlier vengeance upon this neighbouring kingdom might well be wanting. But however this might be, in Moab David sought sanctuary for his father and mother; perilous this decision might be—probably it turned out so in fact—but he was in a great strait, and thought that, in a choice of evils, this was the least.

Now what principle of preference may be imagined to have governed David when he committed his family to the dangerous keeping of the Moabites? Was it a mere matter of chance? It might seem so, as far as appears to the contrary in David's history, given in the Books of Samuel; and if the Book of Ruth had never come down to us, to accident it probably would have been ascribed. But this short and beautiful historical document shows us a *propriety* in the selection of Moab above any other for a place of refuge to the father and mother of David; since it is there seen that the grandmother of Jesse, David's father, was actually a *Moabitess;* Ruth being the mother of Obed, and Obed the father of Jesse [Ruth 4:17.] . And, moreover, that Orpah, the other Moabitess, who married Mahlon at the time when Ruth married Chilon his brother, remained behind in Moab after the departure of Naomi and Ruth, and remained behind with a strong feeling of affection, nevertheless, for the family and kindred of her deceased husband, taking leave of them with tears [Ruth 1:14.] . She herself then, or, at all events, her descendants and friends, might still be alive. Some regard for the posterity of Ruth, David would persuade himself, might still survive amongst them. An interval of fifty years, for it probably was not more, was not likely, he might think, to have worn out the memory and the feelings of the relationship, in a country, and at a period, which acknowledged the ties of family to be long and strong, and the blood to be the life thereof.

Thus do we detect, not without some pains, a certain fitness in the conduct of David in this transaction, which marks it to be a real one. The forger of a story could not have fallen upon the happy device of sheltering Jesse in Moab, simply on the recollection of his Moabitish extraction two generations earlier; or, having fallen upon it, it is probable he would have taken care to draw the attention of his readers towards his device by some means or other, lest the evidence it was intended to afford of the truth of the history might be thrown away upon them. As it is, the circumstance itself is asserted without the smallest attempt to explain or account for it. Nay, recourse must be had to another book of Scripture, in order that the coincidence may be seen.

VIII. DAVID AND MICHAL

Events roll on, and another incident in the life of David now offers itself, which also argues the truth of what we read concerning him. "And Michal, Saul's daughter, loved David," we are told [1 Sam. 18:20.] . On becoming his wife, she gave further proof of her affection for him, by risking the vengeance of Saul her father, when she let David through the window that he might escape, and made an image and put it in the bed, to deceive Saul's messengers [1 Sam. 19:12.] After this, untoward circumstances produced a temporary separation of David and Michal. She remains in her father's custody,—and Saul, who was the tyrant of his family, as well as of his people, gives her "unto Phaltiel, the son of Laish," to wife. Meanwhile David, in his turn, takes Abigail the widow of Nabal, and Ahinoam of Jezreel, to be his wives; and continues the fugitive life he had been so long constrained to adopt for his safety. Years pass away, and with them a multitude of transactions foreign to the subject I have now before me. Saul, however, is slain; but a formidable faction of his friends, and the friends of his house, still survives. Abner, the late monarch's captain, and Ishbosheth, his son and successor in the kingdom of Israel, put themselves at its head.

But David waxing stronger every day, and a feud having sprung up between the prince and this his officer, overtures of submission are made and accepted, of which the following is the substance:—"And Abner sent messengers to David on his behalf, saying, Whose is the land? saying, also, Make thy league with me, and, behold, my hand shall be with thee to bring about all Israel unto thee. And he said, Well, I will make a league with thee; but one thing I require of thee—that is, Thou shalt not see my face, except thou first bring Michal, Saul's daughter, when thou comest to see my face. And David sent messengers to Ish-bosheth, Saul's son, saying, Deliver me my wife Michal, whom I espoused to me. And Ish-bosheth sent and took her from her husband, even from Phaltiel the son of Laish. And her husband went with her along, *weeping behind her to Bahurim.* Then said Abner unto him, Go, return; and he returned." [2 Sam. 3:12–16.] It is probable, therefore, that Michal and Phaltiel parted very reluctantly. She had evidently gained his affections; he, most likely, had won hers: and in the meantime she had been supplanted (so at least she might think), in David's house and heart, by Abigail and Ahinoam. These were not propitious circumstances, under which to return to the husband of her youth. The effect, indeed, they were likely to have upon her conduct is not even hinted at in the remotest degree in the narrative; but they supply us, however, incidentally with the link that couples Michal in her first character, with Michal in her second and later character; for the difference between them is marked, though it might escape us on a superficial glance; and if our attention did not happen to be arrested by the events of the interval, it would almost infallibly escape us. The last act then, in which we left Michal engaged, was one of loyal attachment to David—saving his life, probably at great risk of her own; for Saul had actually attempted to put Jonathan his son to death for David's sake, and why should he spare Michal his daughter [1 Sam. 20:33.] ? Her subsequent marriage with Phaltiel was Saul's business; it might, or might not, be with her consent: an act of conjugal devotion to David was the last scene in which she was, to our knowledge, a voluntary actor. Now let us mark the next—not the next event recorded in order, for we lose sight of Michal for a season,—but the next in which she is a party concerned; at the same time remembering that the Books of Samuel do not offer the slightest explanation of the contrast which her former and latter self present, or the least allusion to the change. David brings the Ark from Kirjath-jearim, where it had been abiding since it was recovered from the Philistines, to his own city. He dances before it, girded with the priestly or prophetical vest, the linen ephod, and probably chanting his own noble hymn, "Lift up your heads, O ye gates! and be ye lift up, ye everlasting doors, and the King of Glory shall come in!" [Psalm

24:7.] Michal, in that hour, no doubt felt and reflected the joy of her husband! She had shared with him the day of adversity—she was now called to be partaker of his triumph! How read we? The reverse of all this. "Then did Michal, Saul's daughter, look through a window, and saw king David leaping and dancing before the Lord, and *she despised him in her heart.*" [2 Sam. 6:16.] Nor did she confine herself to contemptuous silence: for when he had now set up the Ark in the midst of the tabernacle, and had blessed the people, he came unto his own household, prepared, in the joy and devotion of the moment, to bless that also. How then is he received by the wife whom he had twice won at the hazard of his own life, and who had in return shown herself heretofore ready to sacrifice her own safety for his preservation? Thus it was. "Michal came out to meet him, and said, How glorious is the king of Israel to-day in the eyes of the *handmaids* of his servants!—as one of the vain fellows shamelessly uncovereth himself." Here was a burst of ill temper, which rather made an occasion for showing itself, than sought one. Accordingly, David replies with spirit, and with a righteous zeal for the honour of God—not without an allusion (as I think) to the secret, but true cause of this splenetic attack,—"It was before the Lord, which chose me before thy father, and before all his house, to appoint me ruler over the people of the Lord, over Israel: therefore will I play before the Lord. And I will yet be more vile than this, and will be base in mine own sight; and of the *maid-servants which thou hast spoken of, of them shall I be had in honour.*" [2 Sam. 6:21, 22.] In these *handmaids* or *maid-servants*, which are so prominently set forth, I recognise, if I mistake not, Abigail and Ahinoam, the rivals of Michal; and the very pointed rebuke which the insinuation provokes from David, appears to me to indicate, that (whatever she might affect) he felt that the gravamen of her pretended concern for his debasement did, in truth, rest here. And may I not add, that the winding up of this singular incident, "Therefore Michal, the daughter of Saul, had no child unto the day of her death," well accords with my suspicions; and that whether it be hereby meant that God judged her, or that David divorced her, there is still something in the nature of her punishment *appropriate* to the nature of her transgression?

On the whole, Michal is now no longer what Michal was—but she is precisely what, from the new position in which she stands, we might expect her to be. Yet it is by the merest glimpses of the history of David and her own, that we are enabled to account for the change. The fact is not formally explained; it is not even formally asserted. All that appears is a marked inconsistency in the conduct of Michal, at two different points of time; and when we look about for an explanation, we perceive in the corresponding fortunes of David, as compared with her own during the interval, a very natural, though, after all, only a conjectural, explanation.

Herein, I again repeat, are the characters of truth—incidents dropping into their places without care or contrivance—the fragments of an imperfect figure recovered out of a mass of material, and found to be still its component parts, however they might not seem such when *individually* examined.

And here let me remark, (for I have been unwilling to interrupt my argument for the purpose of collateral explanation, and yet without it I may be thought to have purchased the evidence at some expense of the moral,) that the practice of polygamy, which was not from the beginning [Matt. 19:8. On this subject, see Origen, Ep. ad African. § 8.] , but which Lamech first adopted, probably in the hope of multiplying his issue, and so possessing himself of that "seed," which was now the "*desire* of the nations"—a desire which serves as a key (the only satisfactory one, I think) to much of the conduct of the Patriarchs,—the practice of polygamy, I say, thus introduced, continued, in David's time, not positively condemned; Moses having been only commissioned to regulate some of the abuses to which it led; and though his writing of divorcement must be considered as making allowance for the hardness of heart of those for whom he was legislating (our Lord himself so considers it)—a hardness of heart confirmed by a long and slavish residence in a most polluted land; still that writing, lax as it might be, was, no doubt, in itself a *restrictive* law, as matters then stood. The provisions of the Levitical code in general, and the extremely gross state of society they argue, prove that it must have been a *restrictive* law, an *improvement* upon past practices at least. And when the times of the Gospel approached, and a better dispensation began to dawn, the Almighty prepared the world, by the mouth of a Prophet, to expect those restrictions to be drawn closer—Malachi being commanded to proclaim, what had not been proclaimed before, that God "hated putting away." [Mal. 2:16.] And when at length mankind were ripe for a more wholesome decree, Christ himself pronounced it, and thenceforward "A man was to cleave unto his wife," and "they *twain* were to be one flesh," and by none were they "to be put asunder, God having joined them together." [Mark 10:7; 2 Cor. 11:2.] A *progressive* scheme this—agreeable to that general plan by which the Almighty seems to be almost always guided in his government—the development of that same principle by which the law against murder was passed for an age that was full of violence; and was afterwards sublimed into a law against malice: by which the law against adultery was provided for a carnal and grovelling generation; and was afterwards refined into a law against concupiscence: by which the law of strict retaliation, and no more, eye for eye, and tooth

for tooth—a law, low and ungenerous as it may now be thought, nevertheless in advance of the people for whom it was enacted, and better than the
law of the strongest—afterwards gave place to that other and nobler law,
"resist not evil." And it may be observed, that the very case of divorce
(and polygamy is closely connected with it) is actually in the contemplation of our Lord, when He is thus exhibiting to the Jews the more elevated
standard of Christian morals, and is ever contrasting, as He proceeds,—"It
was said by them of old time," with his own more excellent way, "but I
say unto you;" as if in times past, according to the words of the Apostle,
"God suffered nations to walk in their own ways," [Acts 14:16.] for some
wise purpose, and for a while "winked at that ignorance." [Acts 17:30.]

IX. THE ARK OF GOD AT THE HOUSE OF OBED-EDOM

But there is another circumstance connected with this removal of the
Ark of God to Jerusalem, which bespeaks, like the last, the fidelity with
which the tale is told. It was the intention of David to have conveyed this
emblem of God's presence with his people from Kirjath-jearim (from
Ephratah, where they found it in the wood [Ps. 132:6.]) at once to his
own city. An incident, however, of which I shall presently speak, occurred
to shake his purpose and change his plan. "So David," we read upon this,
"would not remove the Ark of the Lord unto him into the city of David;
but David carried it aside into the house of Obed-Edom, the *Gittite*." [2
Sam. 6:10.] Now what regulated David in choosing the house of Obed-
Edom as a resting-place for the Ark? Was it an affair of mere chance? It
might be so; no motive whatever for the selection of *his* house above that
of another man, is assigned—but this we are taught, that "when the cart
which bare the Ark came to Nachon's threshing-floor, Uzzah put forth his
hand and took hold of it, for the oxen shook it—and the anger of the Lord
was kindled against Uzzah, and God smote him there for his error, and he
died by the Ark of God." [2 Sam. 6:6.] It had been commanded, as we find
in the seventh chapter of the Book of Numbers (v. 9.), that the Ark should
be borne on the shoulders of the Levites—David, however, had placed it
in a cart, after the fashion of the Philistines' idols, and had neglected the
Levitical precept. The sudden death of Uzzah, and the nature of his
offence, alarms him, sets him to think, reminds him of his neglect, and he
turns to the house of Obed-Edom, the *Gittite*. The epithet here so incidentally annexed to the name of Obed-Edom, enables us to answer the question, wherefore David chose the house of this man, with some probability
of being right in our conjecture. For we learn from the Book of Joshua,

that *Gath* (distinguished from other towns of the same name, by the addition of Rimmon [Joshua 21:24.]) was one of the cities of the *Levites;* nor of the Levites only, but of the *Kohathites* (v. 20), the very family specially set apart from the Levites, that "they should bear the Ark upon their shoulders." [Num. 7:9.] If, therefore, Obed-Edom was called the Gittite, from *this* Gath, as he doubtless was so called from some Gath or other, then must he have been a *Levite;* and more than this, actually a *Kohathite;* so that he would be strictly in his office when keeping the Ark; and because he was so, he was selected; David causing the Ark to be "carried aside," or out of the direct road (for that is the force of the expression [See Num. 20:17, where the same Hebrew word is used, and 22:23.]), precisely for the purpose of depositing it with a man of an order, and of a peculiar division of that order, which God had chosen for his Ark-bearers. Accordingly, we read in the fifteenth chapter of the first Book of Chronicles,—where a fuller account, in some particulars, is given, than in the parallel passage of Samuel, of the final removal of the Ark from under the roof of Obed-Edom to Jerusalem,—that the profane cart was no longer employed on this occasion, but the more reverential mode of conveyance, and that which the Law enjoined, was now strictly adopted in its stead (v. 15); and, moreover, that Obed-Edom was appointed to take an active part in the ceremonial (v. 18, 24).

This I look upon as a coincidence of some value—(supposing it, of course, to be fairly made out)—of some value, I mean, even independently of its general bearing upon the credibility of Scripture; for it is a touch of truth in the circumstantial details of an event which is in its nature miraculous. This it establishes as a fact, that, for some reason or other, David went out of his way to deposit the Ark with an individual of a family whose particular province it was to serve and bear the Ark. This, I say, is established by the coincidence as a fact—and here, taking my stand with substantial ground under my feet, I can with safety, and without violence, gradually feel my way along through the inconvenience which prompted this deviation from the direct path; this change in the mode of conveyance; this sudden reverence for the laws of the Ark; even up to the disaster which befel the rash and unconsecrated Uzzah, and the caution and alarm it inspired, as being a manifest interposition of God for the vindication of his honour; and when I find the apparently trivial appellation of the *Gittite*, thus pleading for the reality of a marvellous act of the Almighty, I am reminded how carefully we should gather up every word of Scripture, that nothing be lost; and I am led to contemplate the precautions, the superstitious precautions of the Rabbins, if you will, that one jot or one tittle may not be suffered to pass from the text of the Law, not without respect, as if its every letter might contain some hidden treasure, some unsuspected fount from which virtue might happily go out for evidence, for doctrine, or for duty.

X. DAVID AND BATHSHEBA

We are now arrived at another incident in the history of David—for I must still call the attention of my readers to the memoirs of that extraordinary person, as exhibiting marks of truth and reality, numerous, perhaps, beyond those which any other character of the same antiquity presents—an incident which has been accounted, and most justly accounted, the reproach of his life. The province which I have marked out for myself in this work is the evidence for the veracity of the sacred historians, and not the interpretation of the moral difficulties which the history itself may sometimes involve. In the present instance, however, the very coincidence which establishes the trustworthiness of the history, may serve also to remove some stumbling-blocks out of the sceptic's path, and vindicate the ways of God to man.

That the man after God's own heart should have so fallen from his high estate, as to become the adulterer and the assassin, has been ever urged with great effect by unbelievers; and this very consequence of David's sin was foreseen and foretold by Nathan the prophet, when he approached the King, bearing with him the rebuke of God on his tongue, and saying, "By this deed thou hast given great occasion to the enemies of God to blaspheme." Such has indeed been its effect, from the day when it was first done unto this day, and such probably will its effect continue to be unto the end of time. David's transgression, committed almost three thousand years ago, sheds, in some sort, an evil influence on the cause of David's God, even now. So wide-wasting is the mischief which flows from the lapse of a righteous man; so great the darkness becomes, when the light that is amongst us is darkness! But was David the man after God's own heart here? It were blasphemy to suppose it. That the sin of David was fulfilling some righteous judgment of God against Uriah and his house, I doubt not—for God often makes his enemies his instruments, and without sanctifying the means, strikes out of them good. Still a sin it was, great and grievous, offensive to that God to whom the blood of Uriah cried from the ground. And this the Almighty proclaimed even more loudly, perhaps, by suffering David to live, than if, in the sudden burst of his instant displeasure, He had slain him. For, at the period when the King of Israel fell under this sad temptation, he was at the very height of his glory and his strength. The kingdom of Israel had never so flourished before; it was the first of the nations. He had thoroughly subdued the Philistines, that mighty people, who in his youth had compelled all the Israelites to come down to their quarters, even to sharpen their mattocks, so rigid was the exercise of their rule. He had smitten the Moabites, on the other side Jordan, once themselves the oppressors of Israel, making them tributaries. He had subdued the Edomites, a race that delighted in war, and had stationed his troops throughout all their territories. He had possessed himself of the independent kingdom of the Syrians, and garrisoned Damascus their capital. He had extended his frontier eastward to the Euphrates [2 Sam. 8.] , though never perhaps beyond it [See Ezra 6:20.] , and he was on the point of reducing the Ammonites, whose city, Rabbah, his generals were besieging; and thus, the whole of the Promised Land, with the exception of the small state of Tyre, which the Israelites never appear to have conquered, was now his own. Prosperity, perhaps, had blinded his eyes, and hardened his heart. The treasures which he had amassed, and the ease which he had fought for and won, had made him luxurious; for now it was, that the once innocent son of Jesse the Bethlehemite,—he who had been taken from the sheep-folds because an excellent spirit was in him, and who had hitherto prospered in all that he had set his hand unto,—it was now that that man was tempted and fell. And now mark the remainder of his days—God eventually forgave him, for he repented him (as his penitential psalms still most affectingly attest), in the bitterness and anguish of his soul; but God dried up all the sources of his earthly blessings thenceforward for ever. With this sin the sorrow of his life began, and the *curse* which the prophet denounced against him, sat heavy on his spirit to the last; a curse—and I beg attention to this—which has a peculiar reference to the nature of his crime; as though upon this offence all his future miseries and misfortunes were to turn; as though he was only spared from the avenger's violent hand to be made a spectacle of righteous suffering to the world. He had committed murder by the edge of the sword, and therefore the sword was never to depart from his house. He had despised the commandment of the Lord (so Nathan expressly says), and taken the wife of another to be his wife; therefore were his own wives to be taken from him, and given to his neighbour in turn. The *complexion*, therefore, of his remaining years, was set by this one fatal deed of darkness (let none think or say that it was lightly regarded by the Almighty), and having become the man of blood, of blood he was to drink deep; and having become the man of lust, by that same baneful passion in others was he himself to be scourged for ever. Now the manner in which these tremendous threats are fulfilled is very remarkable; for it is done by way of *natural consequence* of the sin itself; a dispensation which I have not seen developed as it deserves to be, though the facts of the history furnish very striking materials for the purpose. And herein lies the coincidence, to which the remarks I have hitherto been making are a needful prologue.

By the *rebellion of Absalom* it was that these menaces of the Almighty Judge of all the earth were accomplished with a fearful fidelity.

Absalom was able to draw after him the hearts of all the people as one man. And what was it that armed him with this moral strength? What was it that gave him the means of unseating his father in the affections of a loyal people?—the king whom they had so greatly loved—who had raised the name of Israel to a pitch of glory never attained unto before—whose praises had been sung by the mothers and maidens of Israel, as the champion to whom none other was like? How could he steal away the hearts of the people from such a man, with so little effort, and apparently with so little reason? I believe that this very sin of David was made the engine by which his throne was shaken; for I observe that the chief instrument in the conspiracy was *Ahithophel.* No sooner has Absalom determined upon his daring deed, than he looks to Ahithophel for help. He appears, for some reason or other not mentioned, to have quite reckoned upon him as well-affected to his cause, as ready to join him in it heart and hand; and he did not find himself mistaken. "Absalom," I read [2 Sam. 15:12.] , "sent for Ahithophel the Gilonite, David's counsellor, from his city, even from Giloh, while he offered sacrifices. And the conspiracy" (it is forthwith added, as though Ahithophel was a host in himself) "was strong; for the people increased continually with Absalom." David, upon this, takes alarm, and makes it the subject of his earnest prayer to God, that "he would turn the counsel of Ahithophel into foolishness." Nor is this to be wondered at, when we are told in another place that "the counsel of Ahithophel, which he counselled in those days, was as if a man had enquired at the oracle of God: so was all the counsel of Ahithophel both with David and with Absalom." [2 Sam. 16:23] He therefore was the sinews of Absalom's cause. Of his character, and the influence which he possessed over the people, Absalom availed himself, both to sink the spirits of David's party, and to inspire his own with confidence, for all men counted Ahithophel to be as a prophet. But independently of the weight of his public reputation, it is probable that certain private wrongs of his own (of which I have now to speak) at once prepared him for accepting Absalom's rebellious overtures with alacrity, and caused him to find still greater favour in the eyes of the people, as being an injured man, whom it was fit that they should avenge of his adversary. For in the twenty-third chapter of the second Book of Samuel, I find in the catalogue of David's guardsmen, thirty-seven in number, the name of "Eliam the son of *Ahithophel the Gilonite*" (v. 34). The epithet of Gilonite sufficiently identifies this Ahithophel with the conspirator of the same name. One, therefore, of the thirty-seven officers about David's person, was a son of the future conspirator against his throne. But, in this same catalogue, I also meet with the name of *Uriah the Hittite* (v. 39). Eliam, therefore, and Uriah must have been thrown much together, being both of the same rank, and being each one of the thirty-seven officers of the King's guard. Now, from the eleventh chapter of the second Book of Samuel, I learn that Uriah the Hittite had for his wife Bath-sheba, the daughter of one *Eliam* (v. 3). I look upon it, therefore, to be so probable, as almost to amount to certainty, that this was the same Eliam as before, and that Uriah (as was very natural, considering the necessary intercourse of the parties) had married the daughter of his brother officer, and accordingly the *grand-daughter of Ahithophel*. I feel that I now have the key to the conduct of this leading conspirator; the sage and prudent friend of David converted, by some means or other, into his deadly foe—for I now perceive, that when David murdered Uriah, he murdered Ahithophel's *grandson* by marriage, and when he corrupted Bath-sheba, he corrupted his *grand-daughter* by blood. Well then, after this disaster and dishonour of his house, might revenge rankle in the heart of Ahithophel! Well might Absalom know that nothing but a fit opportunity was wanted by him, that he might give it vent, and spend his treasured wrath upon the head of David his wrong-doer! Well might he approach him with confidence, and impart to him his treason, as a man who would welcome the news, and be his present and powerful fellow-worker! Well might the people, who, upon an appeal like this, seldom fail to follow the dictates of their better feelings, and to stand manfully by the injured, find their allegiance to a throne defiled with adultery and blood, relaxed, and their loyalty transferred to the rebel's side! And the terms in which Shimei reproaches the King, when he follows after him to Bahurim, *casting stones* at him, not improbably as expressive of the legal punishment of the adulterer, "Come out, come out, thou *bloody* man, and thou man of *Belial*;" [2 Sam. 16:7.] and the meekness moreover with which David bows to the reproach, accepting it as a merited chastisement from God, "So let him curse, because the *Lord hath said unto him*, Curse David" (v. 10); are minute incidents which testify to the same fact—to the popular voice now lifted up against David, and to the merited cause thereof. Well might he find his heart sink within him, when he heard that his ancient counsellor had joined the ranks of his enemies, and when he knew but too well what reason he had given him for turning his arms against himself in that unmitigated and inextinguishable thirst for vengeance which is sweet, however utterly unjustifiable, to all men so deeply injured, and sweetest of all to the children of the East! And in the very first word of exhortation which Ahithophel suggests to Absalom, I detect, or think I detect, the wounded spirit of the man seizing the earliest moment for inflicting a punishment upon his enemy, of a kind that should not only be bitter, but appropriate, the eye for the eye; and when Absalom said, "Give counsel among you what we shall do," and Ahithophel answered, "Go in unto thy father's concubines which he hath left to keep the house," [2 Sam. 16:21.] he was not only moved by the desire that the rebellious son should stand fairly committed to his rebellion by an unpardonable outrage against the majesty of an eastern monarch, but by the desire also to make David taste the bitterness of that cup which he had caused others to drink, and to receive the very measure which he had himself meted withal. And so it came to pass, that Absalom followed his counsel, and they spread for him the incestuous tent, we read, on the top of the house, in the sight of all Israel [2 Sam. 16:22.] , on that very roof, it should seem, on which David at even-tide had walked, when he conceived this his great sin, upon which his life was to turn as upon a hinge [2 Sam. 11:2.] ; and so again it came to pass, and under circumstances of local identity and exposure which wear the aspect of strictly judicial reprisals, that that which he had done secretly (his abduction of another man's wife) God did for him, and more also, as He said He would, before all Israel, and before the sun [2 Sam. 12:12.] .

Thus, having once discovered by the apposition of many passages, that a relation subsisted between Ahithophel and Uriah, a fact which the sacred historian is so far from dwelling upon, that he barely supplies us with the means to establish it at all, we see in the circumstances of the conspiracy, the *natural recoil* of David's sin; and in his punishment, retributive as it is, so strictly retributive, that it must have stricken his conscience as a judgment, even had there been no warning voice concerning it, the accomplishment, by means the most easy and unconstrained, of all that Nathan had uttered, to the syllable.

XI. DAVID AND JOAB

There is another incident connected with this part of the history of David, which I have pondered, alternately accepting and rejecting it, as still further corroborating the opinion I have expressed, that the fortunes of David turned upon this one sin—that having mounted to their high-mark, they henceforward began, and continued to ebb away—this one sin which, according to Scripture, itself eclipsed every other. For though it would not be difficult to name sundry instances of ignorance, of negligence, of inconsideration, of infirmity, in the life of David besides this, it is nevertheless said, that "he did that which was right in the eyes of the Lord, and turned not aside in anything that he commanded him all the days of his life, *save only in the matter of Uriah the Hittite.*" [1 Kings 15:5. See Sanderson, Serm. iv. ad Aulam.] I propose, however, this coincidence for the reason I have said, not without some hesitation; though at the same time, quite without concern for the safety of my cause, it being, as I observed in the beginning of this work, a very valuable property of the argument by which I am endeavouring to establish the credibility of Scripture, that any member of it, if unsound or unsatisfactory, may be detached, without further injury to the whole than the mere loss of that member entails.

This, therefore, I perceive, or think I perceive, that David became thoroughly encumbered by his connexion with *Joab, the captain of his armies;* that he was too suspicious to trust him, and too weak to dismiss him; that this officer, by some chance or other, had established a despotic control over the King; and that it is not unreasonable to believe (and here lies the coincidence), that when *David made him the partner and secret agent of his guilty purpose touching Uriah, he sold himself into his hands;* that in that fatal letter he sealed away his liberty, and surrendered it up to this his unscrupulous accomplice. Certain it is, that during all the latter years of his reign, David was little more than a nominal king.

Joab, no doubt, was by nature a man that could do and dare—a bold captain in bad times. The faction of Saul was so strong, that David could at first scarcely call the throne his own, or choose his servants according to his pleasure; and Joab, an able warrior, though sometimes avenging his own private quarrels at the expense of his sovereign's honour, and thereby vexing him at the heart, was not to be displaced; he was then too hard for David, as the King himself complains [2 Sam. 3:39.] . But as yet, David was not tongue-tied at least. He openly, and without reserve, reprobated the conduct of Joab in slaying Abner, though he had the excuse, such as it was, of taking away the life of the man by whose hand his brother Asahel had fallen. Moreover, he so far asserted his own authority, as to make him rend his clothes, and gird him with sackcloth, and mourn before this very Abner, whom he had thus vindictively laid low; doubtless a bitter and mortifying penance to a man of the stout heart of Joab, and such as argued David, who insisted upon it, to be as yet in his own dominions supreme. Circumstances might constrain him still to employ this famous captain, but he had not at least (young as his authority then was) yielded himself up to his imperious subject. On the contrary, waxing stronger, as he did every day, and the remnant of Saul's party dispersed, he became the king of Israel in fact, as well as in name; his throne established not only upon law, but upon public opinion too, so that "whatsoever the king did," we are told, "pleased all the people." [2 Sam. 3:36.] He was now in a condition to rule for himself, and for himself he did rule (whatever had become of Joab in the mean season); for we presently find him appointing that officer to the command of his army by his own act and deed, simply because he happened to be the man to win that rank when it was proposed by David as the prize of battle to any individual of his whole host, who should first get up the gutter and smite the Jebusites at the storming of Zion [2 Sam. 5:8; 1 Chron. 11:6.] . And whoever will peruse the eighth and tenth chapters of the second Book of Samuel, in which are recorded the noble achievements of David at this bright period of his life, his power abroad and his policy at home, the energy which he threw into the national character, and the respect which he commanded for it throughout all the East, will perceive that he reigned without a restraint and without a rival. Now comes the guilty act; the fatal stumbling-block against which he dashed his foot, and fell so pernicious a height. And hence-forwards I see, or imagine I see, Joab usurping by degrees an authority which he had not before; taking upon himself too much; executing or disregarding David's orders, as it suited his own convenience; and finally conspiring against his throne and the rightful succession of his line. Again, I perceive, if I mistake not, the hands of David tied, his efforts to disembarrass himself of his oppressor feeble and ineffectual: his resentment set at nought; his punishments, though just, resisted by his own subject, and successfully resisted. For I find Joab suggesting to David the recall of Absalom after his banishment, through the widow of Tekoah, in a manner to excite the suspicion of the King [2 Sam. 14:19.] . "Is not the hand of Joab with thee in all this?" were words in which probably more was meant than met the ear. It is not unlikely (though the passage is altogether mysterious and obscure) that there was then some secret understanding between the soldier and the future rebel, which was only interrupted by the impetuosity of Absalom, who resented Joab's delay, and set fire to his barley [2 Sam. 14:30.] ; an injury which he must have had some reason to feel Joab durst not resent, and which, in fact, even in spite of the fury of his natural character, he did not resent. Howbeit, he remembered it in the rebellion which now broke out, and took his personal revenge whilst he was professedly fighting the battle of David, to whom his interest or his passion decided him for this time to be true. "Deal gently for my sake with the young man, even with Absalom," was the parting charge which the King gave to this dangerous champion as he went forth with the host; in the hearing of all the people he gave it, and to all the captains who were with him. It was the thing nearest his heart. For here it may be observed, that David's strong *parental feelings*, of which we have many occasional glimpses, give an *identity* to his character, which, in itself, marks it to be a real one. The fear of the servants to tell him that his infant was dead [2 Sam. 12:18.] ; the advice of Jonadab, "a subtle man," who had read David's disposition right, to Amnon, to feign himself sick, that "*when his father came to see him*," he might prefer to him his request [2 Sam. 13:5.] ; his "weeping so sore" for the death of this son, and then again, his anguish subsided, "his soul longing to go forth" to the other son who had slain him [2 Sam. 13:39.] ; the little trait which escapes in the history of Adonijah's rebellion, another of his children, that "his father had not displeased him at any time, in saying, Why hast thou done so?" [1 Kings 1:6.] are all evidently features of one and the same individual. So these last instructions to his officers touching the safety of Absalom, even when he was in arms against him, are still uttered in the same spirit; a spirit which seems, even at this moment, far more engrossed with the care of his child, than with the event of his battle. "Deal gently for my sake with Absalom." Joab heard, indeed, but heeded not; he had lost all reverence for the King's commands; nothing could be more deliberate than his infraction of this one, probably the most imperative which had ever been laid upon him: it was not in the fury of the fight that he forgot the commission of mercy, and cut down the young man with whom he was importuned to deal tenderly; but as he was hanging in a tree, helpless and hopeless; himself directed to the spot by the steps of another; in cold blood; but remembering perhaps his barley, and more of which we know not, and caring nothing for a king whose *guilty secret he had shared*, he thrust him through the heart with his three darts, and then made his way, with countenance unabashed, into the chamber of his royal master, where he was weeping and mourning for Absalom. The bitterness of death must have been nothing to David, compared with the feelings of that hour when his conscience smote him (as it doubtless did) with the complicated trouble and humiliation into which his deed of lust and blood had thus sunk him down. The rebellion itself, the fruit of it (as I hold); the audacious disobedience of Joab to the moving entreaties of the parent, that his favourite son's life might be spared, rebel as he was, felt to be the fruit of that sin too; for by that sin it was that he had delivered himself and his character, bound hand and foot, to the tender mercies of Joab, who had no touch of pity in him. The sequel is of a piece with the opening; Joab imperious, and David, the once high-minded David, abject in spirit and tame to the lash. "Thou hast shamed this day the faces of all thy servants. Arise, go forth, and speak comfortably unto thy servants; for I swear by the Lord, if thou go not forth, there will not tarry one with thee this night: and that will be worse unto thee than all the evil that befell thee from thy youth until now." [2 Sam. 19:7.] The passive King yields to the menace, for what can he do? and with a cheerful countenance and a broken heart obeys the command of his subject, and sits in the gate. But this is not all. David now sends a message to Amasa, a kinsman whom Absalom had set over his rebel army; it is a proposal, perhaps a secret proposal, to make him captain over his host in the room of Joab. The measure might be dictated at once by policy, Amasa being now the leader of a powerful party whom David had to win, and by disgust at the recent perfidy of Joab, and a determination to break away from him at whatever cost. Amasa accepts the offer; but in the very first military enterprise on which he is despatched, Joab accosts him with the friendly salutation of the East, and availing himself of the unguarded moment, draws a sword from under his garment, smites him under the fifth rib, and leaves him a bloody corpse in the highway. Then he calmly takes upon himself to execute the commission with which Amasa had been charged; and this done, "he returns to Jerusalem," we read, "unto the king," and once more he is "over all the host of Israel."

It is needless to point out how extreme a helplessness on the part of David this whole transaction indicates. Here is the general of his own choice assassinated in an act of duty by his own subject, his commission usurped by the murderer, and David, once the most popular and powerful of sovereigns, saying not a word. The dishonour, indeed, he felt keenly; felt it to his dying day, and in his latest breath gave utterance to it [1 Kings 2:5.] ; but Joab has him in the toils, and extricate himself he cannot. The want of cordiality between them was now manifest enough, however the original cause might be conjectured, rather than known; and when Adonijah prepares his revolt—for another enemy now sprung up in David's own house—to Joab he makes his overtures [1 Kings 1:7.] , having observed him, no doubt, to be a thorn in the King's side; nor are the overtures rejected; and, amongst other facts developed in this second conspiracy, it incidentally appears, that the ordinary dwelling-place of Joab was "*in the wilderness;*" [1 Kings 2:34.] as if, suspicious and suspected, a house within the walls of Jerusalem was not the one in which he would venture to lay his head. It is remarkable that this formidable traitor, from whose thraldom David, in the flower of his age, and the splendour of his military renown, could never, we have seen, disengage himself, fell at once, and whilst whatever popularity he might have with

115

the army must have been fresh as ever, before the arm of Solomon, a stripling, if not a beardless boy; who, taking advantage of a fresh instance of treachery in this hardened adventurer, fearlessly gave command to "fall upon him and bury him, that he might thus take away," as he said, the innocent blood which Joab shed, from him, and from the house of his father; when he fell upon two men more righteous and better than himself, and slew them with the sword, his father David not knowing thereof; to wit, Abner, the son of Ner, captain of the host of Israel, and Amasa, the son of Jether, captain of the host of Judah [1 Kings 2:32.] . But Solomon had as yet a clear conscience, which David had forfeited with respect to Joab; this it was that armed the youth with a moral courage which his father had once known what it was to have, when he went forth as a shepherd-boy against Goliath, and which he afterwards knew what it was to want, when he crouched before Joab, as a king. So true it is, the "wicked flee when no man pursueth, but the righteous is bold as a lion."

And now can any say that God winked at this wickedness of his servant? That the man after his own heart, for such in the main he was, frail as he proved himself, sinned grievously, and sinned with impunity? On the contrary, this deed was the pivot upon which David's fortunes turned; that done, and he was undone; then did God raise up enemies against him for it out of his own house, for "the thing," as we are expressly told, "displeased the Lord;" [2 Sam. 11:27; 12:11.] thenceforward the days of his years became full of evil, and if he lived (for the Lord *caused death to pass* from himself to the child, by a vicarious dispensation [2 Sam. 12:13.] ,) it was to be a king, with more than kingly sorrows, but with little of kingly power; to be banished by his son; bearded by his servant; betrayed by his friends; deserted by his people; bereaved of his children; and to feel all, all these bitter griefs, bound, as it were, by a chain of complicated cause and effect, to this one great, original transgression. This was surely no escape from the penalty of his crime, though it was still granted him to live and breathe—God would not slay even Cain, nor suffer others to slay him, whose punishment, nevertheless, was greater than he could bear—but rather it was a lesson to him and to us, how dreadful a thing it is to tempt the Almighty to let loose his plagues upon us, and how true is He to his word, "Vengeance is mine, I will repay," saith the Lord.

Meanwhile, by means of the fall of David, however it may have caused some to blaspheme, God may have also provided, in his mercy, that many since David should stand upright; the frailty of one may have prevented the miscarriage of thousands; saints, with his example before their eyes, may have learned to walk humbly, and so to walk surely, when they might otherwise have presumed and perished; and sinners, even the men of the darkest and most deadly sins, may have been saved from utter desperation and self-abandonment, by remembering David and all his trouble; and that, deep as he was in guilt, he was not so deep but that his bitter cries for mercy, under the remorse and anguish of his spirit, could even yet pierce the ear of an offended God, and move Him to put away his sin.

XII. DAVID AND THE BATTLE IN THE WOOD OF EPHRAIM

My subject has compelled me to anticipate some of the events of David's history according to the order of time. I must now, therefore, revert to certain incidents in it, which it would before have interrupted my argument to notice, but which are too important, as evidences of its credibility, to be altogether overlooked.

The conspiracy of Absalom being now organized, it only remained to try the issue by force of arms; and here another coincidence presents itself.

In the seventeenth chapter of the second Book of Samuel, we read that "David arose, and all the people that were with him, and they passed over Jordan" (v. 22); and in the same chapter, that "Absalom passed over Jordan, he and all the men of Israel with him" (v. 24); and that "they pitched in the land of Gilead" (26). Now in the next chapter, where an account is given of a review of David's troops, and of their going forth to the fight, it is said, "So the people went out into the field against Israel, and the battle was in the *wood of Ephraim*." [2 Sam. 18:6.] But is not the sacred historian, in this instance, off his guard, and having already placed his combatants on one side the river, does he not now place his combat on the other? Is he not mistaken in his geography, and does he not thereby betray himself and the credit of his narrative? Certain it is, that Absalom had passed over Jordan eastward, and so had David, with their respective followers, pitching in Gilead; and no less certain it is, that the tribe of *Ephraim* lay altogether west of Jordan, and had not a foot of ground beyond it: how then was the battle in the wood of *Ephraim?* By any fabulous writer this seeming difficulty would have been avoided, or care would have been taken that, at least, it should be explained. But the Book of Samuel, written by one familiar with the events he describes, and with the scenes in which they occurred; written, moreover, in the simplicity of his heart, probably without any notion that his veracity could be called in question, or that he should ever be the subject of suspicious scrutiny, contents itself with stating the naked facts, and then leaves it to the critics to reconcile them as they can. Turn we then to the twelfth chapter of the

Book of Judges. There we are told of an attack made by the *Ephraimites* upon Jephthah, in the land of *Gilead*, on pretence of a wrong done them when they were not invited by the latter to take part in his successful invasion of Ammon. It was a memorable struggle. Jephthah indeed, endeavoured to soothe the angry assailants by words of peace, but when he spake of peace, they only made themselves ready for battle. Accordingly, "he gathered together all the men of Gilead, and fought with Ephraim." Ephraim was discomfited with signal slaughter; those who fell in the action, and those who were afterwards put to death upon the test of the word Shibboleth, amounting to forty-two thousand men; almost an extinction of all the fighting men of Ephraim. Now an event so singular, and so sanguinary, was not likely to pass away without a memorial; and what memorial so natural for the grave of a tribe, as its own name for ever assigned to the spot where it fell, the Aceldama of their race?

Thus, then, may we account most naturally for a "*wood of Ephraim*" in the land of *Gilead;* a point which would have perplexed us not a little, had the Book of Judges never come down to us, or, coming down to us, had no mention been made in it of Jephthah's victory; and though we certainly cannot *prove* that the battle of David and Absalom was fought on precisely the same field as this of Jephthah and the Ephraimites some hundred and twenty years before, yet it is highly probable that this was the case, for both the battles were assuredly in *Gilead*, and both apparently in that part of Gilead which bordered upon one of the *fords of Jordan.*

Thus does a seeming error turn out, on examination, to be an actual pledge of the good faith of the historian; and the unconcern with which he tells his own tale, in his own way, never pausing to correct, to balance, or adjust, to supply a defect, or to meet an objection, is the conduct of a witness to whom it never occurred that he had anything to conceal, or anything to fear; or, if it did occur, to whom it was well known that truth is mighty, and will prevail.

XIII. DAVID AND CHIMHAM

David having won the battle, and recovered his throne, prepares to repass the Jordan, and return once more to his capital. His friends again congregate around him, for the prosperous have many friends. Amongst them, however, were some who had been true to him in the day of his adversity; and the aged Barzillai, a Gileadite, who had provided the King with sustenance whilst he lay at Mahanaim, and when his affairs were critical, presents himself before him. He had won David's heart. The King now entreats him to accompany him to his court, "Come thou over with me, and I will feed thee with me in Jerusalem." But the unambitious Barzillai pleads fourscore years as a bar against beginning the life of a courtier, and chooses rather to die in his own city, and be buried by the grave of his father and of his mother. His son, however, had life before him: "Behold thy servant Chimham; let him go over with my lord the king; and do to him what shall seem good unto thee. And the king answered, Chimham shall go over with me, and I will do to him that which shall seem good unto thee." [2 Sam. 19:37.] So he went with the king. Thus begins, and thus ends, the history of Chimham; he passes away from the scene, and what David did for him, or whether he did anything for him, beyond providing him a place at his table, and recommending him, in common with many others, to Solomon before he died, does not appear. Singular, however, it is, and if ever there was a coincidence which carried with it the stamp of truth, it is this, that in the forty-first chapter of Jeremiah, an historical chapter, in which an account is given of the murder of Gedaliah, the officer whom Nebuchadnezzar had left in charge of Judea, as its governor, when he carried away the more wealthy of its inhabitants captive to Babylon, we read that the Jews, fearing for the consequences of this bloody act, and apprehending the vengeance of the Chaldeans, prepared for a flight into Egypt, so "they departed," the narrative continues, "and dwelt in the habitation of *Chimham*, which is by *Bethlehem*, to go to enter into Egypt" (v. 17). It is impossible to imagine anything more incidental than the mention of this estate near *Bethlehem*, which was the habitation of *Chimham*—yet how well does it tally with the spirit of David's speech to Barzillai, some four hundred years before! for what can be more probable, than that David, whose birth-place was this very *Bethlehem*, and whose patrimony in consequence lay there, having undertaken to provide for Chimham, should have bestowed it in whole, or in part, as the most flattering reward he could confer, a personal, as well as a royal, mark of favour, on the son of the man who had saved his life, and the lives of his followers in the hour of their distress; and that, to that very day, when Jeremiah wrote, it should have remained in the possession of the family of Chimham, and have been a land called after his own name?

XIV. HEBRON, THE CITY CALEB INHERITED

There is a coincidence similar to this, which might have been introduced earlier with more chronological propriety, but which I have reserved on account of its being akin to the one I have just named. In the

14th chapter of Joshua, Caleb pleads with Joshua for the fulfillment of Moses' promise to him, which had been delayed for several years, that as a reward for the encouragement he had given the Israelites to go up against the land of Canaan when they were faint-hearted and alarmed, he would assign to him an inheritance it. Accordingly "Joshua blessed him, and gave unto Caleb the son of Jephunneh Hebron for an inheritance. Hebron therefore became the inheritance of Caleb the son of Jephunneh the Kenezite, unto this day."

Now we read in the 30th chapter of the first Book of Samuel, the account of an incident which happened some four hundred years afterwards; when David, pursuing the Amalekites, who had spoiled Ziklag, and carried off the women, met, we are told, with an Egyptian who had been a servant to one of these marauders, and whom his master had left behind sick. From him David learned what the party had been about. "We made an invasion," says the man, "upon the south of the Cherethites, and upon the coast which belongeth to Judah, and," he adds, "upon the south of Caleb."

It is probable in the highest degree that the land which Joshua gave to Caleb, and which certainly lay in this quarter, for Hebron was on the side of Judah which looked towards the Amalekites, was this very district, and had retained the name of Caleb from its original possessor. Yet there is no allusion in the text to any such circumstance; or to Caleb having had any connection with this part of the country, which, but for the passage in Joshua, would have been unknown to us.

XV. DAVID AND ABIATHAR THE PRIEST

I proceed with the history of David, in which we can scarcely advance a step without having our attention drawn to some new, though perhaps subtle, incident, which marks at once the reality of the facts, and the fidelity of the record. No doubt the surface of the narrative is perfectly satisfactory; but beneath the surface, there is a certain substratum now appearing, and presently losing itself again, which is the proper field of my inquiry. Here I find the true material of which I am in search; coincidences shy and unobtrusive, not courting notice—as far from it as possible—but having chanced to attract it, sustaining not only notice, but scrutiny; such matters as might be overlooked on a cursory perusal of the text a hundred times, and which indeed would stand very little chance of any other fate than neglect, unless the mind of the reader had been previously put upon challenging them as they pass. Therefore it is that I feel often incapable of doing justice to my subject with my readers, however familiar they may be with Holy Writ. The full force of the argument can only be felt by him who pursues it for himself, when he is in his chamber and is still; his assent taken captive before he is aware of it; his doubts, if any he had, melting away under the *continual dropping* of minute particles of evidence upon his mind, as it proceeds in its investigation. It is difficult, it is scarcely possible, to impart this sympathy to the reader. And even when I can grasp an incident sufficiently substantial to detach and present to his consideration, I still am conscious that it is not *launched* to advantage; that a thousand little preparations are lacking in order that it may leave the slips (if I may venture upon the expression) with a motion that shall make it win its way; that the plunge with which I am compelled to let it fall, provokes a resistance to which it does not deserve to be exposed. I proceed, however, with the history of David, and to a passage in it which has partly suggested these remarks. When Saul in his fury had slain, by the hand of Doeg, Ahimelech the high-priest, and all the priests of the Lord, "one of the sons of Ahimelech," we read, "named Abiathar, escaped, and fled after David." [1 Sam. 22:20.] David received him kindly, saying unto him, "Abide thou with me, fear not; for he that seeketh my life seeketh thy life; but with me thou shalt be in safeguard." Abiathar had brought with him the ephod, the high-priest's mysterious scarf; and his father being dead, he appears to have been made high-priest in his stead, so far as David had it then in his power to give him that office, and to have attended upon him and his followers [1 Sam. 30:7.] . These particulars we gather from several passages of the first Book of Samuel.

We hear now nothing more of Abiathar (except that he was confirmed in his office, together with a colleague, when David was established in his kingdom) for nearly thirty years. Then he re-appears, having to play not an inconspicuous part in David's councils, on occasion of the rebellion of Absalom. Now here we find, that though he is still in his office of priest, Zadok (the colleague to whom I alluded) appears to have obtained the first place in the confidence and consideration of David. When David sends the Ark back, which he probably thought it irreverent to make the partner of his flight, and delivers his commands to this effect, it may be remarked that he does not address himself to Abiathar, though Abiathar was there, but to *Zadok*—Zadok takes the lead in everything. The king says to *Zadok*, "Carry back the Ark of God into the city:" [2 Sam 15:25.] —and again, "The king said also unto *Zadok* the priest, Art not thou a seer? return into the city in peace;" and when Zadok and Abiathar are mentioned together at this period, Zadok is placed foremost. No doubt Abiathar was honoured by David; there is evidence enough of this (v. 35); but many trifles lead us to conclude that herein he attained not unto his companion.

Now, unquestionably, it cannot be asserted with confidence, where there is no positive document to substantiate the assertion, that Abiathar felt his associate in the priesthood to be his rival in the state, his more than successful rival; yet that such a feeling should find a place in the breast of Abiathar seems most natural, seems almost inevitable, when we take into account that these two priests were the representatives of two *rival houses*, over one of which, a prophecy affecting its honour, and well nigh its existence, was hanging unfulfilled. For Zadok, be it observed, was descended from Eleazar, the eldest of the sons of Aaron; Abiathar from Ithamar, the youngest [1 Chron. 24:3.] , and so from the family of Eli, a family of which it had been foretold, some hundred and fifty years before, that the priesthood should pass from it, Could Abiathar read the signs of his time without alarm? or fail to suspect (what did prove the fact) that the curse which had tarried so long, was now again in motion, and that the ancient office of his fathers was in jeopardy; a curse, too, comprising circumstances of signal humiliation, calculated beyond measure to exasperate the sufferer; even that the house of Eli, which God had once said should walk before Him for ever, should be far from Him; even that He would raise up (that is from another house) a faithful priest that should do according to that which was in his heart and his mind: and that the house of that man should be sure built; and that they of the house of Eli which were left, "should come and crouch to him for a piece of silver and a morsel of bread, and say, Put me, I pray thee, into one of the priests' offices, that I may eat a piece of bread?" [1 Sam. 2:36.] Abiathar must have had a tamer spirit than he gave subsequent proof of, if he could have witnessed the elevation of one in whom this bitter threat seemed advancing to its accomplishment, and in whom it was in fact accomplished, with complacency; if he could see him seated by his side in the dignity of the high-priesthood, and favoured at his expense by the more frequent smiles of his sovereign, without a wounded spirit.

Now having possessed ourselves of this secret key, namely *jealousy of his rival*, a key not delivered into our hands directly by the historian, but accidentally found by ourselves (and here is its value), let us apply it to the incidents of Abiathar's subsequent conduct, and observe whether they will not answer to it. We have seen Abiathar flying from the vengeance of Saul to David; protected by David in the wilderness; made by David his priest, virtually before Saul's death [1 Sam. 23:2–6.] , and formally, when he succeeded to Saul's throne [2 Sam. 8:17.] . We have seen, too, Zadok united with him in his office, and David giving signs of preferring Zadok before him; a preference the more marked, and the more galling, because Abiathar was undoubtedly the *high-priest* (as the sequel will prove), and Zadok his *vicar* only, or sagan [See Lightfoot's Works, Vol. i. 911, 912, fol.] .

This being the state of things, let us now observe the issue. When David was forced to withdraw for a season from Jerusalem, by the conspiracy of Absalom, Zadok and Abiathar were left behind in the capital, charged with the office of forwarding to the King any intelligence which his friends within the walls might communicate to them, that it was for his advantage to know. Ahimaaz, the son of Zadok, and Jonathan, the son of Abiathar (the sons are named after the same order as their fathers), are the secret messengers by whom it is to be conveyed; and on one occasion, the only one in which their services are recorded, we find them acting together [2 Sam. 17:21.] . But I observe that after the battle in which Absalom was slain, a battle which seems to have served as a test of the real loyalty of many of David's nominal friends, Ahimaaz, the son of *Zadok*, and not Jonathan, the son of Abiathar, is at hand to carry the tidings of the victory to David, who had tarried behind at Mahanaim; and this office he solicits from Joab, who had intended it for another, with the utmost importunity, and the most lively zeal for the King's cause [2 Sam. 18:19–22.] . This, it will be said, proves but little; more especially as there is reason to believe that David was, at least, upon terms with Abiathar at a later period than this [2 Sam. 19:11.] . Still there may be thought something suspicious in the absence of the one messenger, at a moment so critical, as compared with the alacrity of the other, their office having been hitherto a joint one; it is not enough to *prove* that the loyalty of Abiathar and his house was waxing cool, though it accords with such a supposition. Let us, however, proceed. Within a few years of this time, probably about eight, another rebellion against David is set on foot by another of his sons. Adonijah is now the offender. He, too, prepares him chariots and horsemen, after the example of his brother. Moreover, he feels his way before he openly appears in arms. And to whom does he make his first overtures? "He confers," we read, "with *Abiathar* the priest," [1 Kings 1:7.] having good reason, no doubt, for knowing that such an application might be made in that quarter with safety, if not with success. The event proved that he had not mistaken his man. "Abiathar," we learn, "*following Adonijah, helped him:*" not so Zadok; he, we are told, "*was not with Adonijah;*" on the contrary, he was one of the first persons for whom David sent, that he might communicate with him in this emergency; his staunch and steadfast friend; and him he commissioned, together with Nathan the prophet, to set the crown upon the head of Solomon, and thereby to confound the councils of the rebels [1 Kings 1:32. 34.] . Nor should we leave unnoticed, for they are facts which coincide with the view I have taken of Abiathar's loyalty, and the cause of it, that one of the first acts of Solomon's reign was to banish the traitor "to his own fields," and to thrust him out of the priesthood, "that he might fulfil" (so it is expressly said in the twenty-seventh verse of the second chapter of the first Book of Kings) "the word of the Lord, which he spake concerning the house of Eli in Shiloh,"— fulfil it, not by that act only, but by the other also, which followed and crowned the prophecy; for "Zadok the priest," it is added, "did Solomon put in *the room of Abiathar;*" [1 Kings 2:35,] or, as the Septuagint translates it still more to our purpose, Zadok the priest did the King make *first priest* in the room of Abiathar; so that Abiathar, as I said, had been hitherto Zadok's superior; his superior in office, and his inferior in honour; a position of all others calculated to excite in him the heart-burnings we have discovered, long smothered, but at last bursting forth—beginning in lukewarmness, and ending in rebellion.

This is all extremely natural; nothing can drop into its place better than the several parts of this history; not at all a prominent history, but rather a subordinate one. Yet manifest as the relation which they bear to one another, is, when they are once brought together, they are themselves dispersed through the Books of Samuel, of Kings, and of Chronicles, without the smallest arrangement or reference one to another; their succession not continuous; suspended by many and long intervals; intervals occupied by matters altogether foreign from this subject; and after all, the integral portions of the narrative themselves defective: there are gaps even here, which I think, indeed, may be filled up, as I have shown, with very little chance of error; but still, that there should be any necessity even for this, argues the absence of all design, collusion, and contrivance in the historians.

XVI. DAVID AND MEPHIBOSHETH

We have now followed David through the events of his chequered life; it remains to contemplate him yet once more upon his death-bed, giving in charge the execution of his last wishes to Solomon his son. Probably in consideration of his youth, his inexperience, and the difficulties of his position, David thought it well to put him in possession of the characters of some of those with whom he would have to deal; of those whom he had found faithful or faithless to himself; that, on the one hand, his own promises of favour might not be forfeited, nor, on the other, the confidence of the young monarch be misplaced. Now it is remarkable, that in this review of his friends and foes, David altogether overlooks Mephibosheth, the son of Jonathan. Joab he remembers, and all that he had done; Shimei he speaks of at some length, and puts Solomon upon his guard against him. The sons of Barzillai, and the service they had rendered him in the day of his adversity, are all recommended to his friendly consideration; but of Mephibosheth, who had played a part, such as it was, in the scenes of those eventful times, which had called forth, for good or evil, a Chimham, a Barzillai, a Shimei, and a Joab, he does not say a syllable. Yet he was under peculiar obligations to him. He had loved his father Jonathan. He had promised to show kindness to his house for ever. He had confirmed his promise by an oath. That oath he had repeated [1 Sam. 20:17.] . On his accession to the throne he had evinced no disposition to shrink from it; on the contrary, he had studiously inquired after the family of Jonathan, and having found Mephibosheth, he gave him a place at his own table continually, for his father's sake, and secured to him all the lands of Saul [2 Sam. 9:6, 7.] .

Let us, however, carefully examine the details of the history, and I think we shall be able to account satisfactorily enough for David's apparent neglect of the son of his friend; for I think we shall find violent cause to suspect that Mephibosheth had forfeited all claims to his kindness.

When David was driven from Jerusalem by the rebellion of Absalom, no Mephibosheth appeared to share with him his misfortunes, or to support him by his name, a name at that moment of peculiar value to David, for Mephibosheth was the representative of the house of Saul. David naturally intimates some surprise at his absence; and when his servant Ziba appears, bringing with him a small present of bread and fruits (the line of the king's flight having apparently carried him near the lands of Mephibosheth), a present, however, offered on his own part, and not on the part of his master, David puts to him several questions, expressive of his suspicions of Mephibosheth's loyalty: "What meanest thou by these? Where is thy master's son?" [2 Sam. 9:6, 7.] Ziba replies in substance, that he had tarried at Jerusalem, waiting the event of the rebellion, and hoping that it might lead to the re-establishment of Saul's family on the throne. This might be true, or it might be false. The commentators appear to take for granted that it was a mere slander of Ziba, invented for the purpose of supplanting Mephibosheth in his possessions. I do not think this so certain. Ziba, I suspect, had some reason in what he said, though probably the colouring of the picture was his own. Certain it is, or all but certain, that the tribe of *Benjamin*, which was the tribe of

Mephibosheth, did, in general, take part with the rebels. When David returned victorious, and Shimei hastened to make his peace with him, a thousand men of Benjamin accompanied him; and it was his boast that he came the first of "all the house of Joseph" to meet the King [2 Sam. 19:17–20.] , as though others of his tribe (for they of Benjamin were reckoned of the house of Joseph, the same mother having given birth to both) were yet behind. Went not then the heart of Mephibosheth in the day of battle with his brethren, rather than with his benefactor? David himself evidently believed the report of Ziba, and forthwith gave him his master's inheritance [2 Sam. 16:4.] . The battle is now fought, on which the fate of the throne hung in suspense, and David is the conqueror. And now, many who had forsaken, or insulted him in his distress, hasten to congratulate him on his triumph, and to profess their joy at his return; Mephibosheth amongst the rest. There is something touching in David's first greeting of him; "Wherefore wentest thou not with me, Mephibosheth?" A question not of curiosity, but of reproach. His ass was saddled, forsooth, that he might go, but Ziba, it seems, had taken it for himself, and gone unto the King, and slandered him unto the King; and meanwhile, "thy servant was lame." The tale appears to be as lame as the tale-bearer. I think it clear that Mephibosheth did not succeed in removing the suspicion of his disloyalty from David's mind, notwithstanding the ostentatious display of his clothes unwashed and beard untrimmed; weeds which the loss of his estate might very well have taught him to put on: for otherwise, would not David, in common justice both to Mephibosheth and to Ziba, have punished the treachery of the latter—the lie by which he had imposed upon the King to his own profit, and to his master's infinite dishonour and damage, by revoking altogether the grant of the lands which he had made him, under an impression which proved to be a mistake, and restoring them to their rightful owner, who had been injuriously supposed to have forfeited them by treason to the crown? He does, however, no such thing. To Mephibosheth, indeed, he gives back half, but that is all; and he leaves the other half still in the possession of Ziba; doing even thus much, in all probability, not as an act of justice, but out of tenderness to a son, even an unworthy son of Jonathan, whom he had loved as his own soul. And then, as if impatient of the wearisome exculpations of an ungrateful man, whose excuses were his accusations, he abruptly puts an end to the parley (the conversation having been apparently much longer than is recorded), with a *"Why speakest thou any more of thy, matters? I have said, Thou and Ziba divide the land."* [2 Sam. 19:29.]

Henceforward, whatever act of grace he received at David's hands was purely gratuitous. His unfaithfulness had released the King from his bond;

and that he lived, was perhaps rather of sufferance, than of right; a consideration which serves to explain David's conduct towards him, as it is reported on an occasion subsequent to the rebellion. For when propitiation was to be made by seven of Saul's sons, for the sin of Saul in the slaughter of the Gibeonites, "the king," we read, "spared Mephibosheth, the son of Jonathan, the son of Saul, *because of the Lord's oath* that was between them, between David and Jonathan the son of Saul;" [2 Sam. 21:7.] as though he owed it to the oath only, and to the memory of his father's virtues, that he was not selected by David as one of the victims of that bloody sacrifice.

Now, under these circumstances, is it a subject for surprise, is it not rather a most natural and veracious coincidence, that David, in commending on his deathbed some of his stanch and trustworthy friends to Solomon his son, should have omitted all mention of Mephibosheth, dissatisfied as he was, and ever had been, with his explanations of very suspicious conduct, at a very critical hour? considering him, with every appearance of reason, a waiter upon Providence, as such persons have been since called—a prudent man, who would see which way the battle went, before he made up his mind to which side he belonged? This coincidence is important, not merely as carrying with it evidence of a true story in all its details, which is my business with it; but also as disembarrassing the incident itself of several serious difficulties which present themselves, on the ordinary supposition of Ziba's treachery, and Mephibosheth's truth; difficulties which I cannot better explain, than by referring my hearers to the beautiful "Contemplations" of Bishop Hall, whose view of these two characters is the common one, and who consequently finds himself, in this instance (it will be perceived), encumbered with his subject, and driven to the necessity of impugning the justice of David. It is further valuable, as exonerating the King of two other charges which have been brought against him, yet more serious than the last, even of indifference to the memory of his dearest friend, and disregard to the obligations of his solemn oath. But these are not the only instances in which the character of David, and indeed of the history itself, which treats of him, has suffered from a neglect to make allowance for omissions in a very brief and desultory memoir, or from a want of more exact attention to the under-current of the narrative, which would, in itself, very often supply those omissions.

XVII. JUDAH AND EPHRAIM

The history of the people of God has thus far been brought down to the reign of Solomon, and its *general* truth and accuracy (I think I may say) established by the application of a test which could scarcely fail us. The great schism of the tribes is now about to divide our attention between the kingdoms of Israel and Judah; but before I proceed to offer some observations upon the effects of it, both religious and political, on either kingdom, observations which will involve many more of those undesigned coincidences which are the subject of these pages, I must say a word upon the progress of events towards the schism itself; for herein I discover combinations, of a kind which no ingenuity could possibly counterfeit, and to an extent which verifies a large portion of the Jewish annals. "By faith, Jacob, when he was a dying, blessed his children." On that occasion, *Judah* and *Ephraim* were made to stand conspicuous amongst the future founders of the Israelitish nation. "Judah," says the prophetic old man, "thou art he whom thy brethren shall praise: thy hand shall be on the neck of thine enemies: thy father's children shah bow down before thee. Judah is a lion's whelp: from the prey, my son, thou art gone up. He stooped down, he crouched as a lion, and as an old lion: who shall rouse him up? The sceptre shall not depart from Judah, nor a lawgiver from between his feet, till Shiloh come; and unto him shall the gathering of the people be." [Gen. 49:8.] All this, and more, did Jacob foretel of this mighty tribe. Again, crossing his hands, and studiously laying the right upon the head of *Ephraim*, the younger of Joseph's children, "Manasseh also shall be a people," he exclaimed, "and he also shall be great; but truly his *younger brother* shall be greater than he, and his seed shall become a multitude of nations. And so he blessed them that day, saying, In thee shall Israel bless, saying, God make thee as *Ephraim* and as Manasseh." [Gen. 48:20.] Thus did these two tribes, Judah and Ephraim, enter the Land of Promise some two hundred and forty years afterwards, with the Patriarch's blessing on their heads; God having conveyed it to them by his mouth, and being now about to work it out by the quiet operations of his hands. As yet, neither of them was much more powerful than his brethren, the latter less so; Judah not exceeding one other of the tribes, at least, by more than twelve thousand men, and Ephraim actually the smallest of them all, with the single exception of Simeon [Num. 26.] . The lot of Ephraim, however, fell upon a fair ground, and upon this lot, the disposing of which was of the Lord, turned very materially the fortunes of Ephraim; it fell nearly in the midst of the tribes; and accordingly, the invasion and occupation of Canaan being effected, at *Shiloh* in *Ephraim*, the Tabernacle was set up, there to abide three hundred years and upwards, *during all the time of the Judges* [Judges 21:19.] . Hither, we read, Elkanah repaired year by year for worship and sacrifice; here the lamp of God was never suffered to go out "in the Temple of the Lord," (the expression is remarkable,) "where the Ark of God was;" [1 Sam. 3:3.] here Samuel ministered as a child, all Israel, from Dan even to Beer-sheba, speedily perceiving that he was established to be a prophet, because all Israel was accustomed to resort annually to Shiloh, at the feasts [1 Sam. 3:20, 21.] . *Shiloh*, therefore, in *Ephraim*, was the great *religious capital*, as it were, from the time of Joshua to Saul, the spot more especially consecrated to the honour of God, the resting-place of his tabernacle, of his prophets, and of his priests [Psalm 132:6; 78:67; 1 Sam. 2:14.] ; whilst at no great distance from it appears to have stood *Shechem* [Judges 21:19; Josh. 24:25, 26.] , once the *political capital* of Ephraim, till civil war left it for a season in ruins, but which, even then, continued to be the gathering point of the tribes [Josh. 24:1; Judges 9:2; 1 Kings 12:1.] ; Shechem, where was Jacob's well [John 4:6.] , and where, accordingly, both literally and figuratively, was the prophecy of that Patriarch fulfilled, "Joseph is a fruitful bough, even a fruitful bough by a *well*, whose branches run over the wall." [See Lightfoot, Vol. i. 49, fol.]

Thus was this district in *Ephraim*, comprising Shiloh and Shechem, probably the most populous, certainly the most important, of any in all the Holy Land during the government of the Judges; and, constantly recruited by the confluence of strangers, Ephraim seems to have become (as Jerusalem became afterwards) what Jacob again foretold, "a multitude of nations."

There are other and more minute incidents left upon record, all tending to establish the same fact. For I observe, that amongst the Judges, many, whether themselves of Ephraim or not, do appear to have repaired paired thither as to the proper seat of government. I find that Deborah "dwelt under the palm-tree, between Ramah and Bethel, in Mount *Ephraim*," and that there the children of Israel went up to her for judgment [Judges 4:5.] . I find that Gideon, who was of Ophrah in Manasseh, where he appears in general to have lived, and where he was at last buried, had, nevertheless, a family at *Shechem* it being incidentally said, that the mother of his son Abimelech resided there, and that there Abimelech himself was born [Judges 8:27–32; 9:1.] : a trifle in itself, yet enough, I think, to suggest, that at Shechem in Ephraim, Gideon did occasionally dwell; the discharge of his judicial functions, like those of Pilate at Jerusalem, probably constraining him to a residence which he might not otherwise have chosen. I find this same Shechem the head-quarters of this same Abimelech, and the support of his cause when he usurped the government of Israel [Judges 9:22.] . And I subsequently find Tola, though a man of Issachar, dwelling in Shamir, in Mount *Ephraim* (Shechem having been recently laid waste), and judging Israel twenty and three years [Judges 10:1.] .

Nor is this all. The comparative importance of Ephraim amongst the tribes during the time of the Judges is further detected in the tone of authority, not to say menace, which it occasionally assumes towards its weaker brethren. Gideon leads several of the tribes against the Midianites, but Ephraim had not been consulted. "Why hast thou served us thus," is the angry remonstrance of the Ephraimites, "that thou calledst us not when thou wentest to fight with the Midianites? And they did chide with him harshly." [Judges 8:1.] Gideon stoops before the storm; he disputes not the vast superiority of Ephraim, his gleaning being more than another's grapes. Jephthah, in later times, ventures upon a similar invasion of the children of Ammon, and discomfits them with a great slaughter, but he, too, without Ephraim's help or cognizance: again the pride of this powerful tribe is wounded, and "they gather themselves together, and go northward, and say unto Jephthah, Wherefore passedst thou over to fight against the children of Ammon, and didst not call us to go with thee? we will burn thine house upon thee with fire." [Judges 12:1.] —All this, the unreasonable conduct of a party conscious that it has the law of the strongest on its side, and, by virtue of that law, claiming to itself the office of dictator amongst the neighbouring tribes. Well, then, might David express himself with regard to the support he expected from this tribe, in terms of more than common emphasis, when at last seated on the throne, his title acknowledged throughout Israel, he reviews the resources of his consolidated empire, and exclaims, *"Ephraim is the strength of my head."* [Psalm 60:7.] Accordingly, all the ten tribes are sometimes expressed under the comprehensive name of Ephraim [2 Chron. 25:6, 7.] ; and the gate of Jerusalem which looked towards Israel appears to have been called, emphatically, the gate of Ephraim [2 Kings 14:13.] ; and Ephraim and Judah together represent the whole of the people of Israel, from Dan to Beer-sheba [Isai. 7:9–17, *et alibi*; Ezek. 37:19.] .

In tracing the seeds of the future dissolution of the ten from the two tribes, I further remark, that whilst Samuel himself remains at Ramah, a border town of Benjamin and Ephraim (for Shiloh and Shechem were probably now in possession of the Philistines), there to sit in judgment on such causes as Ephraim and the northern states should bring before him, he sends his sons to be judges in Beer-sheba [1 Sam. 8:2.] , a southern town belonging to Judah [Josh. 15:28.] , as though there was already some reluctance between these rival tribes to resort to the same tribunal: and the fierce words that passed between the men of *Israel* and the men of *Judah*, on the subject of the restoration of David to the throne, the former claiming ten parts in him, the latter nearness of kin [2 Sam. 19:43.] , still indicate that the breach was gradually widening, and that however sudden was the final disruption of the bond of union, events had weakened it long before. Indeed, humanly speaking, nothing could in all probability have preserved it, but a continuance of the government by judges, under God; who, taken from various tribes, and according to no established order, might have secured the commonwealth from that jealousy which an hereditary possession of power by any one tribe was sure to create, and did create; and which burst out in that bitter cry of Israel, at the critical moment of the separation, "What *portion have we in David?* neither have we inheritance in the son of Jesse—to your tents, O Israel: now see to thine own house, David." [1 Kings 12:16.] And so, by the natural motions of the human heart, did God take vengeance of the people whom He had chosen, for rejecting Him for their sovereign; and a king, indeed, He gave them, as they desired, but He gave him in his wrath.

Thus have we detected, by the apposition of many distinct particulars, a *gradual tendency of the Ten Tribes to become confederate under Ephraim;* an event, to which the local position, numerical superiority, and the seat of national worship, long fixed within the borders of Ephraim, together conspired.

But meanwhile, it may be discovered in like manner, that *Judah* and *Benjamin* were also, on their part, knitting themselves in close alliance; a union promoted by contiguity; by the sympathy of being the only two royal tribes; by the connection of the house of David with the house of Saul (the political importance of which David appears to have considered, when he made it a preliminary of his league with Abner, that Michal should be restored, whose heart he had nevertheless lost [2 Sam. 3:13.]); and finally, and perhaps above all, by the peculiar position selected by the Almighty [1 Chron. 28:11.] , for the great national temple which was soon to rob Ephraim of his ancient honours [Psalm 78:67.] ; for it was not to be planted in Judah only, or in Benjamin only, but on the confines of both; so that whilst the altars, and the holy place, were to stand within the borders of the one tribe, the courts of the temple were to extend into the borders of the other tribe [Comp. Josh. 15:63, and 18:28; and see Lightfoot, Vol. i. p. 1050, fol.] , and thus, the two were to be riveted together, as it were, by a cramp, bound by a sacred and everlasting bond, being in a condition to exclaim, in a sense peculiarly their own, "The Temple of the Lord, the Temple of the Lord are we."

We have thus traced, by means of the hints with which Scripture supplies us (for little more than hints have we had), *the two great confederacies* into which the tribes were gradually, perhaps unwittingly, subsiding; as well as some of the circumstances by which either confederacy was cemented. Let us pursue the subject, but still by means of the under-current of the history only, towards the schism.

And now Ephraim was called upon to witness preparations for the transfer of the seat of national worship from himself to his great rival, with something, we may believe, of the anguish of Phinehas' wife, when she heard that the Ark of God was taken, and Shiloh to be no longer its resting-place; and I-chabod might be the name for the mothers of Ephraim at that hour to give to their offspring, seeing that the glory was departing from among them [1 Sam. 4:21.] . For what desolation and disgrace were felt to accompany this loss may be gathered from more passages than one in Jeremiah, where he threatens Jerusalem with a like visitation, "I will do unto this house" (saith the Lord, by the mouth of the prophet), "which is called by my name, wherein ye trust, and unto the place which I gave to you, and to your fathers, as I *have done to Shiloh.* And I will cast you out of my sight, as I have cast out all your brethren, even the *whole seed of Ephraim.*" And again—"I will make this house *like Shiloh,* and will make this city a curse to all the nations of the earth." [Jer. 7:14, 15; 26:6.] With a heavy heart, then, must this high-spirited and ambitious tribe have found that "the place which God had chosen to set his name there" (so often spoken of by Moses, and the choice suspended so long,)was at length determined, and determined against him; that his expectation (for such would probably be indulged) that God would finally fix his seat where He had so long fixed his Tabernacle, was overthrown; that the Messiah, whom some sanguine interpreters of the prophets amongst his sons had declared should come from between his feet, was not to be of him [See on this subject, Allix, Reflections upon the Four last Books of Moses, p. 180.] ; but that "refusing the tabernacle of Joseph, and not choosing any longer the tribe of *Ephraim,* (mark the patriotic exultation with which the Psalmist proclaims this,) God chose the Tribe of *Judah* and Mount Zion, which he loved." [Psalm 78:67.]

Such was the posture of the nation of Israel, such the temper of the times, "a breach," as it were, "ready to fall, swelling out in a high wall, whose breaking cometh suddenly at an instant," when Solomon began to collect workmen, and to levy taxes throughout all Israel, for those vast and costly structures which he reared, even "the house of the Lord and his own house, and Millo, and the wall of Jerusalem," [1 Kings 9:15.] besides many more; in some of them, indeed, showing himself the pious founder, or the patriot prince; but in some, the luxurious sensualist; and in some, again, the dissolute patron of idolatry [1 Kings 11:7.] . On, however, he went; and as if in small things as well as great, this growing division amongst the tribes (fatal as it was in many respects to prove) was ever to be fostered; as if the coming event was on every occasion to be casting its shadow before, a separate ruler, we read, "was placed over all the charge of *the house of Joseph;*" [1 Kings 11:28.] that is, one individual was made overseer over the work, or the tribute, or both, of the *ten tribes;* for so I understand the phrase, agreeably to its meaning in other passages of Scripture [See 2 Sam. 19:20, and Pole *in loc.* The rights of primogeniture, which Reuben had forfeited, appear to have been divided between Judah and Joseph: to Judah, the headship; to Joseph the double portion of the eldest son, and whatever else belonged to the "birthright." See 1 Chron. 5:2. Thus the people of Israel became *biceps,* and were comprised under the names of the two heads. See Judges 10:9, where the house of Ephraim is synonymous with the house of Joseph. Lightfoot considers Joseph to have been the principal family while the Ark was at Shiloh, and all Israel to have been named after it, as in Ps. 80:1, but that when God refused Joseph, and chose Judah for the chief, Ps. 78:68, 69, then there began, and continued, a difference and distinction betwixt Israel and Judah, Joseph and Judah, Ephraim and Judah, the rest of the tribes being called by all these names, in opposition to Judah.—Lightfoot, i. 66, fol.] . And who was he?—a young man, an industrious man, a mighty man of valour, (for these qualities Solomon made choice of him,) and above all, a man of *Ephraim* [1 Kings 11:26.] ; *Jeroboam* it was.

It is impossible to imagine events working more steadily towards a given point, than here. The knot had already shown itself far from indissoluble, and now, time, opportunity, and a skilful hand, combine to loose it. Here we have a great body of artificers, almost an army of themselves, kept together some twenty years—Ephraimites and their colleagues engaged in works consecrated to the glory and aggrandizement of Judah and Benjamin, rather than to their own—Ephraimites contributing to the removal of the seat of government from Ephraim to Judah—Ephraimites paying taxes great and grievous, not merely to the erection of a national place of worship, (for to this they might have given consent, the command being of God,) but to the construction of palaces for princes, never again to be of their own line; and temples for the idols of those princes, living and dead, which were expressly contrary to the command of God—and lastly, we have an Ephraimite, even Jeroboam, with every talent for mischief, endowed with every opportunity for exercising it, put into an office which at once invested him with authority, and secured him from suspicion, so that his future crown was but the consummation of his present intrigues; the issue of his own subtilty, and the people's discontent. Nor is this matter of conjecture. Is it not written in the Book of Kings (most casually, however), that the people of Israel—I speak of Israel as distinguished from Judah and Benjamin—in the first moment of madness, on the accession of Rehoboam, wreaked their vengeance—upon whom, of all men?—upon Adoniram, the very man whom Solomon his father had appointed to levy men and means throughout Israel, the tax-gatherer for the erection of these stupendous works! and him, the victim of popular indignation, did all Israel stone with stones till he died [1 Kings 5:4; 12:18.] . The wisdom and policy of Solomon, indeed, in spite of his faults and follies, upheld his empire till the last, and saved it from falling in pieces before the time; but how completely the fulness of that time was come is clear, when no sooner was he dead, than his son, and rightful successor, found it expedient to hasten to *Shechem*, there to meet all Israel, conscious as he was, that however his title was admitted by Judah, it was quite another thing whether *Ephraim* would give in his allegiance too; and, as the event proved, his apprehensions were not without a cause [1 Kings. 12:1.] .

And now Jeroboam, a man to seize upon any seeming advantages which his situation afforded him, at once enlisted the ancient sympathies of the people, by forthwith rebuilding *Shechem*, which had been burned by Abimelech [1 Kings 12:25.] , and making it his residence, though he had all the northern tribes among whom to choose; and, with similar policy, he proceeded to provide for them a worship of their own, nor would allow that "in Jerusalem alone was the place where men ought to worship"—a worship, rather, I think, a gross corruption, than an utter abandonment of the true, the idolatry of the second, more than of the first commandment, though the two offences are very closely connected, and almost of necessity run into one another. For I observe, throughout the whole history of the kings of Israel, a distinction made between the sin of Jeroboam and the worship of Baal, somewhat in favour of the former; and that, offensive as they both were to the one Eternal and Invisible God, Baal-worship was the greater abomination. Perhaps, too, it may be added, that this distinction is recognised by the Apostle, whose words are, that, "the glory of the uncorruptible God was,"—not altogether abjured—but "changed into an image made like four-footed beasts." [Rom. 1:23.] But, however this may be, a worship of their own, independent of the temple, and of the regular priesthood, Jeroboam established, still building upon the religious rites of old time, and accommodating the calendar of feasts in some measure to that which had existed before [1 Kings 12:32; Hosea 2:11; 9:5.] ; and whatever might be his reason for selecting Bethel for one of his calves, whether the holy character of the place itself, or its vicinity to the still holier Shiloh [Judges 21:19.] , whither the people had habitually resorted, I discover a very sufficient reason for his choice of Dan for the other, exclusive of all consideration of local convenience, the curious circumstance, that in this town there had already prevailed for ages a form of worship, or of idolatry (I should rather say), very closely resembling that which he now proposed to set up throughout Israel, and furnishing him, if not with a strict precedent, at least with a most suitable foundation on which to work. For in this town stood the teraphim, or images of Micah, whatever might be their shape, which the original founders of Dan had taken with them, and planted there; and a priesthood there was to minister to these images, precisely like that of Jeroboam, not of the sacerdotal order, for they were sons of Manasseh; and thus was there an organized system of dissent from the national church, existing in the town of Dan, "all the time that the House of God was in Shiloh;" [Judges 18:31.] and thus was accomplished, I suspect, that mysterious prediction of Jacob, "Dan shall be a serpent by the way, an adder in the path, that biteth the horse heels, so that his rider shall fall backward." [Gen. 49:17.]

On the present occasion, those *undesigned coincidences*, which are the staple of my argument, have not been presented in so perspicuous a manner as they may have been sometimes; for the attention has, in this instance, been directed not to one point, singled out of several, but to the details of a continuous history. This I could not avoid. At the same time, these details, on a review of them, will be found to involve many minute coincidences, and those just such as constitute the difference between the best-imagined story in the world and a narrative of actual facts. For let this be borne in mind, that the sketch which I have offered of *the gradual development* of the schism between Israel and Judah, is by no means an abridgment of the obvious Scripture account of it—very far from it.—Looking to that part of Scripture which directly relates to this schism, and confining ourselves to that, we might be led to think the rent of the kingdom as sudden and unshaped an event, as the rending of the prophet's mantle, which was its type: for here, as elsewhere, the history is rapid and abrupt. What I have offered is, strictly speaking, a *theory;* a theory by which a great many loose and scattered data, such as Scripture affords to a diligent inquirer, and to no other, are, with much seeming consistency, combined into a whole; it is the pattern which gradually comes out, when the many-coloured threads, gleaned up as we have gone along, are worked into a web.

1. For instance—I can conceive it very possible, without claiming to myself any peculiar sagacity, for a man to read, and not inattentively either, the sacred books from Joshua to Chronicles, and yet never happen to be struck with the fact that Ephraim was a leading tribe—that it was the head, allowed or understood, of an easy confederacy; the thing is scarcely to be discovered but by the apposition of many passages, dispersed through these books, bearing, perhaps, little or no relation to one another,

except that of having a common bias towards this one point. The same may be said of the main cause of this comparative superiority of Ephraim, the accidental, as some would call it,—as we will call it, the providential—establishment of the Tabernacle within its borders. The circumstance of Shiloh being the place whither all Israel went up to worship for three centuries and more, all important as it was to the tribe whom it concerned, is not *put forward* either as accounting for the prosperity of Ephraim above its fellows, whilst in Ephraim the Ark stood; or for the jealousy which it discovered towards Judah, when to Judah the Ark had been transferred; nor yet as being the natural means by which the remarkable words of Jacob were brought to pass, touching the future preeminence of Ephraim and Judah, howbeit, as tribes, they were then but in the loins of their fathers. So far from this, when in the Book of Joshua we are told that the Tabernacle was set up in *Shiloh*, not a syllable is added by which we can guess where Shiloh was, whether in Ephraim or elsewhere [Josh. 18:1.] ; and it is only after some investigation, and by inference at last, that in Ephraim we can fix it.

2. The same is true of the league between Benjamin and Judah. What were the sympathies beyond mere proximity, which cemented them so firmly, is altogether a matter for ourselves to unravel, if unravel it we can. We see them, indeed, acting in concert, as we also see the other tribes acting, but the books of Scripture enter into no explanations in either case. Nevertheless, I find in one place, that Saul, the first king, was of Benjamin, and in another, that David, the second king, was of Judah, with a prospect of a continuance of the succession in that line; and here I perceive a mutual sympathy likely to spring out of the exclusive honours of the two royal tribes. Elsewhere, I find that the two royal houses of Saul and David were united by marriage, and here I detect a further approximation. I look again, and learn that a temple was built for national worship in a city, which one text places in Judah, and a parallel text in Benjamin, leaving me to infer (as was the fact) that the city was on the confines of both, and that upon the confines of both (as was also the fact) the foundations of the temple were laid. In these, and perhaps in other similar matters, which might be enumerated, I certainly do discover *elements* of union, however the writers, who record them, may never speak of them as such.

3. Again, the motives which operated with Jeroboam in the selection of Shechem for his residence, or of Dan for his idolatry, are not even glanced at, though, in either instance, reasons there were, we have seen, to make the choice judicious. And whilst we are told that he fled from Solomon, when the conspirator was detected in him, or when Ahijah's prophecy

awakened the monarch's fears, and went into Egypt, and that from Egypt, at the death of Solomon, he hasted back to take his part in those stirring times, no hint, the most remote, is thrown out, that his sojourn in that idolatrous land, and the peculiar nature of its idolatry, influenced him in the choice of a *calf* for the representative of his own God, though the one fact does very curiously corroborate the other, and still adds credibility to the whole history.

In all this I discover much of coincidence, nothing of design. I see an extraordinary revolution asserted, and, then my eyes being opened, I perceive that the seeds of it, not however described as such, and often so small as to be easily overlooked, had been cast upon the waters generations before. I see coalitions and convulsions in the body politic of Israel, and I find, not without some pains-taking, and after all but in part, attractive or repulsive principles at work in that body, which, without being named as causes, do account for such effects. I see both in persons and places, so soon as I become intimately acquainted with their several bearings, something appropriate to the events with which they are connected, though I see nothing of the kind at first, because no such propriety appears upon the surface. These I hold to be the characters of truth, and the history upon which they are stamped I accordingly receive, nothing doubting—meanwhile, not failing to remark, and to admire, the silent transition of event into those very channels which Jacob in spirit had declared ages before; and to acknowledge, without attempting fully to understand, the mysterious workings of that Controlling Power, which can make men its instruments without making them its tools; at once compelling them to do his will, and permitting them to do their own; proving Himself faithful, and leaving them free.

XVIII. ISRAEL AND JUDAH AND THE CITY OF RAMAH

The next coincidences I have to offer will turn on the condition of the two kingdoms of Israel and Judah, whether political or religious, as it was affected by their separation; and will supply *evidence* to the truth of the history.

"And Baasha, king of Israel," we read, "went up against Judah, and built *Ramah*, that he might not suffer any to go out or come in to Asa, king of Judah." [1 Kings 15:17.]

Ramah seems to have been a border town, between the kingdoms of Israel and Judah, and to have stood in such a position as to be the key to either. The King of *Israel*, however, was the party anxious to fortify it, not the King of Judah; indeed, the latter, as we learn from the Chronicles, [1 Kings 15:17.] did his best to frustrate the efforts of Baasha, and succeeded, apparently not desirous of having Ramah converted into a place of strength, though it should be in his own keeping; for Asa having contrived to draw Baasha away from this work, does not seize upon it and complete it for himself, but contents himself with carrying off the stones and the timber, and using them elsewhere. It is evident, therefore, that it was an object with the kings of Israel, that this strong frontier-post should be established,—with the kings of Judah, that it should be removed. Now this is singular, when we remember, that after the schism the numerical strength lay vastly on the side of Israel, one hundred and eighty thousand men being all that Judah could then count in his ranks [1 Kings 12:21.] , whereas eight hundred thousand were actually produced a few years afterwards by Jeroboam, and even then he was not what he had been [Judges 21:19.] . It was to be expected, therefore, that the fear of invasion would have been upon Judah alone, the weaker state, and that, accordingly, Judah would have gladly taken and kept possession of a fortress which was the bridle of the kingdom on that side, and have made it strong for himself. Yet, as we have seen, the fact was quite the other way. How is this to be explained? By a single circumstance, which accounts for a great deal besides this; though the explanation presents itself in the most incidental manner imaginable, and without the smallest reference to the particular case of Ramah.

In the twelfth chapter of the first Book of Kings, I read (v. 20), that "Jeroboam said in his heart, Now shall the kingdom return to the house of David, if this people go up to sacrifice in the house of the Lord at Jerusalem;" and that accordingly he set up a worship of his own in Bethel and Dan.

In the eleventh chapter of the second Book of Chronicles, I read (v. 14), that "he cast off the Levites" (as indeed it was most natural that he should) "from executing the priest's office," and ordained him priests after his own pleasure. I read further, that in consequence of this subversion of the Church of God, "the priests and the Levites that were in all *Israel* resorted unto Judah out of all their coasts;" nor they only, the ministers of God, who might well migrate, but that "after them out of *all the tribes of Israel*, such as set their hearts to seek the Lord God of their fathers; so they strengthened" (it is added) "the kingdom of Judah, and made Rehoboam, the son of Solomon, strong" (v. 16, 17). The son of Nebat was a great politician in his own way, but he had yet to learn, that by righteousness is a nation really exalted, and that its righteous citizens are those by whom the throne is in truth upheld. These he was condemned to lose; these he and his ungodly successors were to see gradually waste away before their eyes; depart from a kingdom founded in iniquity, and transfer their allegiance to another and a better soil. Hence the natural solicitude of *Israel* to put a stop to the alarming drainage of all that was virtuous out of their borders, and the clumsy contrivance of a fortification at Ramah for the purpose; as though a spirit of uncompromising devotion to God, happily the most unconquerable of things, was to be coerced by a barrier of bricks. Hence, too, the no less natural solicitude of Judah to remove this fortification, Judah being desirous that no obstacle, however small, should be opposed to the influx of those virtuous Israelites, who would be the strength of any nation wherein they settled. Here I find a coincidence of the most satisfactory kind, between the *building of Ramah by Israel, the overthrow of it by Judah, and the tide of emigration which was setting in from Israel towards Judah*, by reason of Jeroboam's idolatry. Yet the relation of these events to one another is not expressed in the history, nor are the events named under the same head, or in the same chapter.

XIX. THE INCREASE OF JUDAH AND DECREASE OF ISRAEL

Nor is this all. Still keeping in mind this single consideration, that the more godly of the people of the ten tribes were disgusted at the calves, and retired, we may at once account for the progressive *augmentation* of the armies of Judah, and the corresponding *decrease* of the armies of Israel, which the subsequent history of the two kingdoms casually, and at intervals, displays.

Immediately after the separation, Rehoboam assembled the forces of his two tribes, and found them, as I have said, one hundred and eighty thousand men. Some eighteen years afterwards, Ahijah, his son, was able to raise against Jeroboam (who still, however, was vastly stronger) four hundred thousand. [2 Chron. 13:3.] This is a considerable step. Some six or seven years later, Asa, the son of Ahijah, is invaded by a countless host of Æthiopians. On this occasion, notwithstanding the numbers which must have fallen already in the battle with Jeroboam, he brings into the field five hundred and eighty thousand: so rapidly were the resources of Judah on the advance. About two and thirty years later still, the army of Jehoshaphat, the son of Asa, consists of one million one hundred and sixty thousand men [2 Chron. 17:14–18.] ; a prodigious *increase* in the population of the kingdom of Judah.

On the other hand, we may trace (the act, it must be observed, is altogether our own, no such comparison being instituted in the history,) the gradual decay and *depopulation* of the kingdom of Israel. Jeroboam himself, we have found, was eight hundred thousand strong. The continual diminution of this national army, we cannot, in the present instance, always trace from actual numbers, as we did in the former; but, from circumstances which transpire in the history, we can trace it by inference. Thus, Ahab, one of the successors of Jeroboam, and contemporary with Jehoshaphat, whose immense armaments we have seen, is threatened by Benhadad and the Syrians. Benhadad will send men to take out of his house, and out of the houses of his servants, whatever is pleasant in their eyes [1 Kings 20:6.] . It is the insolent message of one who felt Israel to be weak, and being weak, to invite aggression. Favoured by a panic, Ahab triumphs for the once; but at the return of the year Benhadad returns. Ahab is warned of this long before. "Go strengthen thyself," is the friendly exhortation of the prophet (v. 22);—no doubt he did so, to the best of his means, but after all, "when the children of Israel were numbered, and were all present, and went against them, the children of Israel pitched before the Syrians like *two little flocks of kids*, but the Syrians filled the country" (v. 27). And in Joram's days, the son and successor of Ahab, such was the boldness of Syria, and the weakness of Israel, that the former was constantly sending marauding parties, "companies," as they are called, or "bands," [2 Kings 5:2; 6:23; 13:21.] into Israel's quarters, sometimes taking the inhabitants captive, and sometimes even laying siege to considerable towns [2 Kings 6:14.23.] . And in the reign of Jehu, the next king, Syria, with Hazael at its head, crippled Israel still more terribly, actually seizing upon all the land of Jordan eastward, Gilead, the Gadites, the Reubenites, and the Manassites, from Aroer to Bashan [2 Kings 10:33.] . And to complete the picture, the whole army of Jehoahaz, the next in the royal succession of Israel, consisted of fifty horsemen, ten chariots, and ten thousand foot, Syria having exterminated the rest [2 Kings 13:7.] : so gradually was Israel upon the decline.

Now it must be remembered, in order that the force of the argument may be felt, that no parallel of the kind we have been drawing is found in the history itself; no invitation to others to draw one. The materials for doing so it does indeed furnish, dispersed, however, over a wide field, and less definite than might be wished, were our object to ascertain the relative strength of the two kingdoms with exactness: that, however, it is not; and the very circumstance, that the gradual growth of Judah and declension of Israel are sometimes to be gathered from other facts than positive numerical evidence, is enough in itself to show that the historian could have no *design* studiously to point out the coincidence of facts with his casual assertion, that the Levites had been supplanted by the priests of the calves, and that multitudes had quitted the country with them, in just indignation.

XX. GIBBETHON AND SUBURBS, THE CITY OF THE LEVITES

There is still another coincidence which falls under the same head.

In the fifteenth chapter of the first Book of Kings, (v. 27) I read that "Baasha the son of Ahijah, of the house of Issachar, conspired against him (*i. e.* Nadab the son of Jeroboam) at *Gibbethon*, which belonged *to the Philistines;* for Nadab and all Israel laid siege to Gibbethon."

It appears, then, that Gibbethon, situated in the tribe of Dan, had by some means or other fallen into the hands of the Philistines, and that the forces of Israel were now engaged in recovering possession of it. It may seem a very hopeless undertaking, at this time of day, to ascertain the circumstances of which an enemy availed himself, in order to gain possession of a particular town in Canaan, near three thousand years ago. Yet, perhaps, the investigation, distant as it is, is not desperate; for in the twenty-first chapter of Joshua (v. 23), I find Gibbethon and her suburbs mentioned as a city of the *Levites*. Now Jeroboam, we have heard, drove all the Levites out of Israel: what, then, can be more probable, than that Gibbethon, being thus suddenly evacuated, the Philistines, a remnant of the old enemy, still lurking in the country, and ever ready to rush in wherever there was a breach, should have spied an opportunity in the defenceless state of Gibbethon, and claimed it as their own [That the Philistines were thus dispersed over the land may be gathered from many hints in Scripture; even in the kingdom of Judah they were to be found, much more in Israel. "Some of the Philistines brought Jehoshaphat presents, and tribute silver," 2 Chron. 17:11. Probably the miscreants mentioned 1 Kings 15:12, whom Asa expelled, and those mentioned 22:46, whom Jehoshaphat his son drove out, and those again mentioned 2 Kings 23:7, who were established even at Jerusalem, whom Josiah cast out, were all of this nation. And there still were Hittites somewhere at hand, who had even kings of their own, 1 Kings 10:29; 2 Kings 7:6; and we read of a land of the Philistines, where the Shunammite sojourned during the famine, 2 Kings 8:2; and, indeed, the Philistines are one of the nations against whom Jeremiah prophesies as about to be destroyed by Nebuchadnezzar, (47:4,) all evident tokens that a considerable body of the primitive inhabitants of Palestine still dwelt in it.] ? It is, indeed, far from improbable that this story of Gibbethon is that of many other *Levitical* cities throughout Israel; that this is but a glimpse of much similar confusion, misery, and intestine tumult, by which that kingdom was now convulsed; and, though a solitary fact in itself, a type of many more;—and thus, in another way, did the profane act of Jeroboam operate to the downfall of his kingdom, and fatally eat into its strength.

Whether I am right in this conjecture, it is impossible to tell; the case does not admit of positive decision either way; but, certainly the grounds upon which it rests are, to say the least, very specious; and if they are sound, as I think they are, I cannot imagine a point of harmony more complete, or more undesigned, than that which we have found between these half-dozen words touching Gibbethon, a Levitical city, lapsing into the hands of the Philistines, and the expulsion of the Levites out of Israel by the sin of Jeroboam.

XXI. ELIJAH ON THE RUN FROM JEZEBEL

Nor is this all. There is another and a still more valuable coincidence yet, connected with this part of my subject; more valuable, because involving in itself a greater number of particulars, and, therefore, more liable to a flaw, if the combination was artificial. When Elijah has worked his great miracle on the top of Carmel, and kindled the sacrifice by fire from heaven, he has to fly from Jezebel for his life, who swears that, by the morrow, she will deal with him as he had dealt with the prophets of Baal her god, and slay him [1 Kings 18:40; 19:2.] . Now when it was so common a practice, as we have seen, for the godly amongst the people of Israel to betake themselves to Judah in their distress, there to worship the God of their fathers without scandal and without persecution, it seems obvious that this was the place for Elijah to repair unto; the most appropriate, for it was because he had been very jealous for the Lord, that he was banished—the most convenient, for no other was so near; he had but to cross the borders, one would think, and he was safe. Yet neither on this occasion, nor yet during the three preceding years of drought, when Ahab sought to lay hands upon him, did Elijah seek sanctuary in *Judah*. First he hides himself by the brook Cherith, which is before Jordan [It is true that there is great difference of opinion as to the situation of this brook Cherith; but from the direction given to Elijah being to turn *Eastward*, when he was to go there, he being at the time in Samaria, it is clear that it could not be in Judah.—Consult Lightfoot, Vol. ii. 318, fol.] ; then at "Zarephath which belongs to Zidon;" and though he does at last, when his case seems desperate, and his hours are numbered by Jezebel's sentence, "come in haste to Beer-Sheba, which belongeth to *Judah*," [1 Kings 19:3.]

still it is after a manner which bespeaks his reluctance to set foot within that territory, even more than if he had evaded it altogether. Tarry he will not; he separates from his servant, probably for the greater security of both; goes a day's journey into the wilderness, and for-lorn, and spirit-broken, and alone, begs that he may die; then he wanders away, being so taught of God, forty days and forty nights, till he comes to Horeb, the Mount of God, and there conceals himself in a cave. Now all this is at first sight very strange and unaccountable; strange and unaccountable that the Prophet of God should so studiously avoid Judah, the people of God, governed as it then was by Jehoshaphat, a prince who walked with God [1 Kings 22:43.] ,—Judah being, of all others, a shelter the nearest and most convenient. How is it to be explained?

I doubt not by this fact; that Jehoshaphat, king of Judah, had already married, or was then upon the point of marrying, his son Jehoram to *Athaliah, the daughter of this very Ahab, and this very Jezebel*, who were seeking Elijah's life [2 Kings 8:18; 2 Chron. 18:1.] ; his, therefore, was not now the kingdom in which Elijah could feel that a residence was safe; for by this ill-omened match (such it proved) the houses of Jehoshaphat and Ahab were so strictly identified, that we find the former, when solicited by Ahab to join him in an expedition against Ramoth-gilead, expressing himself in such terms as these: "I am as thou art, my people as thy people, my horses as thy horses;" [1 Kings 22:4.] and in allusion, as it should seem, to this fraternity of the two kings, Jehoshaphat is in one place actually called "King of Israel." [2 Chron. 21:2.]

It may be demonstrated that this fatal marriage (for such it was in its consequences) was, at any rate, contracted not later than the tenth or eleventh of Ahab's reign, and it might have been much earlier; whilst these scenes in the life of Elijah could not have occurred within the first few years of that reign, seeing that Ahab had to fill up the measure of his wickedness after he came to the throne, before the Prophet was commissioned to take up his parable against him. I mention these two facts, as tending to prove that the exile of Elijah could not have fallen out long, if at all, before the marriage; and therefore that the latter event, whether past or in prospect, might well bear upon it. I say that it may be proved that this marriage was not later than the tenth or eleventh of Ahab—for

1. Ahaziah, the fruit of the marriage, the son of Jehoram and Athaliah, began to reign in the *twelfth* year of Joram, son of Ahab, king of Israel [2 Kings 8:25, 26.] .

2. But Joram began to reign in the *eighteenth* year of Jehoshaphat, king of Judah [2 Kings 3:1.].

3. Therefore, the twelfth of Joram would answer to the *thirtieth* of

Jehoshaphat (had the latter reigned so long; it did, in fact, answer to the seventh of Jehoram, the son of Jehoshaphat [Comp. 2 Kings 3:1; 8:16. 1 Kings 22:42.]; but there is no need to perplex the computation by any reference to this reign); and accordingly Ahaziah must have begun his reign in what would correspond to the thirtieth of Jehoshaphat.

4. But he was twenty-two when he began it. Therefore he must have been born about the *eighth* year of Jehoshaphat; and consequently the marriage of Jehoram and Athaliah, which gave birth to him, must have been contracted at least as early as the sixth or seventh of Jehoshaphat.

5. Now Jehoshaphat began to reign in the *fourth* of Ahab, king of Israel; therefore the marriage must have been solemnized as early as the tenth or eleventh of Ahab—how much earlier it was solemnized, in fact, we cannot tell; but the result is extremely curious; and without the most remote allusion to it on the part of the sacred historian, as being an incident in any way governing the movements of Elijah, it does furnish, when we are once in possession of it, a most satisfactory explanation of the shyness of Elijah to look for a refuge in a country where, almost under any other circumstances, it was the most natural he should have sought one; and, where, at any other time, since the division of the kingdoms, he certainly would have found not only a refuge, but a welcome.

XXII. ELIJAH AND THE BARRELS OF WATER

I have already advanced several arguments for the truth of that remarkable portion of Scripture which tells the history of the great prophet Elijah, and showed, that, on comparing some of the reputed events of his life with the political and domestic state of his country at the time, the reality of those events was established beyond all reasonable doubt. But I have not yet done with this part of my subject; and I press on the notice of my readers once again, as I have repeatedly pressed it before, the consideration that these casual indications of truth, found in the very midst of miracles the most striking, give great support to the credibility of those miracles; that the portions of the history on which these seals of truth are set, combine with the other and more extraordinary portions so intimately, that if the former are to be received, the latter cannot be rejected without extreme violence, and laceration of the whole; that standing or falling, they must stand or fall together.

I spoke before of the flight of Elijah, and gave my reasons for believing it. I speak now of a trifling incident in that magnificent scene which is said to have been the prologue to his flight. This it is. Twelve barrels of water, at the command of the prophet, are poured upon the sacrifice, and fill the trench. But is it not a strange thing, that at a moment of drought so intense, when the king himself and the governor of his house, trusting the business to no inferior agent, actually undertook to examine with their own eyes the watering-places throughout all the land, dividing it between them, to see if they could save the remainder of the cattle alive [1 Kings 18:5.] ; when the prophet had been long before compelled to leave Cherith, because the brook was dried up, and for no reason else, and to crave at the hands of the widow-woman of Zarephath, whither he had removed, though a land of danger to him, a little water in a vessel that he might drink; is it not, I say, a gross oversight in the sacred writer, to make Elijah, at such a time, give order for this wanton waste of water above all things, whereof scarcely a drop was to be found to cool the tongue; and not only so, but to describe it as forthcoming at once, apparently without any search made, an ample and abundant reservoir [Bishop Hall in his Contemplations shows himself aware of the difficulty in this passage, but not of its probable solution. B. xviii. Contempl. 7.] ? How can these things be? Let us but remember the local position of Carmel, that it stood upon the *coast*, as an incidental remark in the course of the narrative testifies; that the water was therefore probably *seawater;* and all the difficulty disappears. But the historian does not trouble himself to satisfy our surprise, being altogether unconscious that he has given any cause for it; he, honest man as he was, tells his tale, a faithful one as he feels, and the objection which we have alleged, and which a single word would have extinguished, he leaves to shock us as it may, nothing heeding. But would not an impostor have preserved the keeping of his picture better, and been careful not to violate seeming probabilities by this prodigal profusion of water, whilst his action was laid in a miraculous drought, for the removal of which, indeed, this very sacrifice was offered—or, if of these twelve barrels he must needs speak, by way of silencing all insinuation, that the whole was a scene got up, and that fire was secreted, would he not have studiously told us, at least, that the water was from the sea which lay at the foot of Carmel, and thus have guarded himself against sceptical remarks? Now when I see this momentous period of Elijah's ministry compassed in on every side with tokens of truth so satisfactory; when I see so much in his history established as matter of fact, am I to consider all that is not so established, merely because materials are wanting for the purpose, as matters of fiction only? Or, taking my stand upon the good faith with which his flight, at least, is recorded, an event which, in itself, I look upon as proved beyond all reasonable doubt by a former coincidence; or upon the good faith with which his challenge at Carmel is recorded, an event not unsatisfactorily confirmed by this coincidence; or rather upon the veracity of both facts, shall I not feel my way along from the prophet's recoil on setting foot in Judah, to the anger of Jezebel, with whom Judah was then in close alliance; from this anger of hers, to the cause assigned for it in the slaughter of her priests; from the slaughter of her priests, to the authority by which he did the deed, himself a defenceless individual, in a country full of the inveterate worshippers of the God of those priests; and thus, finally, shall I not ascend to the mighty miracle by which that authority was conveyed to him, God in pledge thereof touching the mountain that it smoked?

XXIII. ELIJAH AT ZAREPHATH

Towards the end of the famine caused by this drought, Elijah is commanded by God to "get him to *Zarephath*, which *belongeth to Zidon*, and dwell there;" where a widow-woman was to sustain him [1 Kings 17:9.] . He goes; finds the woman gathering sticks near the gate of the city; and asks her to fetch him a little water and a morsel of bread. She replies, "As the Lord thy God liveth, I have not a cake, but an handful of meal in a barrel, and a little *oil* in a cruse: and, behold, I am gathering two sticks, that I may go in and dress it for me and my son, that we may eat it, and die." [1 Kings 17:12.]

This widow-woman then, it seems, dwelt at *Zarephath*, or Sarepta, which belongeth to *Zidon*. Now, from a passage in the book of Joshua, [Josh. 19:28.] we learn that the district of Zidon, in the division of the land of Canaan, fell to the lot of Asher. Let us, then, turn to the thirty-third chapter of Deuteronomy, where Moses blesses the Tribes, and see the character he gives of this part of the country: "Of Asher he said, Let Asher be blessed with children; let him be acceptable to his brethren, and let him dip *his foot in oil;*" [Deut. 33:24.] indicating the future fertility of that region, and the nature of its principal crop. It is likely, therefore, that at the end of a dearth of three years and a half, *oil* should be found there, if anywhere. Yet this symptom of truth occurs once more as an ingredient in a miraculous history—for the oil was made not to fail till the rain came. The incident itself is a very minute one; and, minute as it is, only discovered to be a coincidence by the juxtaposition of several texts from several books of Scripture. It would require a very circumspect forger of the story to introduce the mention of the oil; and when he had introduced it, not be tempted to betray himself by throwing out some slight hint why he had done so.

XXIV. ELISHA AND THE SHUNAMITE WOMAN

Not long after this period, the history of Elisha furnishes us with a coincidence characteristic, I think, of truth. It appears that "a great woman" of Shechem had befriended the prophet, finding him and his servant, from time to time, as they passed by that place, food and lodging. In return for this he sends her a message: "Behold, thou hast been careful for us with all this care; what is to be done for thee? *wouldest thou be spoken for to the king, or to the captain of the host?*" [2 Kings 4:13.] Now we should have gathered from previous passages in Elisha's history, that Jehoram, who was then king of Israel, was not one with whom he was upon such terms as this proposition to the Shunammite implies. Jehoram was the son of Ahab, his old master Elijah's enemy, and apparently no friend of his own; for when the three kings, the king of Israel, the king of Judah, and the king of Edom, in their distress for water, in their expedition against Moab, wished to inquire of the Lord through Elisha, his answer to the king of Israel was, "As the Lord of hosts liveth, before whom I stand, surely, were it not that I regard the presence of Jehoshaphat the king of Judah, *I would not look toward thee, nor see thee.*" [2 Kings 3:14.] What, then, had occurred in the interval betwixt this avowal, and his proposal to the Shunammite to use his influence in her favour at court, which had changed his position with respect to the king of Israel? It may be supposed that it was the sudden supply of water, which he had furnished these kings with, by God's permission, thus saving the expedition; and the defeat of the enemy, to which it had been instrumental [2 Kings 3:16, 17.] . This would naturally make Elisha feel that the king of Israel was under obligations to him and that he could ask a slight favour of him without seeming to sanction the character of the man by doing so. And this solution of the case appears to be the more probable, from Elisha coupling the *"captain of the host"* with the king; as though his interest was equally good with him too, which he might reasonably consider it to be, when he had done the army such signal service; and it is further confirmed by another incident related of this same Shunammite in a subsequent chapter. For having fled from the seven years' famine into another country, she lost her house and land in her own, on which she appealed to king Jehoram. Accordingly, "the king talked with Gehazi, the servant of the man of God, saying, *Tell me, I pray thee, all the great things Elisha hath done;*" [2 Kings 8:4.] Elisha having now, no doubt, actually recommended her case to the king. And when Gehazi had named some of these miracles, "the king appointed to her a certain officer, saying, Restore all that was hers;" so that the event shows that Elisha on the former occasion had not miscalculated his powers, or the grounds on which he might challenge the king's favours.

XXV. THE REIGN OF AHAZIAH AND JEHORAM, AHAB'S SONS

A word upon the marriage of which I spoke in a former paragraph. Evil was the day for Judah when the son of Jehoshaphat took for a wife the daughter of Ahab, and of Jezebel ten times the daughter. Singular, indeed, is the hideous resemblance of Athaliah to her mother, though our attention is not at all directed to the likeness; and were the fidelity of the history staked upon the few incidents in it which relate to this female fiend, it would be safe—so characteristic are they of the child of Jezebel: the same thirst for blood; the same lust of dominion, whether in the State or the household; the same unfeminine influence over the kings their husbands; Jezebel the setter-up of Baal in Israel; Athaliah in Judah;—those bitter fountains from which disasters innumerable flowed to either kingdom, [Hosea 13:1.] preparing the one for a Shalmanezer, the other for a Nebuchadnezzar. But this by the way. Whatever might be the motive which induced so good a prince as Jehoshaphat to sanction this alliance; whether, indeed, it was of choice, and in the hope of re-uniting the tow kingdoms, which is probable; or whether it was of compulsion, the act of an impetuous son, and not his own—for the subsequent history of Jehoram shows how little he was disposed to yield to his father's will, when his own was thwarted by it [2 Chr 21:3, 4.]—certain it is, that it proved a sad epoch in the fate and fortunes of Judah; a calamity almost as withering in its effects upon that kingdom, as the sin of Jeroboam had been upon his own. Up to the time of Jehoshaphat, Judah had prospered exceedingly; henceforward there is a taint of Baal introduced into the blood royal, and a curse for a long time, though not without intermissions, seems to rest upon the land. The even march with which the two kingdoms now advance hand in hand is early seen; they were now bent upon grinding at the same mill; and a remarkable instance of coincidence without design here presents itself, which the general observations I have been making may serve to introduce.

1. *Ahaziah*, the son of Ahab, I read, [1 Kings 22:51.] began to reign over Israel in Samaria, in the *seventeenth* year of Jehoshaphat king of Judah.

2. But Jehoram, the son of Ahab, began to reign over Israel in Samaria, in the eighteenth year of Jehoshaphat king of Judah, his brother Ahaziah being dead. [2 Kings 3:1.]

3. Elsewhere, however, it is said that this Jehoram, the son of Ahab, began to reign in the second year of Jehoram son of Jehoshaphat king of Judah. [2 Kings 1:17.]

4. Therefore, the second year of Jehoram son of Jehoshaphat must have corresponded with the eighteenth of Jehoshaphat; or in other words, *Jehoram* son Jehoshaphat must have begun to reign in the *seventeenth* of Jehoshaphat.

It is obvious that the maze of dates and names thus brought together from various places in Scripture, through which the argument is to be pursued, renders all contrivance, collusion, or packing of facts, for the pupose of supporting a conclusion, utterly impossible. Now the result of the whole is this—that *Ahaziah*, the son of Ahab king of Israel, and *Jehoram*, the son of Jehoshaphat king of Judah, both began to reign in *the same year*, in the respective kingdoms of their fathers, *their fathers being nevertheless themselves alive, and active sovereigns at the time*. Is there anything by which this simultaneous adoption of these young men to be their fathers' colleagues can be accounted for? An identity so remarkable in the proceedings of the confederate kingdoms can scarcely be accidental. Let us, then, endeavour to ascertain what event was in progress in the *seventeenth year of Jehoshaphat*, the year in which the two appointments were made.

Now Jehoshaphat began to reign in the fourth of Ahab. But Ahab died in the great battle against Ramoth-gilead, having reigned twenty-two years; he died therefore in the eighteenth of Jehoshaphat.

Accordingly, in the *seventeenth* of that monarch, the year in which we are concerned, the two kings were preparing to go up against Ramoth—a measure upon which they did not venture without long and grave deliberation, concentration of forces, application to prophets touching their prospects of success.

But when they approached this hazardous enterprise in a spirit so cautious, can anything be more probable than that each monarch should then have made his son a partner of his throne, in order that, during his own absence with the army, there might be on left behind to rule at home, and in case of the father's death, in battle (Ahab did actually fall), to reign in his stead? There can be little or no doubt that this is the true solution of the case, though the text itself of the narrative does not contain the slightest intimation that it is so.

XXVI. AMAZIAH AND JOASH

Such arrangements, indeed, were not unusual in those days and in those countries. Here is a further proof of it, and at the same time a coincidence which is a companion to the last.

1. "In the thirty-seventh year of Joash king of Judah, began Jehoash, the son of Jehoahaz, to reign over Israel in Samaria." So we are told in one passage [2 Kings 13:10.] . But, in another [2 Kings 14:1.] , that, "In the second year of Joash (Jehoash), the son of Jehoahaz, king of Israel, reigned Amaziah, the son of Joash, king of Judah.

2. Therefore, Amaziah, king of Judah, reigned in the *thirty-ninth* of Joash, king of Judah.

3. Now we learn from a passage in the second Book of Chronicles [2 Chron. 24:1.] , that "Joash reigned *forty* years in Jerusalem."

4. Therefore Amaziah must have begun to reign one year at least before the death of his father Joash.

Can we discover any reason for this? The clue will be found in a parenthesis of half a line, which the following paragraph in the Chronicles presents: "And it came to pass at the end of the year, that the host of Syria came up against him (Joash); and they came to Jerusalem, and destroyed all the princes of the people ... And when they were departed from him *(for they left him in great diseases)*, his own servants conspired against him, for the blood of the sons of Jehoiada the priest, and slew him on his bed, and he died." [2 Chron. 24:23. 25.]

The *great diseases*, therefore, under which, it seems, Joash was labouring at the moment of the Syrian invasion, presents itself as the probable cause why Amaziah his son, then in the flower of his age, was admitted to a share in the government a little before his time. Yet how circuitously do we arrive at this conclusion! The Book of Kings alone would not establish it; the Book of Chronicles alone would not establish it. From the former, we might learn when Amaziah began to reign; from the latter, when Joash, the father of Amaziah, died; and accordingly, a comparison of the two dates would enable us to determine that the reign of Amaziah began before that of Joash ended; but neither document asserts the fact that the son did reign conjointly with the father. We infer it: that is all. Neither does the Book of Kings make the least allusion to any accident whatever which rendered this co-partnership necessary; nor yet the Book of Chronicles directly, only an incidental parenthesis, a word or two in length, intimates that at the time of the Syrian invasion Joash was sick.

I have adduced this coincidence, strong in itself, chiefly in illustration and confirmation of the principles upon which the last proceeded; the simultaneous and premature assumption of the sceptre by the sons of Jehoshaphat and Ahab, as compared with the date of the combined expedition of those two kings against Ramoth-gilead. But I must not dismiss the subject altogether without calling your attention to the *undesignedness* manifested in either case. Nothing can be more latent than the congruity, such as it is, which is here found; either history might be read a thousand times without a suspicion that any such congruity was there; investigation is absolutely necessary for the discovery of it; patient disembroilment of a labyrinth of names, many being identical, where the parties are not the same; scrutiny and comparison of dates, seldom so given as to expedite the labours of the inquirer. All this must be done, or these singular tokens of truth escape us, and many, I doubt not, do escape us after all. What imposture can be here? What contrivers could be prepared for such a sifting of their plausible disclosures? What pretenders could be provided with such vouchers; or, having provided them, would bury them so deep as that they should run the risk of never being brought to light at all, and thus frustrate their own end in the fabrication?

Once more I commit to my readers facts which speak, I think, to the truth of Scripture, as things having authority; facts, which afford proof infallible that there is a mine of evidence, "*deep* things of God," in this sense, in the sacred writings, which they who look upon them with a hasty and impatient glance—and such very generally is the manner of sceptics, and almost always the manner of youthful sceptics,—leave under their feet unworked; a treasure hid in a field which they only who will be at the pains to dig for it will find.

But if an investigation, such as this that we are conducting, leads to such a conclusion—to a conclusion, I mean, that there is a substratum of truth running through the Bible, which none can discover but he who will patiently and perseveringly sink the well at the bottom of which it lies—and such is the conclusion at which we must arrive—is it not a lamentable thing to hear, as we are sometimes condemned to hear it, the superficial objection, or supercilious scoff, proceeding from the mouth of one whose very speech betrays that he has walked over the surface of his subject merely, if even that, and who nevertheless pretends and proclaims that truth he finds not?

XXVII. AHAB AND JEZEBEL

In considering the political and religious condition of the two kingdoms after the division, I have looked at the establishment of the calves at Bethel and Dan by Jeroboam as a great national epoch; as a measure pregnant with consequences far more numerous and more important, fetching a much larger compass, and affecting many more interests, than its author probably contemplated. I have now to fix upon another event, the wide-wasting effects of which I have already hinted as another national crisis, one which, in the end, most materially influenced the fortunes both of Israel and Judah; the thing in itself apparently a trifle; "but God," says Bishop Hall, "lays small accidents as foundations for greater designs;" I speak of the *marriage between Ahab and Jezebel*. It is thus announced: "And it came to pass, as if it had been a light thing for him to walk in the sins of Jeroboam the son of Nebat, that he took to wife Jezebel, the daughter of Ethbaal, king of the Zidonians, and went and served Baal, and worshipped him. And he reared up an altar for Baal in the house of Baal, which he had built in Samaria. And Ahab made a grove; and Ahab did more to provoke the Lord God of Israel to anger than all the kings of Israel that were before him." [1 Kings 16:31.] Here we have the beginning of a new and more pestilent idolatry in Israel. This Zidonian queen corrupts the country, to which she is unhappily translated, with her own rooted heathenish abominations; and priests of Baal, and prophets of Baal, being under her own special protection and encouragement, multiply exceedingly; and so seductive did the voluptuous worship prove, that, with the exception of seven thousand persons, all Israel had, more or less, partaken in her sin. Jeroboam's calf had been a base and sordid representative of God, but a representative still; Jezebel's Baal was an audacious rival. Nevertheless, Israel could not find in their hearts to put away the God of their fathers altogether; and accordingly we hear Elijah exclaim, "How long halt ye between two opinions? if the Lord be God, follow him; but if Baal, then follow him." [1 Kings 18:21.] I do not think sufficient notice has been taken of the curious manner in which this sudden ejaculation of the prophet corresponds with a number of unconnected incidents, characteristic of the times, which lie scattered over the Books of Kings and Chronicles. I shall collect a few of them, that it may be seen how well their confronted testimony agrees together, and how strictly, but undesignedly, they all coincide with that state of public opinion upon religious matters which the words of Elijah express—a *halting opinion*.

Thus, in the scene on Mount Carmel, we find, that after the priests of Baal had in vain besought their god to give proof of himself, and it now became Elijah's turn to act, "he *repaired* the altar of the Lord that was broken down," [1 Kings 18:30.] as though here, on the top of Carmel, were the remains of an altar to the true God (one of those high places tolerated, however questionably, by some even of the most religious kings), which had been superseded by an altar to Baal, since Ahab's reign had begun; the prophet not having to build, it seems, but only to renew. And agreeably to this, we have Obadiah, the governor of Ahab's own house, represented as a man "who feared the Lord greatly, and saved the prophets of the Lord;" he, therefore, no apostate, but Ahab, in considera- tion of his fidelity, winking at his faith; perhaps, indeed, himself not so much sold to Baal-worship, as sold into the hands of an imperious woman, who would hear of no other. And so "Ahab served Baal a *little*," said Jehu, his successor [2 Kings 10:18.] , another of the equivocal tokens of the times; whilst the command of this same Jehu, that the temple of Baal should be searched before the slaughter of the idolaters began, lest there should be there any of the *worshippers of the Lord*, instead of the *worshippers of Baal* only, still argues the prevalence of the same half measure of faith. Moreover, the character of the four hundred prophets of Ahab, which, by its contradictions, has so much perplexed the commenta- tors; their number corresponding with that of those who ate at Jezebel's table; their parable, nevertheless, taken up in the *Lord's name;* still their veracity suspected by Jehoshaphat, who asks if "there be no prophet of the *Lord* besides;" and the mutual ill-will which manifests itself between them and Micaiah; are all very expressive features of the same doubtful mind [1 Kings 18:19; 22:6–24; 2 Chron. 18:10–23.] . Then the pretence by which Ahab, through Jezebel, takes away the life of Naboth, is "*blas- phemy* against God and the king," against the true God, no doubt, the tyrant availing herself of a clause in the Levitical law [Levit. 24:16.] ; a law which was still, therefore, as it should seem, the law of the land, even in the kingdom of Israel, howbeit standing in the anomalous position of deriving its authority from an acknowledgment of Jehovah alone, and yet left to struggle against the established worship of Baal, too; enough in itself to confound the people, to compromise all religious distinctions, and to ensure a *halting* creed in whatever nation it obtained. Thus, whilst I see the prophets of the Lord cut off under the warrant of Jezebel, and the government of the Lord virtually renounced; at another time I see, as I have said, a man condemned to death for blasphemy against the Lord, under the warrant of Leviticus; and the two sons of an Israelitish woman sold to her creditor for bondsmen, under the same law [2 Kings 4:1; Levit. 25:39.] ; and the lepers shut out at the gate of Samaria, still under the same [2 Kings 7:3; Levit. 13:46; 14:3; Num. 5:2, 3.] , and contrary, as it should appear, to the Syrian practice; for Naaman, though a leper, does not seem to have been an outcast, but to have had servants about him, and to have executed the king's commands, and even to have expected Elisha to come out to him, and put his hand upon the place. What can argue the embarrassment under which Israel was labouring in its religious relations more clearly than all this?—the law of Moses acknowledged to be valid, and its provisions enforced, though its claim to the obedience of the people only rested upon having God for its author; that God whom Baal was supplanting. Here, I think, is truth: it would have been little to the purpose to produce *flagrant* proofs that the worship of God and the worship of Baal prevailed together in Israel; those might have been the result of contrivance; but it is coincidence, and undesigned coincidence, to find a prophet exclaiming, in a moment of zeal, "How long *halt* ye," and then to find indications, some of them grounded upon the merest trifles of domestic life, that the people did halt.

XXVIII. JEHORAM AND ATHALIAH

But this marriage of Ahab and Jezebel, so ruinous to Israel, was scarcely less so to Judah; for in Judah the same miserable alliance was to be acted over again in the next generation, and with the very same consequences.

Ahab, king of Israel, had taken to himself Jezebel, a heathen, for his wife, and Israel, through her, became a half-heathen nation. Jehoram, king of Judah, had taken to himself Athaliah, the daughter of Jezebel, worthy in all respects of the mother who bore her, to be his wife; and now Judah, in like manner, and for the like cause, fell away. Of Ahab it is said, "But there was none like unto Ahab, who did sell himself to work wickedness in the sight of the Lord, *whom Jezebel his wife stirred up.*" [1 Kings 21:25.] Such were the bitter fruits of his marriage. Of Jehoram, it is said, "And he walked in the ways of the kings of *Israel*, as did the house of Ahab, for the *daughter of Ahab was his wife*, and he did evil in the sight of the Lord." [2 Kings 8:18.] Such in turn was this ill-omened union to him and his. Either of these women, therefore, was the curse of the kingdom over which her husband ruled; and as we have already seen some of the mischief brought into Israel (faulty enough before) by Jezebel, so shall we now see still more brought into Judah (hitherto a righteous and prosperous people) by Athaliah, the daughter of Jezebel. I, however, shall not enter into the subject further than to draw from it what I can of evidence.

And here, before I proceed further, let me notice a circumstance, trivial in itself, which tends, however, to establish this reputed alliance of the houses of Jehoshaphat and Ahab as a matter of fact. There is no more cause, indeed, for calling this in question, than any other historical incident of an indifferent nature; but still, I am unwilling to let any opportunity pass of drawing out these tokens of truth, whether significant or not: be the gifts great or small, which are cast into the treasury of evidence, they contribute to swell the amount; they contribute to justify the general conclusion, that truth is still the pervading principle of the sacred writings, in minute as well as in momentous matters, in things which are, or which are not, of a kind to provoke investigation.

I am told, then, that a son of the King of Judah marries a daughter of the King of Israel. Now, agreeably to this, for some time afterwards, I discover a marked *identity* of names in the two families; so much so, as to render, whilst it lasts, the contemporary history of the two kingdoms extremely complicated and embarrassing. Thus, Ahab is succeeded by a son *Ahaziah* [1 Kings 22:49.] , on the throne of Israel; and Jehoram is also succeeded by a son *Ahaziah* (the nephew of the other), on the throne of Judah [2 Chron. 22:1.] . Again, Ahaziah, king of Israel, dies, and he is succeeded by a *Jehoram* [2 Kings 1:17; 3:1.] ; but a *Jehoram*, the brother-in-law of the former, is at the same moment on the throne of Judah, as his father's colleague [2 Kings 1:17.] . How much longer this mutual inter-change of family names might have continued, it is impossible to tell, for Ahab's house was cut off in the next generation by Jehu, and a new dynasty was set up; but the thing itself is curious; and however our patience may be put to the proof, in disengaging the thread of Israel and Judah at this point of their annals, we have the satisfaction of feeling that the intricacy of the history at such a moment is a very strong argument of the truth of the history. For, although no remark is made upon this identity of names, nor the least hint given as to the cause of it, we at once perceive that it may very naturally be referred to the union which is said to have taken place between the houses, and which many circumstances tend to show, however extraordinary it may seem, was a cordial union.

XXIX. THE PUBLIC CONSEQUENCES OF JEHORAM'S MARRIAGE

I now proceed to consider some of the public consequences of this marriage to Judah.

In the eighteenth verse of the eighth chapter of the second Book of Kings, we are informed of Jehoram's wickedness, and at whose instiga-tion it was wrought. In the twenty-second verse, we find it said (after some account of a rebellion of the Edomites), "then *Libnah* revolted at the same time." No cause is assigned for this revolt of Libnah; the few words quoted are incidentally introduced, and the subject is dismissed. But in the Chronicles [2 Chron. 21:10.] a cause is assigned, though still in a manner very brief and inexplicit; "the same time, also," (so the narrative runs,) "did Libnah revolt from under his hand; *because he had forsaken the Lord God of his fathers;*" that is, because, at the persuasion of

Athaliah—for she, we have found [2 Kings 8:18.] , was his state-adviser—Jehoram did what Ahab, his father-in-law, had done at the persuasion of the mother of Athaliah, set up a strange god in his kingdom, even Baal. Thus, this supplementary clause, short as it is, may serve, I think, as a clue to explain the revolt of Libnah; for Libnah, it appears from a passage in Joshua, was one of the cities of Judah, given to the *priests*, the sons of Aaron [Josh. 15:42; 21:13.] . No wonder, therefore, that the citizens of such a city should be the first to reject with indignation the authority of a monarch, who was even then setting at nought the God whose servants they especially were, and who was substituting for him the abomination of the Zidonians. This is the explanation of the revolt of Libnah. Yet, satisfactory as it is, when we are once fairly in possession of it, the explanation is anything but obvious. Libnah, it is said, revolts, but that revolt is not expressly coupled with the introduction of Baal into the country as a god; nor is that pernicious novelty coupled with the marriage of Athaliah; nor is any reason alleged why *Libnah* should feel peculiarly alive to the ignominy and shame of such an act; for where Libnah was, or what it was, or whereof its inhabitants consisted, are things unknown to the readers of Kings and Chronicles, and would continue unknown, were they not to take advantage of a hint or two in the Book of Joshua.

XXX. THE REVOLT OF LIBNAH

I am confirmed in the supposition that the revolt of Libnah is correctly ascribed to the indignation of the *Priests* at the worship of Baal, by other circumstances in the history of those times; for many things conspire to show, on the one side, the reckless idolatry of the royal house of Judah (so true to their God till the blood of the house of Ahab began to run in their veins); and, on the other side, the general disaffection of the ministers of God, and the desperate condition to which they were reduced. For when the Temple of Jerusalem was to be repaired, which was done by Joash, the grandson of Athaliah [2 Chron. 24:4.] , the effects of her wicked misrule incidentally come out. Not only had the utensils of the Temple been removed to the house of Baal, but its very walls had in many places been broken up, the ample funds put into the hands of the young king being principally devoted, not to decorations, but to the purchase of substantial materials, timber and stones; and from a casual expression touching the rites of the Temple, that "there were offered burnt-offerings in the House of the Lord *continually all the days of Jehoiada*," [2 Chron. 24:14.] it is pretty evident that, whilst Athaliah was in power, even these had been discontinued; that even Judah, the tribe of God's own choice, even Zion, the hill which he loved, paid him no longer any public testimony of allegiance, the faithful city herself became an harlot. So wanton was the defiance of the Most High God, during the reigns of Jehoram, Ahaziah, and the subsequent usurpation of Athaliah, when these, her husband, and her son, were dead.

On the other hand, Joash, the rightful possessor of the throne of Judah, an infant plucked from among his slaughtered kindred by an aunt, and saved from the murderous hands of a grandmother, grew up unobserved—where, of all places?—in *the Lord's House*, contiguous as it was to the palace of Athaliah, who little dreamed that she had such an enemy in such a quarter; the High Priest his protector; the Priests and Levites his future partizans; so that when events were ripe for the overthrow of Athaliah, the child was set up as the champion of the Church of God, so long prostrate before Baal, but still not spirit-broken—cast down, but not destroyed; and by that Church, and no party else, was he established; and the unnatural usurper was hurled from her polluted throne, with the shriek of treason upon her lips; and having lived like her mother, like her mother she died, killed under her own walls, and among the hoofs of the horses [2 Kings 11:16.] . This, I say, is a very consistent consummation of a resistance, of which the revolt of Libnah, some fourteen years before, was the earnest: in the revolt of Libnah, a city of the Priests, the disaffection of the Priests prematurely breaks out; in the dethronement of Athaliah, achieved by the Priests, that same disaffection finds its final issue; the interval between the two events having sufficed to fill up the iniquity of Baal's worshippers, and to organize a revolt upon a greater scale than that of Libnah, which restored its dues to the Church, and to God his servants, his offerings, and his house.

But will any man say that the sacred historian so ordered his materials, that such incidents as these which I have named should successively turn up—that he guided his hands in all this wittingly—that he let fall, with consummate artifice, first a brief and incidental notice (a mere parenthesis) of the revolt of a *single* town, suppressing meanwhile all mention of its peculiar constitution and character, though such as prepared it above others for revolt—that then, after abandoning not only Libnah, but the subject of Judah in general, and applying himself to the affairs of Israel in their turn, he should finally revert to his former topic, or rather to a kindred one, and lay before us the history of a *general* revolt, organized by the Priests; and all in the forlorn hope that the uniform working of the same principle of disaffection in the same party, and for the same cause, in two detached instances, would not pass unobserved; but that such consistency would be detected, and put down to the credit of the narrative at large? This surely is a degree of refinement much beyond belief.

Thus having traced this singular people through a long and most diversified history, we are come to see planted in both kingdoms of Israel and Judah the idolatrous principle which was shortly to be the downfal of both. God usually works out his own ends in the way of natural consequence, even his judgments being in general the ordinary fruits of the offences which called for them; and in this instance the calves of Jeroboam and the groves of Baal were the sin; and from the sin were made to flow, as a matter of course, the disgust of all virtuous Israelites, and the intestine divisions resulting from it; the interruption or suspension of all public worship; the mischiefs of a perpetual conflict between a national code of laws still in force, and national idolatry, no less actually established than the laws; the depravity of morals which that idolatry encouraged, and which served to sap the people's strength; all, elements of ruin which only wanted to be developed in order to be fatal, and which in a very few generations did their work.

It is curious to observe how the origin, the progress, and the consummation of the devastating principle, correspond in the two kingdoms.

Israel is the first to offend, both by the sin of Jeroboam and the sin of Ahab; and Israel is the first to have illustrious Prophets sent to him to counteract the evil, if it were possible—whom, however, he persecutes or slays; and Israel is the first to be carried into captivity.

Judah, after some years, follows the example of his rival. Idolatry, even the worst, that of the same Baal, is brought into Judah. Prophets, many and great, are now in turn sent to warn him of the evil to come; but now he too has declared for the groves; and those Prophets he stones, in one instance even between the porch and the altar; and, accordingly, by nearly the same interval as Judah followed Israel in his idolatries, did he follow him in his fate, and went after him to sit down and weep by the waters of Babylon. There is something very coincident in this relative scale of sin and suffering.

It was the office of those Prophets of whom I spoke, not only to foretel things to come, but also to denounce the sins of the times in which they lived; they were censors, as well as seers. Of the earlier race, Ahijah, Elijah, Elisha, and others, we have no writings at all, otherwise they would have doubtless offered, in their province as moralists, a mirror of their own age, in their own nation of Israel. Of the latter race, Isaiah, Jeremiah, and more, we possess the records, and in those records not unfrequently a picture of the condition of either kingdom; of Judah more especially. Here, therefore, a new scene opens before us; a new, though limited field of argument, such as I have been exploring, presents itself. It remains to produce a few such allusions to contemporary transactions as are blended with the prophecies—to examine how they tally with facts, as we find them set forth elsewhere by the sacred historians; and thence to derive vouchers for the veracious character of the Prophets themselves, such as may promote a disposition to give them at least a favourable hearing.

Part III

The Veracity of the Prophetical Scriptures

Thus far I have been applying the test of coincidence without design to the historical Scriptures; I will now do the same by some of the prophetical, founding the argument chiefly on a comparison of these latter writings with those details relating to the period in which the Prophet is said to have lived, given in the concluding chapters of the Books of Kings and Chronicles. It is possible that these coincidences may be thought proportionally fewer in number than those which other parts of Scripture have been found to supply; but it must be remembered, that the Books of the Prophets are not of any great bulk, and that the chapters in the Books of Kings and Chronicles which furnish materials for checking them, are neither long nor many. Moreover, which is the chief consideration, that the language of Prophecy, as might be expected, is commonly framed in terms so general, and often so dark and figurative, that it is easy to overlook a latent allusion to an event of the day which it may really contain, even where some notice of that event does happen also to be left on record in the contemporary history. With regard to such coincidences as we do find, it may be observed,

1. *First*, that the argument they furnish has a twofold value; since it not only demonstrates the Historian and the Prophet to be veracious—the one, in the narrative of facts, the other, in such allusions to them as blend with passages more strictly prophetical—but that it also serves to determine the date of the Prophet himself—a date which, when once obtained, fixes many other events of which he clearly seems to tell, far in futurity with respect to him, and so ministers to our conviction that it could not be of human knowledge that he spoke. We indeed, on whom the ends of the

world are come, may be supposed to stand less in need of such a confirmation of our faith in the Prophets; for since the objects of their prophecy are two: the more immediate events which were coming upon several kingdoms of the world, and especially those of Israel and Judah; and the more distant Advent of the Messiah; the evidence for the genuineness of their claim to the prophetical character arising out of this latter province, where they appear as heralds of the gospel, is strong to us, because we do see the actual circumstances of Jesus Christ and his coming, correspond in so express a manner with the sketch made of them, by Isaiah, for example (as nobody in this instance can dispute), so many hundred years before. But their contemporaries, or the generations who lived next to them (and these were the persons who admitted their writings into the prophetical canon), were cut off from this ground of confidence in their message; they must have rested their belief in them upon the accomplishment of their political prophecies alone, such being the only ones of which they lived to see the completion. Although therefore the mere fact of the Jews having of old agreed to acknowledge them as Prophets, is enough to show that such evidence alone sufficed for them, they being the best judges of what was sufficient; still if we have the means of convincing ourselves that these remarkably exact prophecies (claiming at least so to be), which related to the Assyrian invasions, the captivity, and the like, were certainly delivered long before the events arose, we shall have a further reason, over and above an experience of the fulfilment of those concerning the Messiah, for putting our trust in them, and considering them Prophets indeed.

2. Nor is this all. For, *Secondly*, it may be observed, that the effect of this evidence from coincidence without design is to show, that the prophet sometimes occupied a considerable range of years in the delivering of his predictions—thus, that the whole Book of Isaiah was not struck off at a heat, was no extempore effusion, but a collection of many distinct predictions (claiming to be such) uttered from time to time, as events, or the heart hot within the prophet, prompted them; that it was in truth, as the title describes it, "the vision which he saw concerning Judah and Jerusalem, in the days of Uzziah, Jotham, Ahaz, and Hezekiah, kings of Judah." Now this is an important consideration, because it argues that the prophet did not deliver himself of some happy oracle for the once, and earn the reputation of a seer by an accident, but maintained that character through a life— a circumstance which goes very far in itself to exclude the possibility of imposture, nothing being so fatal to fraud of this kind as time.

Having made these preliminary remarks, I shall now address myself to the argument itself.

I. ISAIAH AND THE CONDUIT OF THE UPPER POOL

In the seventh chapter of Isaiah we read that Ahaz king of Judah was threatened with invasion by the confederate armies of Syria and Israel, and that Isaiah the prophet was commissioned by God to foretel to Ahaz the result of this invasion; and not only so, but the disastrous end of one of those kingdoms, if not both of them, after a period of threescore and five years. And the charge is thus given to Isaiah: "Go forth now to meet Ahaz, thou and Shear-jashub thy son, at the end *of the conduit of the upper pool*, in the highway of the fuller's field" (v. 3). Here was to be the scene of the prophecy; and, accordingly, here it professes to have been actually spoken. To this point I would draw the attention of my readers, because the incidental mention of the place where it was to be delivered, furnishes us with the means of showing with great probability that a prophecy it was. For, why at the *end of the conduit of the upper pool?* No reason whatever is assigned, or even hinted for the choice of this particular spot, rather than the palace of Ahaz, or the city gate. But on turning to the thirty-second chapter of the second Book of Chronicles, in which are described the preparations made by king Hezekiah some thirty years afterwards against a similar invasion of Jerusalem by Sennacherib and the Assyrians, I find this to be amongst the number, that "he took counsel with his princes and his mighty men to stop the waters of the *fountains* which were *without the city;* and they did help him. So there was gathered much people who stopped *all the fountains*, and the brook that ran through the midst of the land, saying, Why should the kings of Assyria come, and find much water?" [2 Chron. 32:3–5.]

Here, then, in this passage of Hezekiah's history, have we the key to the passage in the history of Ahaz, which is now engaging our inquiry, and in which the prophecy of Isaiah is involved. "Isaiah was to *go forth* to meet Ahaz, at the *end of the conduit of the upper pool;*" to go forth—the conduit of the upper pool, therefore, was without the walls, open to the use of the enemy. Ahaz, therefore, we may *conjecture*, was employed, as we *know*, though not from Isaiah, Hezekiah under similar circumstances afterwards was employed, with a number of his people in providing a defence for the city by stopping the fountains, of which the enemy might get possession. The place, therefore, was *appropriate* to the subject of the message with which Isaiah was charged, namely, that their labours were needless, for that God would take care of their city; and it was *convenient* for the publication of it, because the work interested and occupied both the sovereign and the people, and consequently a multitude were there gathered together ready to hear it. Now it appears to me, that this casual mention of Ahaz, being for some reason or other to be found by the prophet at the conduit of the upper pool, to which he was to go *forth*, without one word of note or explanation why he should be found there, or what was its exact site, or why it should be a fit place for delivering the message, coupled with the satisfactory cause for his being there, which most incidentally we are enabled of ourselves to supply from another quarter, does establish it as a fact, that Ahaz was occupied with concerting measures of defence for the city when Isaiah hailed him. But if so, Isaiah's message must have necessarily been delivered when the invasion was only threatened, when there was yet time for making provision to meet it, and when the result of it, of which he speaks, must have been as yet in futurity; whilst events still beyond it, to which his words extend too, must have been in a futurity yet more distant; *i.e.* Isaiah must have been a *prophet.* Certainly it is a small matter of fact which lays the foundation for a great conclusion: but its seeming insignificance is just that which gives it extraordinary value for the purpose for which I use it; since it is impossible to believe that a forger of pretended prophecies, written after the event, would have hit upon such an expedient for stamping his imposture with a mark of truth, as to make the scene of this prediction a conduit outside the walls, without adding the most remote hint about the inference he meant to be drawn from it.

II. ISAIAH, URIAH THE PRIEST, AND ZECHARIAH

There is another coincidence, or at least a probable coincidence, between a passage in Isaiah (viii. 2), and other passages in the Books of Kings (2 Kings 16:10, 18:2), and Chronicles (2 Chron. 29:1), which goes to determine that the prophet was contemporary with Ahaz; thus identifying the age of Isaiah and the date of his prophecying, with a period a hundred and forty years before the Babylonish captivity, of which event nevertheless he is full to overflowing. The following is the coincidence I suppose.

It appears to have been an object with this prophet to warn Judah from depending upon Assyria for help against Syria and Israel.—He saw by the spirit, more to apprehend in the ally than in the adversary (opposed as this opinion was to the judgment of a generation who did not allow for the ambition of Assyria, and especially of Assyria when absorbed in the Babylonish empire [See Lightfoot, Vol. i. p. 114, fol. Hosea 5:13; 7:11.] , in its present profession of amity; nor the approaching downfall of Syria and Israel, in their actual strength). However, to impress this his prophetical view of things upon Ahaz the more effectually (the policy of that monarch having been to court Assyria [2 Chron. 28:16.]), he takes his pen, and writes in a great roll, again and again, after the manner of his age and nation, when symbolical teaching prevailed, one word of woe, Maher-shalal-hashbaz—"hasting to the spoil he hasteth to the prey"—which, being interpreted, spake of Assyria, that so it should come to pass, touching the havoc about to be wrought by Assyria; first, on the kingdoms of Syria and Israel; and eventually, when merged in the Chaldean kingdom, on Judah itself. And to render this act more emphatic, or to impress it the more memorably on the King, he calls in two witnesses, Uriah the priest, and Zechariah the son of Jeberechiah (Isa. 8:2) [Lightfoot, Vol. i. p. 101.] .

Now who are they? Names, it may be said, of unknown individuals perhaps; nay, possibly mere names; the whole being a figure, and not a fact. Yet I discern, on turning to the sixteenth chapter of the second Book of Kings, that one Uriah, he also a priest, was a person with whom king Ahaz was in close communication, using him as a tool for his own unlawful innovations in the worship of his country; "when he introduced into the temple the fashion of the altar which he had seen at Damascus:" in all which, we are told, "Uriah the priest did according to all that king Ahaz commanded" (v. 16). If therefore this was the same Uriah (for the coincidence turns on that), we have one witness taken from the confidential servants of the King. And with respect to Zechariah, the other witness, I learn from the eighteenth chapter of the same Book of Kings, that twenty and five years old was Hezekiah when he began to reign, and that "he reigned twenty and nine years in Jerusalem," and that "his mother name was Abi, the daughter of *Zechariah*" (v. 2). It should seem, therefore, that Ahaz, who was father of Hezekiah, was son-in-law of one Zechariah; if therefore this was the same Zechariah—for the coincidence again turns on that—we have a second witness taken from amongst the immediate connections of the King; and it may be added, that the probability of these parties mentioned in Isaiah being the same as those of the same names mentioned in the Book of Kings, is increased by their being *two* in number: had *Uriah* alone been spoken of in Isaiah, or *Zechariah* alone, and a single person of the same name been met with in the Book of Kings, as about the person of Ahaz, the identity of the two might have admitted of more dispute than when Uriah and Zechariah are *both* produced by the prophet, and are *both* found in the history. If the names had been twenty instead of two, and all had been found to agree, no doubt whatever of the identity could have been entertained.

Here, then, we can account for the choice of Isaiah, who wished the transaction in which he was engaged to be enforced upon the attention of Ahaz with all the advantages he could command, and so selected two of the King's bosom friends to testify concerning it.

This, I say, induces the belief that the prophet really was contemporary with Ahaz; for how can we suppose, that if his pretended prophecy had been a forgery of after times, so happy, because so trivial an evidence of its genuineness, should have been introduced, and the names of his witnesses have been selected, according so singularly with those of two men certainly about the person of Ahaz whilst he lived? And how difficult it is to imagine that a forger, even admitting that he adopted those names by a fortunate or astute device, should have stopped where he did, and not have taken care to make it *clear* that by them he meant the Uriah who was the priest of Ahaz, and the Zechariah who was his relation, instead of leaving the matter (as it is left) open to dispute [It is scarcely necessary to remark that Uriah (Isaiah 8:2) and Urijah (2 Kings 16:16) are the same word in the Hebrew.—Dr. Lightfoot takes for granted that the parties named in Isaiah and in Kings are the same. Vol. i. p. 101, fol.]!

III. THE ASSYRIAN ARMY, AND THE PROPHECY OF BABYLONIAN CAPTIVITY

The next coincidence which I shall lay before you is one which tends to establish two facts of the utmost importance; the one, that the Assyrian army under Sennacherib perished in some remarkable manner; the other, that the Babylonish Captivity was distinctly foretold, when Babylon was as yet no object of fear to Jerusalem.

With respect to the first, indeed, the sudden destruction of the Assyrian host, it was to be expected that if such a catastrophe did occur, it would be an epoch in the times, an event that would fill the whole East with its strangeness; and accordingly, the allusions to it, direct and indirect, which are to be met with in the writings of Isaiah, are very many. His mind seems much possessed by it; and this is indeed an argument for the truth of the fact, not feeble in itself—but the one I have to propose to you is more definite and precise.

In the thirty-ninth chapter of Isaiah, I read as follows: "At that time Merodach-baladan, the son of Baladan, king of Babylon, sent letters and a present to Hezekiah; for he had heard that he had been sick, and was recovered. And Hezekiah was glad of them, and showed them the house of his precious things, the silver, and the gold, and the spices, and the precious ointment, and all the house of his armour, and all that was found in his treasures; there was nothing in his house, nor in all his dominion, that Hezekiah showed them not. Then came Isaiah the prophet to king

Hezekiah, and said unto him, What said these men? and from whence came they unto thee? And Hezekiah said, They are come from a *far country* unto me, even from *Babylon*. Then said he, What have they seen in thy house? And Hezekiah answered, All that is in mine house have they seen; there is nothing among my treasures that I have not showed them. Then said Isaiah to Hezekiah, Hear the word of the Lord of hosts: Behold, the days come, that all that is in thine house, and that which thy fathers have laid up in store until this day, shall be carried to Babylon: nothing shall be left, saith the Lord. And of thy sons that shall issue from thee, which thou shalt beget, shall they take away; and their shall be eunuchs in the palace of the king of Babylon."

1. Now the first thing I would observe is this: that the embassy from the King of Babylon to Hezekiah was to congratulate him on his recovery from his sickness; which sickness must have befallen him in the year of Sennacherib's invasion, and immediately previous to it—in *that year*, because he is to said to have reigned twenty and nine years; [2 Kings 18:2.] and the invasion of Judah is said [2 Kings 18:13] to have occurred in the fourteenth year of his reign; leaving him still fifteen years to reign, which was precisely the period by which his life was prolonged beyond his sickness;—*immediately previous to that invasion*, because the prophet, in the same breath that he assures him from God of his recovery, assures him also that God would deliver the city out of the hand of the *King of Assyria*, and would defend the city (Is. 38:6), as though the danger was imminent [This clearly fixes the order of the two events, and shows that in 2 Chron. 32:21–24, the order is not observed.] . The recovery, therefore, of Hezekiah, and the destruction of the Assyrians, were events close upon one another in point of time. And after a short interval, allowing for the news of Hezekiah's recovery to reach Babylon, and an embassy to be prepared, that embassy of congratulation was despatched; or, in other words, the embassy from Babylon must have been close upon the destruction of the Assyrian army,

Now we are told, that upon the eve of the invasion of Jerusalem itself, and whilst Sennacherib was already in the country taking the fenced cities of Judah before him [2 Kings 18:13, 14.] , Hezekiah in his alarm endeavoured to buy off the King of Assyria: "That which thou puttest on me," said he, "will I bear"—"And the king of Assyria appointed unto Hezekiah three hundred talents of silver, and thirty talents of gold,"—a sum which completely exhausted the means of Hezekiah; insomuch that after he had given him all the silver that was found in the house of the Lord, and in the treasures of the King's house, he was reduced to the necessity of actually cutting off the gold from the doors of the temple, and from the pillars which he had overlaid, to give to the King of Assyria. Nothing, therefore, could be more complete than the *exhaustion of his resources*, whether those of the palace or of the temple, immediately before the advance of Sennacherib's army on the capital—for in spite of this cowardly sacrifice on the part of the Jews, the Assyrians broke faith with them, and marched on Jerusalem.

But from the passage in Isaiah (ch. 39.) which I have extracted, where the embassy from Babylon is mentioned, and the date of which has been already fixed (to the utmost probability at least), we gather that Hezekiah was then in possession of *a treasury singularly affluent;* so much so, indeed, as to lead him to make a vainglorious display of his vast magazines to these strangers—"he was glad of them, and shewed them the house of his precious things, the silver, and the gold, and the spices, and the precious ointments, and all the house of his armour, and all that was found in his treasures: there was nothing in his house, nor in all his dominion, that he showed them not." [Isaiah 39:2.]

Here there seems a strange and unaccountable contradiction to the penury he had exhibited so shortly before. A very brief interval had elapsed (as we have proved) since he had scraped the gilding from the very doors and pillars, to make up a sum to purchase the forbearance of the enemy; and now his store is become so ample as to betray him into the vanity of exposing it before the eyes of these suspicious strangers. There is no attempt made to account for the discrepancy. A passage, however, of a very few lines, and very incidentally dropping out in the thirty-second chapter of the second Book of Chronicles (v. 22, 23), and nowhere else, supplies the explanation of this extraordinary and sudden mutation. There, after a short account of the discomfiture of the Assyrians by the angel, it is added, "Thus the Lord saved Hezekiah and the inhabitants of Jerusalem from the hand of Sennacherib the king of Assyria, and from the hand of all other, and guided them on every side. And *many brought gifts unto the Lord to Jerusalem, and presents to Hezekiah king of Judah; so that he was magnified in the sight of all nations from thenceforth.*"

This fact clears up at once the apparent contradiction, though certainly introduced for no such purpose; no man can imagine it; indeed, the order of these several events is confounded in this chapter of Chronicles, and their mutual dependence (on which my argument rests) deranged: so free from all suspicion of contrivance is this combination of incidents in the narrative.

For only let us recapitulate the several particulars of the argument. From a passage in the second Book of Kings (18:13, 14), I learn that Hezekiah spent his resources to the very last to bribe the Assyrian to forbearance; but, as it proved, in vain.

By a comparison of a passage in 2 Kings (18:13, 14), with another in Isaiah (38:1–6), I learn, that the sickness of Hezekiah was immediately before the invasion of Jerusalem by the Assyrians.

By another passage in Isaiah (39:1), I learn that an embassage of congratulation was sent to Hezekiah from Babylon, on his recovery from his sickness. By the same, that these ambassadors found him then in possession of a treasury full to overflowing.

I am at a loss to account for this, nor does the Scripture take any pains to do it for me; but I find, incidentally, a passage in the second Book of Chronicles, which says (32:22, 23) that many had brought gifts to the Lord at Jerusalem, and presents to Hezekiah; so that he was thenceforth magnified in the sight of all nations.

This explains the change of circumstances I had observed for *myself*. The several particulars, therefore, of the history, gleaned from this quarter and that, perfectly cohere; are evidently component parts of one trustworthy narrative; and no reasonable doubt will remain upon our minds, that Hezekiah was greatly straightened before the invasion, and was suddenly replenished after it; but then the truth of these facts bears upon the truth of the wonderful event which is said to have accompanied and terminated that invasion; not indeed *proving* the truth of it, but very remarkably agreeing with the supposition of its truth. For certainly this extraordinary and voluntary influx of gifts to Jerusalem from the nations round about, sinking as Judah had long been in its position amongst those nations, indicates some strong re-action or other in its favour at that time; as indeed does this embassage from a *far country* (such is the description of it), a country then comparatively but little known. The dignity of Israel seems to have once more asserted itself; and though it is not to be affirmed as a positive fact (at least on the authority of the Book of Kings or of Isaiah, though the Book of Chronicles, howbeit, in other parts of this transaction so defective, does seem to imply it), that the *miraculous* destruction of the Assyrian army was the event which had caused this strong sensation in the countries round about; yet such an event, to say the least, is very consistent with it; and accordingly, the passage of Chronicles to which I refer (32:23), tells us, that "many brought gifts to the *Lord* at Jerusalem," as well as "presents to Hezekiah," in testimony, it may be presumed, of the work being the Lord's doing, and not the act of man; *i.e.* that the Assyrian host fell by an infliction from heaven, and not by any ordinary defeat; and if it should suggest itself, that a part of these treasures might have been derived from the spoils of the Assyrian host, and that the amount of gifts from the surrounding nations might have been augmented by the sacking of the tents of the enemy; even as "all the way was full of garments and vessels" (we are told on another occasion of the sudden overthrow of an army of a different nation) "which the Syrians had cast away in their haste;" [2 Kings 7:15.] the argument remains still the same.

2. Neither is this all. Hitherto, we have merely derived from the coincidence an argument for the truth of the *miracle*.

But it also confirms the *prophecy* touching the captivity to Babylon; and shows the words to have been spoken very long before the event.

For the aptness with which the several independent particulars we have collected fit into one another, when brought into juxtaposition, without being packed for the purpose, viz., the threat of the Assyrian invasion; the impoverishment of the exchequer of Hezekiah to avert it; the overthrow of the Assyrian host; the influx of treasure to Jerusalem from foreign nations, or from the enemy's camp; the recovery of Hezekiah; the arrival of the embassage of congratulation from Babylon; the wealth he now exhibits to that embassage, even to ostentation; the harmony, I say, with which these several incidents concur, both in details and dates, is such as could only result from the truth of the whole and of its parts. If we take therefore this fact as a basis, as a fact established, for so I regard it, that at that time Merodach-baladan, the son of Baladan, sent letters and a present to Hezekiah; for he had heard that he had been sick and was recovered; and that Hezekiah showed the messengers all that was found in his treasures, &c., the warning of Isaiah to which Hezekiah's vanity gives occasion, rises so naturally out of the premises, is so entirely founded upon them, and so intimately combined with them, that it is next to impossible not to accept it as a fact too. The folly of the King, and the reproof of the prophet, must stand or fall together: the one prompts the other; the truth of the one sustains the truth of the other; the date of the one fixes the date of the other. But this warning, this reproof of Isaiah, and this confession of the King, runs thus:—"What said these men? and from whence came they unto thee?" To which Hezekiah made answer, "They are come from a far country unto me, even from Babylon. Then said he, What have they seen in thine house? And Hezekiah answered, All that is in mine house have they seen; there is nothing among my treasures that I have not shewed them. Then said Isaiah to Hezekiah, Hear the word of the Lord of hosts: Behold, the days come, that all that is in thine house, and that which thy fathers have laid up in store until this day, shall be carried to Babylon, and nothing shall be left, saith the Lord." [Isaiah 39.]

Thus the period of Hezekiah's display of his finances being determined to a period soon after the downfall of the Assyrians, this rebuke of the prophet which springs out of it is determined to the same. Then the rebuke was a prophecy; for as yet it remained for Esar-haddon, the son of Sennacherib, to annex Babylon to Assyria by conquest—it remained for the two kingdoms to continue united for two generations more—it remained for Nabopolassar, the satrap of Babylon, to revolt from Assyria, and set up that kingdom for itself—and it remained for Nebuchadnezzar his son to succeed him, and by carrying away the Jews to Babylon, accomplish the words of Isaiah. But this interval occupied a hundred years and upwards; and so far, therefore, must the spirit of prophecy have carried him forward into futurity; and that, too, contrary to all present appearances; for Babylon was as yet but a name to the people of Jerusalem—it was a far country, and was to be swallowed up in the great Assyrian empire, and recover its independence once more, before it could be brought to act against Judah.

The only objection to this argument which I can imagine is, that the prophetical part of the passage might have been grafted upon the historical part by a later hand; but the seaming, I think, must in that case have appeared. Whereas the prophecy is in the form of a rebuke; the rebuke inseparably connected with Hezekiah's vainglorious display of his treasures; his possession of those treasures to display, at the peculiar crisis when the embassy arrived, though shortly before his poverty was excessive, confirmed as a matter of fact beyond all reasonable doubt, by an undesigned coincidence. The premises, then, being thus established in truth, and the consequences flowing from them being so close and so natural, it is less easy to suppose them fictitious than prophetical.

IV. SENNACHERIB'S INVASION

There is another ingredient in the details of this invasion of Sennacherib which, when compared with a passage in Isaiah, furnishes, I think, a probable coincidence; and tends to hem round the wonderful event which is said to have attended that invasion, with still more evidence of truth.

When the King of Assyria sent his host against Jerusalem on this occasion, the persons deputed by Hezekiah to confer with his captains, were, we read, "Eliakim, the *son* of Hilkiah, which was over the household, and Shebna the scribe, and Joah the *son* of Asaph the recorder." [2 Kings 18:18.] Their names occur more than once [2 Kings 19:2; Isa. 36:3.] , and still with this distinction, namely, that the parentage of Eliakim and of Joah is given, but not that of Shebna: of the two former it is told whose sons they were, as well as what offices they held; whilst Shebna is designated by his office only.

Now is there a reason for this, or is it merely the effect of accident? The omission certainly may be accidental, but I will suggest a ground for thinking it not so, and will leave my readers to be the judges of the matter.

In the twenty-second chapter of Isaiah (15, *et seq.*) we find the prophet delivering a message of wrath against one Shebna, in the following terms: "Thus saith the Lord God of hosts, Go, get thee unto this treasurer, even unto Shebna, which is over the house, and say, *What hast thou here? and whom hast thou here*, that thou hast hewed thee out a *sepulchre here*, as he that heweth him out a sepulchre on high, and that graveth an habitation for himself in a rock? Behold, the Lord will carry thee away with a mighty captivity, and will surely cover thee. He will surely violently turn and toss thee like a ball into a large country: there shalt thou die, and there the chariots of thy glory shall be the shame of thy lord's house. And I will drive thee from thy station, and from thy state shall he pull thee down." The purport of which rebuke is that, whereas Shebna was busily engaged in constructing for himself a sumptuous sepulchre at Jerusalem, as though he and his posterity were to have that for their burial-place for ever, he might spare himself the pains, for that God, for some transgression of his which is not mentioned, was about to depose him from the post of honour which he held, and banish him from his city, and leave him to die in a strange land.

It is true that Shebna is here called the "treasurer," whereas the Shebna mentioned in the Book of Kings, with whom the coincidence requires that he should be identified, is called "the scribe," but the two periods are not necessarily the same, and he might have been "the treasurer," at the one, and "the scribe," at the other; for that he is the same man I can have no doubt, not merely from Shebna in either case belonging clearly to the King's court, which greatly limits the conditions; but from Eliakim the son of Hilkiah being again spoken of immediately in connection with him, in the passage of Isaiah (5:20), as he had been in the passage of the Book of Kings. It being presumed, then, that the Shebna of Isaiah and the Shebna of the Book of Kings is the same person, I account for the omission of his parentage in the history from the circumstance of his being a *foreigner* at Jerusalem, whilst Eliakim and Joah were native Jews whose genealogy was known; and this fact I conclude from the expression in Isaiah which I have printed in Italics, "*What hast thou here, and whom hast thou here*, that thou hast hewed thee out a *sepulchre here?*" Jerusalem not having been the burial-place of his family, because he did not belong to Jerusalem.

V. HEPHZI-BAH AND BEULAH

In the 62nd chapter of this same prophet Isaiah; reference is made to the future restoration of the Jewish Church; in the first sense, perhaps, and as a frame-work of more, its restoration from Babylon; in a second, its eventual restoration to Christ, and the coming in of the Jew and Gentile together. "Thou shalt no more be termed *Forsaken*,"—so Isaiah here expresses himself concerning Jerusalem,—"neither shall thy land any more be termed *Desolate;* but thou shalt be called *Hephzi-bah*, and thy land *Beulah:* for the Lord *delighteth* in thee, and thy land shall be married." (v. 4.)

The figure here employed is that of a marriage: there is to be a marriage between God and his Church: that divorce from God, which the sins of Jerusalem had effected, was to be done away, and the nuptial bond be renewed. Jerusalem was to be no longer as a widow, *Forsaken* and *Desolate*, but to be as a bride, and to be called *Hephzi-bah, i.e.,* "in her is my delight," and "*Beulah," i.e.,* married. The verse immediately following the one I have produced, still continues the same figure: "For as a young man marrieth a virgin, so shall thy sons marry (or again live with) thee; and as the bridegroom rejoiceth over the bride, so shall thy God rejoice over thee" (ver. 5). Now it is impossible to read the prophets with the least attention, and not discover that the incidents upon which they raise their oracular superstructure are in general real matters of fact which have fallen in their way. When they soar even into their sublimest flights, they often take their spring from some solid and substantial footing. Our Lord was acting quite in the spirit of the older prophets when He advanced from his observations on the temple before him, and the desolation it was soon to suffer, to the final consummation of all things, and the breaking up of the universal visible world; and the commentary of those who would endeavour to construe the whole by a reference to the destruction of Jerusalem only is not imbued with the spirit of the prophets of ancient times.

From the passage before us, then, it should seem that some nuptial ceremony was the accident of the day which gave the prophet an opportunity of uttering his parable concerning the future fortune of Jerusalem. Can we trace any such event in the history of those days, likely from its importance to arrest public attention, and thus to furnish Isaiah with this figure? I do not say positively that we can; nevertheless the name of *Hephzi-bah*, which he assigns to this his new Jerusalem, may throw some light upon our inquiry; for in the twenty-first chapter of the second Book of Kings I read that "Manasseh" (the son of Hezekiah) "was twelve years old when he began to reign, and reigned fifty and five years in Jerusalem, and his mother's name was *Hephzi-bah*." [2 Kings 21:1.] It is not improbable, therefore, that the royal nuptials of Hezekiah occurred about the time of this prophecy; and that Isaiah, after the manner of the prophets in general, availed himself of the passing event, and of the name of the bride, as a vehicle for the tidings which he had to communicate. This, too, may seem the more likely, because this prophecy of Isaiah does not appear to have been spoken at an early period of his mission, but subsequently to the sickness and recovery of Hezekiah (if the prophecies at least are arranged at all in the order in which they were delivered); neither is it probable that the marriage of Hezekiah was contracted till after that same sickness and recovery, seeing that his son and successor was but *twelve* years old at his father's death, which happened, we know, fifteen years after his illness.

VI. ISAIAH CONTEMPORARY WITH UZZIAH, JOTHAM, AHAZ AND HEZEKIAH

But it is not by single and separate coincidences only, that the authority of these prophecies is upheld: there are some coincidences of a more comprehensive and general kind, that argue the same truth. Thus, the scenes amongst which Isaiah seems to write, indicate the commonwealth of Israel to be yet standing. He remonstrates, in the name of God, with the people for a hypocritical observance of the Fast-days (ch. 58:3); for exacting usurious profits nevertheless; for prolonging unlawfully the years of bondage (v. 6); for profaning the Sabbaths (v. 13); for confounding all distinction between clean and unclean meats (ch. 65:4; 66:17). He makes perpetual allusions, too, to the existence of false prophets in Jerusalem, as though this class of persons was very common whilst Isaiah was writing; the most likely persons in the world to be engendered by troubled times. And above all, he reviles the people for their gross and universal idolatry; a sin, which in all its aspects, is pursued from the fortieth chapter to the last with a ceaseless, inextinguishable, unmitigated storm of mockery, contempt, and scorn. With what position of the prophet can these, and many similar allusions, be reconciled, but with that of a man dwelling in Judea before the captivity, during a period, which, as historically described in the latter chapters of the Books of Kings and Chronicles, presents the express counterpart of those references in the prophet? Hezekiah and Josiah, the two redeeming princes of that time, serving, as breakers, to make manifest the fury with which the tide of abominations of every kind was running. I say, to what other period, and to what other position of the writer, does the internal evidence of Isaiah point? indirectly, indeed, but not on that account, in a manner the less conclusive. Had he taken up his parable during the Babylonish bondage, would there not have been frequent and inadvertent allusions to the circumstances of Babylon? Could his style have escaped the contagious influence of the scenes around him? even as the case actually is with Daniel, whose dwelling was at Babylon. Yet in Isaiah there are no allusions of this nature. It is of Jerusalem, and not of Babylon, that his roll savours throughout; of the land of Israel, and not of Chaldea. Moreover, it is of Jerusalem before the captivity; for after that trying furnace through which the Jewish nation was condemned to pass, it was disinfected of idolatry. Nay, a horror of idolatry succeeded, great as had been the propensity to it aforetime; the whole nation baring their necks to the sword, rather than admit within their walls even a Roman Eagle: whilst the ritual observances of the law, so far from falling into desuetude and contempt, were now kept with even a superstitious scrupulosity.

I think, then, that the several undesigned coincidences between passages in Isaiah, and others in the Books of Kings and Chronicles, which have been now adduced, are enough to prove that the prophet was contemporary with Uzziah, Jotham, Ahaz, and Hezekiah, and saw his vision in their days, even as its title declares. The mere introduction of the names of these princes into the pages of Isaiah, is not the argument on which I rely. It might be said, however improbably, that an author of a date much lower, might have admitted these names, and fragments of history connected with them, into his rhapsody, in order to give it a colouring of fact; but it is the indirect coincidences between the prophet and the history, which verifies the date of the former—allusions, mere allusions, to obscure servants of these sovereigns (known to be such); to a marriage of the day; to the stopping of a well; to the foolish exhibition of a treasure—allusions, indeed, in some cases so indistinct, that the full drift of the prophet would have escaped us, but for the historian. Such an argument ought to satisfy us that Isaiah was as surely alive, and dead, long before the Babylonish captivity, which he so accurately foretold, even to the deliverance from it—a still further reach into futurity—as that Ahaz and Hezekiah lived and died long before it; an argument, therefore, which justifies the Jews in their enrolment of his name amongst the most distinguished of the prophets, though they had no other ground for so doing than their knowledge of his exact prediction of the events of those days; and which must leave us without excuse in our incredulity, born as we are after the advent of that Messiah which forms so principal a subject of Isaiah's writings besides; and whose character and Gospel we have found to correspond in so remarkable a manner to the description of both which they contain. For it is not the least singular or the least satisfactory feature in the writings of Isaiah that they should thus relate to two distinct periods, separated by a wide interval of time, and be found to be so exact in both; that they should have first taken for their field the events preceding and accompanying the captivity, foretelling them so faithfully as to convince the Jew that he was one of the greatest of his prophets: that some hundreds of years should then be allowed to elapse, of which they are silent; and that then they should break out again on the subject of a second and altogether different series of incidents, so deeply interesting to the Christian, and be found by him, in his turn, to be so wonderfully true to them—so wonderfully true to them, that he cannot but be surprised that the Jew, whose acceptance of the prophet was even already secured by the previous stage of his prophecy, of which we have been now examining the evidence, should still be unable to see in him the prophet of Jesus Christ of Nazareth too.

VII. NO QUEEN FOR THE JEHOIACHIN?

We next come to the writings of Jeremiah, which do not, however, supply many arguments of the kind I am collecting, nor perhaps any so persuasive in their character as some which I have produced from Isaiah. Still there are several which at least deserve to be brought before my readers.

In the midst of a denunciation of evils to come upon Jerusalem for her wickedness, which we find in the thirteenth chapter of Jeremiah,—a denunciation for the most part expressed in general terms, and in a manner not conveying any very exact allusions,—we read at the eighteenth verse, "Say unto the King and to the *Queen*, Humble yourselves, sit down: for your principalities shall come down, even the crown of your glory." Jeremiah does not here tell us the name either of the king or the queen referred to; but as the queens of Israel do not figure prominently in the history of that nation, except where there is something peculiar in their characters or condition to bring them out, it may be thought there was something of the kind in this instance: and accordingly we have mention made in the twenty-fourth chapter of the second Book of Kings of an invasion of the Chaldeans, attended by circumstances corresponding to what we might expect from this exclamation of Jeremiah. It was the second of the three invasions which occurred at that time within a few years of one another, to which I allude [2 Kings 24:1. 10; 25:1.] ; an invasion made by the servants of Nebuchadnezzar, followed by Nebuchadnezzar himself in person. On this occasion it is said, that "Jehoiachin the king of Judah, went out to the king of Babylon, he, and his *mother*, and his servants, and his princes, and his officers: and the king of Babylon took him in the eighth year of his reign" (v. 12): and again, "And he carried away Jehoiachin to Babylon, and the king's *mother*, and the king's wives, and his officers, and the mighty of the land, those carried he into captivity from Jerusalem to Babylon." (v. 15.)

As Jehoiachin was at that time only eighteen years old, and had reigned no more than three months (v. 8), the queen dowager was no doubt still a person of consequence, possibly his adviser, at any rate an influential person as yet, so short a period having elapsed since the death of her husband the last king; and thus an object of pity to the prophet, and one that called for express notice and remark.

VIII. "WEEP FOR HIM THAT GOETH AWAY, FOR HE SHALL NOT RETURN"

Jeremiah 22:10–12, furnishes us with another instance of coincidence without design, calculated to establish our belief in that prophet. We there read, "Weep ye not for the *dead*, neither bemoan him: but weep for *him that goeth away;* for he shall return no more, nor see his native country. For thus saith the Lord touching Shallum the son of Josiah, king of Judah, which reigned instead of Josiah his father, which went forth out of this place; He shall not return thither any more: but he shall die in the place whither they have led him captive, and shall see this land no more."

Now this passage evidently relates to several events familiar to the minds of those whom the prophet was addressing. It is a series of allusions to circumstances known to them, but by no means sufficiently developed to put us in possession of the tale without some further key. It should appear that there had been a great public mourning in Jerusalem: but it is not distinctly said for whom; it might be supposed for Josiah, whose name occurs in the paragraph;—that another calamity had come upon its heels very shortly afterwards, calling, as the prophet thought, for expressions of national sorrow which might even supersede the other; a prince, the son of Josiah, led away captive into a foreign land; but whither he was thus led, or by whom, is not declared. The whole is evidently the discourse of a man living amongst the scenes he touches upon, and conscious that he has no need to do more than touch upon them to make himself understood by his hearers.

Now let us turn to the thirty-fifth and thirty-sixth chapters of the second Book of Chronicles, where certain historical details of the events of those times are preserved, and the key will be supplied. In the former chapter I find that the death of Josiah, a king who had been a blessing to his kingdom, and who was slain by an arrow, as he fought against the Egyptians, was in fact an event that filled all Jerusalem with consternation and grief: "he died, and was buried in one of the sepulchres of his fathers. And all Judah and Jerusalem mourned for Josiah. And Jeremiah lamented for Josiah: and all the singing men and the singing women spake of Josiah in their lamentations unto this day, and made them an ordinance in Israel: and, behold, they are written in the lamentations." [2 Chron. 35:24, 25.] Here we have the first feature in Jeremiah's very transient sketch completed.

I look at the continuation of the history in the next chapter, and I there find that the son of Josiah, Jehoahaz by name (and not called Shallum in the Chronicles), "began to reign, and he reigned *three months* in Jerusalem; and the king of Egypt put him down at Jerusalem, and condemned the land in a hundred talents of silver and a talent of gold. And the king of Egypt made Eliakim his brother king over Judah and Jerusalem, and turned his name to Jehoiakim. And Necho *took Jehoahaz his brother, and carried him to Egypt.*" Here we have the other outlines of Jeremiah's picture filled up. The second calamity did come, it appears, on the heels of the first, for it was only after an interval of three months. The King of Egypt, we now find, was the conqueror who carried the prince away, and Egypt was the country to which he was conducted. And though the victim is called Jehoahaz in the history, and Shallum in the prophet, the facts concerning him tally so exactly, that there can be no doubt of the identity of the man; whilst the absence of all attempt on either side to explain or reconcile this difficulty about the name, is a clear proof that neither passage was written in reference to the other: though it may be conjectured, that as Necho gave a new name to Eliakim [2 Kings 23:34.] , the one brother, so he might have done the like by the other, and called him Shallum instead of Jehoahaz.

But there is a further hint. "Weep ye not," says Jeremiah, "for the dead: but weep for him that goeth away: for he shall return no more." This should imply that the prince of whom Jerusalem was thus bereft, was *acceptable to his people;* more acceptable than he who was to supply his place. The thing to be lamented was that he would return no more. It is true that for the little time Jehoahaz reigned, he did evil in the sight of the Lord [2 Kings 23:32.] ; but so did Jehoiakim [2 Chron. 36:5.] ; so that in this respect there was nothing to choose; and in the condition of the Jews at that time, an irreligious prince (for that would be the meaning of the term) would not necessarily be an unpopular one. I repeat, therefore, that the words of Jeremiah seem to indicate that the prince who had been carried away was more acceptable than the one who was left in his stead. I now turn, once again, to the thirty-sixth chapter of the second Book of Chronicles (v. 1), or to the twenty-third chapter of the second Book of Kings (v. 30), and I there discover (for the incident is not obvious) a particular with regard to this prince who was carried away captive by Necho, and to his brother who was appointed to reign in his stead, very remarkably coinciding with these inuendos of Jeremiah. For in the former reference it is said, that on the death of Josiah, "*the people of the land took Jehoahaz,*" (the Shallum of the Prophet) "the son of Josiah, and made him king in his father's stead at Jerusalem. Jehoahaz," it continues, "was twenty and three years old when he began to reign." Then comes the history of his deposal, abduction, and of the substitution of his brother Eliakim to reign in Jerusalem in his place, under the name of Jehoiakim: "and Jehoiakim," it is added, "was twenty and five years old when he began to reign." Now inasmuch as Jehoahaz had reigned only three months, Jehoahaz must have been younger than Jehoiakim by nearly two years: how then came the younger son to succeed his father on the throne in the first instance? "*The people of the land took him,*" we have read: *i.e.,* he was the more popular character, and therefore they set him on the throne in spite of the superior claims of the firstborn. And a phrase which occurs in the latter of the two references confirms this view; for the people are there said not only to have taken him, but to have "*anointed him*"—a ceremonial, which, whether invariably observed or not in cases of ordinary descent of the crown, never seems to have been omitted in cases of doubtful succession [See 2 Kings 9:3, and Patrick in loc. and also on 2 Kings 23:30.] .

This history, it will be seen, supplies with great success the particulars which are incidentally omitted in the prophecy, though clearly constructed with no such intention; and fixes the date of Jeremiah to a period long before several of the events which he foretells.

IX. THE MEDO-PERSIAN EMPIRE

Daniel 5:30 "In that night was Belshazzar the king of the Chaldeans slain. And Darius the Median took the kingdom, being about threescore and two years old."

6:1. "It pleased Darius to set over the kingdom *an hundred and twenty princes, which should be over the whole kingdom.*" Thus the Medo-Persian empire consisted at this time of a *hundred and twenty provinces.*

In Daniel 8:4, where the vision, though occurring to Daniel before the capture of Babylon, relates to the progress of events after that conquest, and when the Medo-Persian empire was established, we read: "I saw the ram" (which had two horns, the Medo-Persian empire) *"pushing westward, and northward, and southward;* so that no beasts might stand before him, neither was there any that could deliver out of his hand; but he did according to his will, and became great." The obvious meaning of which passage is, that the Medo-Persian empire was enlarged soon after its first creation; that the hundred and twenty provinces of which it originally consisted, received an accession.

Now let us turn to the Book of Esther, which relates to the same empire, and evidently to a somewhat later period of it, be Ahasuerus who he may. There we are told, 1:1, 2, 3: "Now it came to pass in the days of Ahasuerus, (this is Ahasuerus, which reigned, from India even unto Ethiopia, *over an hundred and seven and twenty provinces:)* that in those days, when the king Ahasuerus sat on the throne of his kingdom, which was in Shushan the palace, in the third year of his reign, he made a feast unto all his princes and his servants; the power of Persia and Media, the nobles and princes of the provinces, being before him."

Here it appears that the number of the provinces was a *hundred and twenty-seven.* Thus, by comparing the latter of these two epochs with the former—an interval of seventeen years according to Archbishop Usher's chronology—we find that seven provinces had been added to the empire: the Book of Esther incidentally establishing the conclusion which the Book of Daniel as incidentally put us in search of.

X. DEARTH IN THE DAYS OF THE KINGS OF JUDAH

Of Hosea, we read that he prophesied "in the days of *Uzziah*, Jotham, Ahaz, and Hezekiah, kings of Judah." 1:1.

In the course of this prophecy we find frequent incidental allusions to a *scarcity of food* in the land of Israel.

"Therefore will I return, and take away my corn in the time thereof, and my wine in the season thereof," 2:9. "I will destroy her vines and her fig-trees," 12. "Therefore shall the land mourn, and every one that dwelleth therein shall languish, with the beasts of the field, and with the fowls of heaven; yea, the fishes of the sea also shall be taken away," 4:3. "They have not cried unto me with their heart, when they howled upon their

180

beds: they assembled themselves for corn and wine, and they rebel against me," 7:14. "They have sown the wind, and they shall reap the whirlwind: it hath no stalk: the bud shall yield no meal:" 8:7. "The floor and the winepress shall not feed them, and the new wine shall fail in her." 9:2.

Again, Amos is said to have prophesied concerning Israel "in the days of *Uzziah*, king of Judah, and in the days of Jeroboam the son of Joash, king of Israel." 1:1.

In this prophet also, in like manner, as in the former, we find incidental allusions to *dearth* in the land. "The habitations of the shepherds shall mourn, and the top of Carmel shall wither," 1:2. "I also have given you cleanness of teeth in all your cities, and want of bread in all your places, yet have ye not returned unto me, saith the Lord. And also I have withholden the rain from you, when there were yet three months to the harvest: ... So two or three cities wandered unto one city, to drink water; but they were not satisfied:... I have smitten you with blasting and mildew: when your gardens, and your vineyards, and your fig-trees, and your olive-trees increased, the palmerworm devoured them:... they shall call the husbandman to the mourning.... And in all vineyards shall be wailing;" 4:6–9; 5:16, 17.—With more to the same effect in both these prophets.

Now, if we turn to 2 Chronicles 26:10, where we have a brief history of the reign of this same king *Uzziah*, under whom we have seen they lived, we shall find a feature of it recorded, which seems to tally extremely well with this representation of the condition of Israel. For it is there told of him, amongst other things, that "he built towers in the desert, and digged many wells: for he had much cattle, both in the low country, and in the plains: husbandmen also, and vine dressers in the mountains, and in Carmel: *for he loved husbandry*." As though the precarious state of the supply of food in the country had turned the King's attention in a particular manner to the improvement of its agriculture.

XI. AMOS THE HERDSMAN

It has been remarked, with respect to the Prophet Amos, that the style in which his prophecies are written, and the images with which they abound, are in strict harmony with his calling and occupation. Yet, whatever coincidence of this kind there may be, is evidently casual.

Thus in chap. 7:14, we read, "Then answered Amos, and said to Amaziah, I was no prophet, neither was I a prophet's son; but I was an *herdman, and a gatherer of sycomore fruit:* And the Lord took me as *I followed the flock*, and the Lord said unto me, Go, prophesy unto my people Israel."

Compare this with the following passages, all found in the compass of nine chapters, for the Book of Amos consists of no more, and those short ones.

Ch. 1:2. "And the habitations of the *shepherds* shall mourn, and the top of Carmel shall wither."

3. "For three transgressions of Damascus, and for four, I will not turn away the punishment thereof; because they have *threshed* Gilead with *threshing instruments* of iron:"

2:9. "Yet destroyed I the Amorite before them, whose height was like the height of the *cedars*, and he was strong as the *oaks*; yet I destroyed his *fruit* from above, and his *roots* from beneath."

13. "Behold, I am pressed under you, as *a cart is pressed that is full of sheaves*."

3:4. "Will a *lion roar in the forest*, when he hath no prey? will a young lion cry out of his den, if he have taken nothing?"

5. "Can a *bird fall in a snare* upon the earth, where no gin is for him? shall one take up a snare from the earth, and have taken nothing at all?"

12. "As the *shepherd taketh out of the mouth of the lion two legs, or a piece of an ear;* so shall the children of Israel be taken out."

4:3. "And ye shall go out at the breaches, *every cow at that which is before her*."

5:11. "Forasmuch therefore as your treading is upon the poor, and *ye take from him burdens* of *wheat,* " &c.

16. "Alas! alas! and they shall call *the husbandman* to mourning, ... and in all *vineyards* shall be wailing."

19. "As if a man did flee from a *lion*, and a *bear* met him."

6:4. They "that lie upon beds of ivory, and stretch themselves upon their couches, and *eat the lambs out of the flock, and the calves out of the midst of the stall*."

12. "Shall *horses run upon the rock? will one plough there with oxen?*"

7:1. "And, behold, he formed grasshoppers in the beginning of the *shooting up of the latter growth; and, lo! it was the latter growth after the king's mowings*."

8:1. "Thus hath the Lord God shewed unto me: and behold a *basket of summer fruit.*

2. "And he said, Amos, what seest thou? and I said, A basket of summer fruit."

5. "When will the new moon be gone, that we may sell *corn?* and the sabbath, that we may set forth *wheat? ...*"

6. "Yea, and sell the refuse of the *wheat?*"

9:9. For, lo! I will command, and I will sift the house of Israel among all nations, *like as corn is sifted in a sieve, yet shall not the least grain fall upon the earth.*"

13. "Behold, the days come, saith the Lord, that the *plowman shall overtake the reaper, and the treader of grapes him that soweth seed; and the mountains shall drop sweet wine....*"

14. "... And they shall *plant vineyards, and drink the wine thereof;* they shall also make gardens, and eat the fruit of them. And I will *plant* them upon their land, and they shall no more be *pulled up* out of their land."

I do not press this argument beyond a point. All I mean to say is, that the occupation of the prophet being accidentally made known to us, his language throughout his prophecy is just what might be expected to result from it.

XII. AMOS THE PROPHET

The following is an example of a case where the hints which transpire in the prophet agree very well with particulars recorded in the history; but perhaps that is all that can be said of it with safety: the language of the prophet not being sufficiently specific to fix the coincidence to a certainty. The reader must judge for himself of the value of the argument in this particular instance.

We read in Amos (7:10, 11) as follows: "Then Amaziah the priest of Beth-el sent to Jeroboam king of Israel, saying, Amos hath conspired against thee in the midst of the house of Israel: *the land is not able to bear all his words.* For thus Amos saith, Jeroboam shall die by the sword, and Israel shall surely be led away captive out of their own land."

We have here a priest of Beth-el, *i.e.*, of the calves, denouncing to the King of Israel the prophet Amos, as one who was unsettling the minds of the people by his prophecies—prophecies which "*the land was not able to bear.*" It would seem then, from this phrase, that the state was in a critical condition; such a condition as gave double force to a prediction which went to deprive it of its king, and to consign its children to bondage. It was ill able to spare Jeroboam, or bear up against evil forebodings. This we gather from the passage of Amos.

Let us now turn to the fourteenth chapter of the second Book of Kings. There we read, first of all, of Jeroboam, that "he departed not from all the sins of Jeroboam the son of Nebat, who made Israel to sin" (v. 23)—*i.e.*, that he strenuously supported the worship of the calves. This fact, then, makes it highly probable that Amaziah, a priest of Beth-el, would find in Jeroboam a ready listener to any sinister construction he might put upon the words of a prophet of the Lord, like Amos.

We further learn, that this same Jeroboam was one of the most success-ful princes that had sat upon the throne of Israel; restoring her coasts, and recovering her possessions by force of arms (v. 25, 28): a sovereign, therefore, to be missed by the nation he ruled, whenever he should be removed; and especially if there was nobody forthcoming calculated to replace him. Let us see how this was. Jeroboam reigned forty-one years (2 Kings 14:23), but in the twenty-seventh of Jeroboam, Azariah (or Uzziah as he is called in the Chronicles, 2 Chron. 26:1), began to reign in Judah (2 Kings 15:1); *i.e.*, Jeroboam's reign expired in the fifteenth of Azariah. But his son and successor Zachariah, for some reason or other, and owing to some impediment, which does not transpire, did not begin his reign over Samaria till the thirty-eighth of Azariah (ib. 8). Therefore the throne of Samaria must have been in some sort vacant twenty-three years: nor did the anarchy cease even then, for Zachariah having at length ascended the throne, after a reign of six months was murdered publicly "before the people;" and Shallum, the usurper who succeeded him, shared the same fate, after a reign of a single month (ib. 13); and Menahem, the successor of Shallum, was reduced to the necessity of buying off an invasion of the Assyrians (the first incursion of that people) under Pul (ib. 19); Assyria having in the meanwhile grown great, and now taking advantage of the ruinous condition of Israel, consequent on the death of Jeroboam, to come against him [This is the first mention of the kingdom of Assyria since the days of Nimrod (Gen. 10:11). It seems to have been inconsiderable when the eighty-third Psalm was penned, in which Assur is represented as help-ing the children of Lot (v. 8).] .

Amaziah, therefore, might well declare that the land was not able to *bear the words* of Amos, for in all probability he could foresee, from the actual circumstances of the country, the troubles that were likely to ensue whenever Jerobam's reign should be brought to an end.

Here, then, I say, the language of the prophet is at least very consistent with the crisis of which he speaks, as represented in the Book of Kings.

I could add several other examples of this class, *i.e.*, where allusions in the prophets are very sufficiently responded to by events recorded in the historical Books of Scripture, but still the want of precision in the terms makes it difficult to affirm the coincidence between the two documents with confidence: and therefore I have thought it better to suppress such instances, as not possessing that force of evidence which entitles them to a place in these pages; as for the same reason I drew no contingent to my argument from a comparison between the Psalms and the Books of Samuel; for though many of the Psalms concur very well with the circumstances in which David is represented to have been actually placed from time to time, in the Books of Samuel; and though the Psalms are often headed with a notice that this was written when he was flying before Saul, and that when he was reproached by Nathan; yet the internal testimony is not so strong as to carry conviction along with it, of such being really the case; and this failing, it is folly to weaken a sound argument by a fanciful extension of it.

Part IV

The Veracity of the Gospels and Acts

I now proceed to apply the same test of truth, the test of coincidence without design, which the Scriptures of the Old Testament have sustained so satisfactorily, to the Gospels and Acts of the Apostles; and I am pleased that my first coincidence in order happens to be one of the class where a miracle is involved in the coincidence.

I. THE CALL OF FISHERMEN BY JESUS

In the fourth chapter of St. Matthew we read thus:—"And Jesus, walking by the sea of Galilee, saw two brethren, Simon called Peter, and Andrew his brother, casting a net into the sea: for they were fishers. And he saith unto them, Follow me, and I will make you fishers of men. And they straight-way left their nets, and followed him. And going on from thence, he saw other two brethren, James the son of Zebedee, and John his brother, in a ship with Zebedee their father, *mending their nets;* and he called them. And they immediately left the ship and their father, and followed him."

Now let us compare this with the fifth chapter of St. Luke. "And it came to pass, that, as the people pressed upon him to hear the word of God, he stood by the lake of Gennesaret, And saw two ships standing by the lake: but the fishermen were gone out of them, and were washing their nets. And he entered into one of the ships, which was Simon's, and prayed him that he would thrust out a little from the land. And he sat down, and taught the people out of the ship. Now when he had left speaking, he said unto

Simon, Launch out into the deep, and let down your nets for a draught. And Simon answering said unto him, Master, we have toiled all the night, and have taken nothing: nevertheless at thy word I will let down the net. And when they had this done, they inclosed a great multitude of fishes; and *their net brake;* And they beckoned to their partners which were in the other ship, that they should come and help them. And they came, and filled both the ships, so that they began to sink. When Simon Peter saw it, he fell down at Jesus' knees, saying, Depart from me; for I am a sinful man, O Lord. For he was astonished, and all that were with him, at the draught of the fishes which they had taken: And so was also James, and John, the sons of Zebedee, which were partners with Simon. And Jesus said unto Simon, Fear not; from henceforth thou shalt catch men. And when they had brought their ships to land, they forsook all, and followed him."

The narrative of St. Luke may be reckoned the supplement to that of St. Matthew; for that both relate to the same event I think indisputable. In both we are told of the circumstances under which Andrew, Peter, James, and John, became the decided followers of Christ; in both they are called to attend Him in the same terms, and those remarkable and technical terms; in both the scene is the same, the grouping of the parties the same, and the obedience to the summons the same. By comparing the two Evangelists, the history may be thus completed:—Jesus teaches the people out of Peter's boat, to avoid the press; the boat of Zebedee and his sons, meanwhile, standing by the lake a little further on. The sermon ended, Jesus orders Peter to thrust out, and the miraculous drought of fishes ensues. Peter's boat not sufficing for the fish, he beckons to his partners, Zebedee and his companions, who were in the other ship. The vessels are both filled and pulled to the shore; and now Jesus, having convinced Peter and Andrew by his preaching, and the miracle which he had wrought, gives them the call. He then goes on to Zebedee and his sons, who having brought their boat to land were mending their nets, and calls them. Such is the whole transaction, not to be gathered from one, but from both the Evangelists. The circumstance to be remarked, therefore, is this: that of the miracle, St. Matthew says not a single word; nevertheless, he tells us, that Zebedee and his sons were found by our Lord, when He gave them the call, "*mending their nets.*" How it happened that the nets wanted mending he does not think it needful to state, nor should we have thought it needful to inquire, but it is impossible not to observe, that it perfectly harmonises with the incident mentioned by St. Luke, that in the miraculous drought of fishes the *nets brake.* This coincidence, slight as it is, seems to me to bear upon the truth of the miracle itself. For the "mending of the nets," asserted by one Evangelist, gives probability to the "breaking of the nets," mentioned by the other—the breaking of the nets gives probability to the large draught of fishes—the large draught of fishes gives probability to the miracle. I do not mean that the coincidence *proves* the miracle, but that it marks an attention to truth in the Evangelists; for it surely would be an extravagant refinement to suppose, that St. Matthew designedly lets fall the fact of the mending of the nets, whilst he suppresses the miracle, in order to confirm the credit of St. Luke, who, in relating the miracle, says, that through it the nets brake.

Besides, though St. Matthew does not record the miraculous draught, *yet the readiness of the several disciples on this occasion to follow Jesus* (a thing which he does record), agrees, no less than the mending of the nets, with that extraordinary event; for what more natural than that men should leave all for a master whose powers were so commanding?

Footnote:

[The identity of the event here recorded by St. Matthew and St. Luke is questioned, and upon the following grounds:

1. In St. Matthew, "Jesus walks by the sea of Galilee." In St. Luke, "the people press upon him to hear the word as he stood by the lake." The quiet walk has nothing in common with the press of the multitude. But how do we know that the walk was a quiet one? It is not, indeed, asserted that it was otherwise, but the omission of a fact is not the negation of it. Nobody would suppose, from St. John's account of the crucifixion, that nature was otherwise than perfectly still; yet there was an earthquake, and rending of rocks, and darkness over all the land.

2. In St. Matthew, "Jesus saw two brethren, Simon and Andrew," and addressed them both, "Follow me." In St. Mark (1:17, who *certainly* describes the same incident as St. Matthew), he says, "Come ye." In St. Luke, Simon only is named; and "Launch out," is in the singular. But though Simon alone is named, it is evident that there was some other person with him in the boat; for no sooner is it needful to let down the nets (an operation which probably required more than one pair of hands) than the number becomes plural. Who the coadjutor was, is not hinted at; but it strikes me that there is a coincidence, and not an idle one, between the intimation of St. Luke, that though Simon only is named, he was nevertheless not alone in the boat, and the direct assertion of St. Matthew and St. Mark, that Andrew was with him; indeed the plural is used in all the remainder of St. Luke's narrative—"they inclosed"—"they beckoned"—not meaning Jesus and Simon, but Simon and some one with him, as is manifest from Jesus himself saying, "Let *ye* down the nets," for so the translation ought to have run. And though it is true that in St. Luke the call is expressly directed to Simon alone, "*thou* shalt catch men," it was

evidently considered to apply to others; for "*they* forsook all and followed him;" amongst whom Andrew might well be included.

3. In St. Matthew, Simon and Andrew receive one call, James and John another. In St. Luke one call serves for all. But where the two calls were to the same effect, and so nearly at the same time, I do not think it inconsistent with the nature of the rapid memoranda of an Evangelist to combine them into one, any more than that the cure of the *two* blind men near Jericho of St. Matthew, should be comprised in the cure of one by St. Mark; for the identity of these miracles, in spite of some trifling differences, I cannot doubt.

4. In St. Matthew, James and John are leisurely mending their nets. In St. Luke, they are busily engaged in helping Simon. But to draw a contradiction from this, it is necessary to show first of all, that St. Matthew and St. Luke both speak to the same instant of time. The mending of the nets does not imply that they had not been helping Simon, nor does the helping Simon imply that they would not presently mend their nets.

5. It is further objected that, if the mending of the nets of St. Matthew was subsequent to the breaking of the nets of St. Luke, or the miraculous draught, Simon and Andrew casting their nets into the sea was also subsequent to it, for that v. 18 and v. 21 (Matt. 4.) relate to events all but simultaneous. It may be so, for my impression is, that when Simon and Andrew cast their net into the sea, it was for the purpose of *washing the net* after the fishing was over, and not of fishing: βαλλοντας αμφιβληστρον is the expression, and perhaps *plunging* the net would be the better translation; and I feel confirmed in this by the fact that, whatever the operation was, it was *done close to shore, if not on shore,* whilst Jesus was talking to them on the land. Whereas, for fishing, it was necessary to move out to sea: "Launch out into the *deep,*" says our Lord when he wants them to let down their nets for a draught.

6. It is said, that according to St. Luke, Simon's net brake, and that, therefore, Simon and his companion were the persons to mend it; whereas, according to St. Matthew, Zebedee and his sons were the parties employed. But they were all partners, and therefore the property was, probably, common property; and that as the "hired servants" were with Zebedee and his sons, it is not unlikely, but the contrary, that the labour of mending the nets would devolve upon them (Mark 1:20).

7. The last objection which remains is, that a comparison of St. Mark, 1:23–39, with St. Luke iv, 31–44, shows the call in St. Mark (which is certainly that of St, Matthew) to have been *prior* to the call in St. Luke. So it does, if St. Luke observes strictly the order of events in his narrative; but I see no sufficient reason for believing that what is related in ch. 4:31–44,

happened before what is related in ch. 5:1–11. In the former passage St. Luke tells us that "Jesus came down to Capernaum, and taught them on the *Sabbath-days,* " and he then goes on to mention some Sabbath-day occurrences, concluding the whole, "and he preached in the synagogues of Galilee." This had carried him too much in medias res, and therefore in ch. 5. he brings up some of the work-day events, which a wish to pursue his former subject without interruption had led him to withhold for awhile, though of prior date. And only let us observe how clumsily the narrative would proceed upon any other supposition—Jesus calls Andrew and Peter, James and John, as he was walking by the sea-side—then he goes to Capernaum—heals Peter's wife's mother, performs other cures, and retires to a solitary place (Mark 1:16–36). Then, supposing St. Luke here to take up the parable (ch. 4:42), he goes again to the sea-side, and again calls Peter, James, and John; which would surely be one call too much.

I doubt not, therefore, the identity of the events described.] .

II. ZEBEDEE'S DEATH?

Matth. 4:21.—"And going on from thence, he saw other two brethren, James the son of Zebedee, and John his brother, in a ship *with Zebedee their Father.*"

Ch. 8:21.—"And another of his *disciples* said unto him, Lord, suffer me first to go and *bury my father.*"

Ch. 20:20.—"Then came to him the *mother of Zebedee's children* with her sons, worshipping him, and desiring a certain thing of him."

Ch. 27:55, 56.—"And many women were there beholding afar off, which followed Jesus from Galilee, ministering unto him. Among which was Mary Magdalene, and Mary the mother of James and Joses, and the *mother of Zebedee's children.*"

When the coincidence which I shall found upon these passages first occurred to me, I felt some doubt whether, by producing it, I might not subject myself to a charge of over-refinement. On further consideration, however, I am satisfied that the conjecture I hazard (for it is nothing more) is far from improbable; and I am the less disposed to withhold it from having observed, when I have chanced to discuss any of these paragraphs with my friends, how differently the importance of an argument is estimated by different minds; a point of evidence often inducing conviction in one, which another would find almost nugatory.

Whoever reads the four verses which I have given at the head of this Number in juxtaposition, will probably anticipate what I have to say. The coincidence here is not between several writers, but between several detached passages of the same writer. From the first of these verses it appears that, at the period when James and John received the call to follow Christ, *Zebedee their father was alive.* They obeyed the call, and left him. From the last two verses it appears, in my opinion, that, at a subsequent period of which they treat, *Zebedee was dead.* Zebedee does not make the application to Christ on behalf of his sons, but the *mother of Zebedee's children* makes it. Zebedee is not at the crucifixion, but the *mother of Zebedee's children.* It is not from his absence on these occasions that I so much infer his death, as from the expression applied to Salome; she is not called the wife of Zebedee, she is not called the mother of James and John, but the *mother of Zebedee's children.* The term, I think, implies that she was a widow.

Now from the second verse, which relates to a period *between these two*, we learn that one of Jesus' disciples asked him permission "*to go and bury his father.*" The interval was a short one; the number of persons to whom the name of *disciple* was given, was very small (see Matthew 9:37); a single boat seems to have contained them all (8:23). In that number we know that the sons of Zebedee were included. My inference therefore is, that the death of *Zebedee* is here alluded to, and that St. Matthew, without a wish, perhaps, or thought, either to conceal or express the individual (for there seems no assignable motive for his studying to do either), betrays an event familiar to his own mind, in that inadvertent and unobtrusive manner in which the truth so often comes out.

The data, it must be confessed, are not enough to determine the matter with certainty either way; it is a *conjectural* coincidence. They who are not satisfied with it may pass it over: I am persuaded, however, that nothing is wanted but more copious information to multiply such proofs of veracity as these I am collecting to a great extent. It is impossible to examine the historical parts of the New Testament or Old in detail, without suspicions constantly arising of facts, which, nevertheless, cannot be substantiated for want of documents. We have very often a glimpse, and no more. A hint is dropped relating to something well known at the time, and which is not without its value even now, in evidence, by giving us to understand that it is a fragment of some real story, of which we are not in full possession. Of this nature is the circumstance recorded by St. Mark (14:51), that when the disciples forsook Jesus, "there followed him a certain young man, having a linen cloth east about his naked body, and the young men laid hold on him; and he left the linen cloth, and fled from them naked." This is evidently an imperfect history. It is an incident altogether detached, and alone: another narrative might give us the supplement, and together with that supplement indications of its truth. As another example of the same kind, may be mentioned an expression in the beginning of the second chapter of the Gospel of St. John, "and the *third day* there was a marriage in Cana of Galilee" (v. i); the Apostle clearly having some other event in his mind which does not transpire, from which this *third day* dates. Meanwhile let us but apply ourselves diligently to comparing together the four witnesses which we have, instead of indulging a fruitless desire for more, and if consistency without design be a proof that they are "true men," I cannot but consider that it is abundantly supplied.

III. JESUS AND THE CENTURIONS

Matth. 8:5.—"And when Jesus was entered into Capernaum, there came unto him a *centurion*, beseeching him."

It has been remarked that favourable mention is made of the Centurions throughout the whole of the New Testament. In the present instance, the centurion is represented as merciful, anxious for the care of his servant; as humble-minded, "I am not worthy that thou shouldest come under my roof;" as having great faith, "speak the word only." In the corresponding case of the centurion in Luke 7:2 (if we suppose the party not the same), there are still exhibited the same virtues; with the addition that he "loved the nation of the Jews, and had built them a synagogue."

In Matthew 27:54, the centurion at the Crucifixion appears to advantage; "Now when the centurion, and they that were with him, watching Jesus, saw the earthquake, and those things that were done, they feared greatly, saying, Truly this was the Son of God:" in St. Luke's account, 23:47, to still greater; "Now when the centurion saw what was done, he glorified God, saying, Certainly this was a righteous man."

In Acts 10:1, 2, we find the same honourable mention made of a centurion. Cornelius was "a devout man, and one that feared God with all his house, which gave much alms to the people, and prayed to God alway."

In Acts 22:25, When Paul had been rescued from the populace at Jerusalem, by the guard, and the chief officer having lodged him in the castle, commanded that he should be examined by scourging; "Paul said unto the centurion that stood by, Is it lawful for you to scourge a man that is a Roman, and uncondemned?" And accordingly he found in the centurion a reasonable man, who at once reported his case to his superior, and the sentence was not carried into execution.

And in the sequel of this transaction, when it had come to Paul's knowledge through his sister's son, that forty persons had entered into a conspiracy to kill him, he at once "called for one of the centurions," as though confident that he would see him protected, and desired him to take his informant to the chief captain, which he at once did (23:17).

In Acts 27:1, we read of another centurion, Julius, and still to the credit of his character—"He courteously entreated Paul, and gave him liberty to go unto his friends to refresh himself"(3); and when in the wreck, "the soldiers' counsel was to kill the prisoners;" "the centurion, wishing to save Paul, kept them from their purpose."(43.)

It appears, therefore, as I have said, that often as a centurion is presented to us in the Gospels, it is uniformly to his praise.

I think there is truth at the bottom of this consistency, which is evidently undesigned. It is impossible to suppose that notices thus incidental, occurring from time to time, at distant intervals, and moreover exhibiting the centurion under a variety of circumstances calculated to test him in different ways, should have been constructed on a plan; should have been contrived for the purpose of giving a colouring of veracity to the narrative. The detection of such a token by the reader could not have been reckoned upon with certainty. It is probable that to most of those who may peruse these pages, the fact of such consistency had not presented itself before: it had not to myself, till my attention was recently called to it [By Mr. Humphry's Commentary on Acts 10:3.] . I may not be able to account for it, but that does not make the argument the worse. Perhaps in the well-regulated Roman armies, the more intelligent and orderly soldiers were promoted to this command. Perhaps, too, their rank and position, not much removed from that of the teachers of the Gospel, might lead these officers to sympathize with them and their cause. Certain it is, that the Evangelists have no theory whatever on the subject. Their testimony would be less valuable for the purpose I use it, if they had. They simply make statements; the inference drawn from them is altogether our own.

IV. PETER HAD A WIFE

Matth. 8:14.—"And when Jesus was come into Peter's house, he saw his *wife's mother* laid, and sick of a fever."

The coincidence which I have here to mention does not strictly fall within my plan, for it results from a comparison of St. Matthew with St. Paul; if, however, it be thought of any value, the irregularity of its introduction will be easily overlooked.

In this passage of the Evangelist, then, we discover, in a manner the most oblique, that Peter was a *married* man. It is a circumstance that has nothing whatever to do with the narrative, but is a gratuitous piece of information, conveyed incidentally in the designation of an individual who was the subject of it.

But that Peter actually was a married man, we learn from the independent testimony of St. Paul: "Have we not power," says he, "to lead about a sister, a *wife*, as well as other Apostles, and as the brethren of the Lord and *Cephas?*" 1 Cor. 9:5. Where it may be remarked that the difference in name, Cephas in the one passage, Peter in the other, is in itself an argument that the one passage was written without any reference to the other—that the coincidence was without design. Here again, be it observed, as in former instances, the indication of veracity in the Apostle's narrative, is found where the subject of the narrative is a miracle; for Christ having "touched her hand, the fever left her, and she arose and ministered unto them," v. 15.

I cannot but think that any candid sceptic would consider this coincidence to be at least decisive of the *actual existence* of such a woman as Peter's wife's mother; of its being no imaginary character, no mere person of straw, introduced with an air of precision, under the view of giving a colour of truth to the miracle. Yet, unless the Evangelist had felt quite sure of his ground, quite sure, I mean, that this remarkable cure would bear examination, it is scarcely to be believed that he would have fixed it upon an individual who certainly did live, or had lived, and who therefore might herself, or her friends might for her, contradict the alleged fact, if it never had occurred.

V. JESUS HEALS AFTER THE SABBATH

Matth. 8:16.—"*When the even was come,* they brought unto him many that were possessed with devils; and he cast out the spirits with his word, and healed all that were sick."

The undesignedness of many passages in the Gospels is overlooked in our familiar acquaintance with them. They have been so long the subject of our reading and of our reflection, that the evidence they furnish of their own veracity does not always present itself to us with that freshness which is necessary to give it its due effect. We often, no doubt, fill up an ellipsis and complete a meaning almost instinctively, without being aware how strongly the necessity for doing this, marks the absence of all caution, contrivance, and circumspection in the writers. For instance, why did they bring the sick and possessed to Jesus *when the even was come?* I turn to the parallel passages of St. Mark (1:21) and St. Luke (4:31), and

find that the transaction in question took place on the *Sabbath-day*. I turn
to another passage in St. Matthew (12:10), wholly independent, however,
of the former, and find that there was a superstition amongst the Jews that
it "was not lawful to *heal* on the Sabbath-day."I put these together, and at
once see the reason why no application for a cure was made to Jesus till
the Sabbath was past, or in other words, till the even was come. But. St.
Matthew, meanwhile, does not offer one syllable in explanation. He states
the naked fact—that when the even was come, people were brought to be
healed; and, for aught that appears to the contrary, it might have been any
other day of the week. Suppose it had happened that St. Matthew's Gospel
had been the only one which had descended to us, the value of these few
words, *"when the even was come,"* would have been quite lost as an argument for the veracity of his story; for how could it have been conjectured
that the thought which was influencing St. Matthew's mind at the moment
when they escaped him, was this, that these things were done on the
evening of a *Sabbath-day?* There is no one circumstance in the previous
narrative of the events of that day as given by this Evangelist, to point to
such a conclusion. Jesus had entered into Capernaum—he had healed the
centurion's servant—he had healed Peter's wife's mother of a fever—how
could it be known from any of these acts that the day was the Sabbath? Or
suppose we had been in possession of the other three Evangelists, but that
the Gospel of St. Matthew had just been discovered among the
manuscripts at Milan, I ask whether such an argument as this would not
have had much weight in establishing its authority?

I am not concerned about the perfect intelligibility of this passage in St.
Matthew. Its meaning is obvious, and it would be a waste of words to
offer what I have done, as commentary—all that I am anxious to do is to
point out the *undesignedness* apparent in it, which is such, I think, as a
writer of an imaginary narrative could not possibly have displayed.

VI. MATTHEW'S HOUSE

Matth. 9:9, 10.—"And as Jesus passed forth from thence, he saw a man,
named Matthew, sitting at the receipt of custom; and he saith unto him,
Follow me; and he arose and followed him. And it came to pass, as Jesus
sat at meat *in the house* , behold, many publicans and sinners came and
sat down with him."

How natural for a man, speaking of a transaction which concerned
himself, to forget for a moment the character of the historian, and to talk
of Jesus sitting down in *the* house, without telling his readers whose

house it was! How natural for him not to perceive that there was vagueness and obscurity in a term, which to himself was definite and plain! Accordingly, we find St. Mark and St. Luke, who deal with the same incident as historians, not as principals, using a different form of expression. "And as he passed by," says St. Mark, "he saw Levi the son of Alpheus sitting at the receipt of custom, and said unto him, Follow me: and he arose and followed him. And it came to pass, that as Jesus sat at meat in *his* house." 2:15.

"And Levi," says St. Luke, "made him a great feast in *his own* house." v. 29.

It may be further remarked, that a number of *publicans* sat down with Jesus and his disciples upon this occasion; a fact for which no reason is assigned, but for which we discover a very good reason in the occupation which St. Matthew had followed.

I think the odds are very great against the probability of a writer preserving consistency in trifles like these, were he only *devising* a story. I can scarcely imagine that such a person would hit upon the phrase "in *the* house," as an artful way of suggesting that the house was in fact his own, and himself an eye-witness of the scene he described; still less, that he would refine yet further, and make the company assembled there to consist of publicans, in order that the whole picture might be complete and harmonious. It may be added, that Capernaum, which was the scene of St. Matthew's call, was precisely the place where we might expect to meet with a man of his vocation—it being a station where such merchandize as was to be conveyed by water-carriage, along the Jordan southwards, might be very conveniently shipped, and where a custom-house would consequently be established. There is a similar propriety in the habitat of Zaccheus (Luke 19:2); he was a "chief among the publicans," and Jesus is said to have fallen in with him near *Jericho*. Now Jericho was the centre of the growth, preparation, and export, of balsam, a very considerable branch of trade in Judea; and therefore a town which invited the presence of the tax-gatherers. These are small matters, but such as bespeak truth in those who detail them.

VII. MATTHEW'S HUMILITY

Akin to this is my next instance [In this argument I am indebted to Nelson (Festivals and Fasts, p. 229), who advances it, however, for a different end, to prove the *humility*, not the *veracity*, of St. Matthew.] of consistency without design.

Matth. 10:2.—"Now the names of the twelve Apostles are these: the first, Simon, who is called Peter, and Andrew his brother; James, the son of Zebedee, and John his brother; Philip, and Bartholomew; *Thomas*, and *Matthew the publican;* James, the son of Alpheus, and Lebbeus, whose surname was Thaddeus; Simon the Canaanite, and Judas Iscariot, who also betrayed him."

This order, as far as regards Thomas and Matthew, is inverted in St. Mark and St. Luke. "Philip and Bartholomew, and *Matthew and Thomas,* " is the succession of the names in those two Evangelists (Mark 3:18; Luke 6:15); and by neither of them is the odious, but distinctive, appellation of "the publican" added. This difference, however, in St. Matthew's catalogue, from that given by St. Mark and St. Luke, is precisely such as might be expected from a modest man when telling his own tale: he places his own name after that of a colleague who had no claims to precedence, but rather the contrary, and, fearful that its obscurity might render it insufficient merely to announce it, and, at the same time, perhaps, not unwilling to inflict upon himself an act of self-humiliation, he annexes to it his former calling, which was notorious at least, however it might be unpopular. I should not be disposed to lay great stress upon this example of undesigned consistency were it a solitary instance, but when taken in conjunction with so many others, it may be allowed a place; for though the order of names and the annexed epithet might be accidental, yet it must be admitted that they would be accounted for at least as well by the veracity of the narrative.

VIII. MARY DESIRES TO SPEAK WITH HER SON

Matth. 12:46.—"While he yet talked, behold, his mother and his brethren stood without, *desiring to speak with him.*"

What his mother's communication might be the Evangelist does not record. It seems to have been made privately and apart, and was probably not overheard by any of his followers. But in the next chapter, St. Matthew very undesignedly mentions, that "when he *was come into his own country*, he taught them in the synagogue" (13:54). Hence, then, we see, that the interview with his mother and brethren was shortly succeeded by a visit to their town. The visit might, indeed, have nothing to do with the interview, nor does St. Matthew hint that it had anything whatever to do with it (for then no argument of veracity, founded upon the *undesigned* coincidence of the two facts, could have been here advanced), but still there is a fair presumption that the visit was in obedience to his mother's wish, more especially as the disposition of the inhabitants of Nazareth, which must have been known to Christ, was unfit for his doing there any mighty works.

IX. THE DEATH OF JOSEPH, MARY'S HUSBAND

The *death of Joseph* is nowhere either mentioned, or alluded to, by the Evangelists; yet, *from all four of them it may be indirectly inferred to have happened whilst Jesus was yet alive;* a circumstance in which, had they been imposing a story upon us, they would scarcely have concurred, when the concurrence is manifestly not the effect of scheme or contrivance. Thus in the passage from St. Matthew, quoted in the last paragraph, we find his mother and brethren seeking Jesus, but not his reputed father. In St. Mark we have the whole family enumerated, but no mention made of Joseph. "Is not this the carpenter, the son of Mary, the brother of James, and Joses, and of Juda, and Simon? and are not his sisters here with us?" 6:3.

"Then came to him," says St. Luke, "his mother and his brethren, and could not come at him for the press," 8:19. "After this," says St. John, "he went down to Capernaum; he, and his mother, and his brethren, and his disciples." 2:12.

Neither do we meet with any notice of Joseph's attendance at the Feast of Cana, or at the Crucifixion; indeed, in his last moments Jesus commends his mother to the care of the disciple whom he loved, and that "disciple took her to his own home." Nor at a scene which occurred very shortly after his Crucifixion, though one in which all the immediate friends as well as family of Jesus are described as taking part; "And when they were come in, they went up into an upper room, where abode both Peter, and James, and John, and Andrew, Philip, and Thomas, Bartholomew, and Matthew, James the son of Alpheus, and Simon Zelotes, and Judas, the brother of James.

"These all continued with one accord in prayer and supplication, with the women, and Mary the mother of Jesus, and with his brethren;" Acts 1:13, 14; the last time in which Mary herself is named in Scripture.

Such a harmony as this cannot have been the effect of concert. It is not a direct, or even an incidental agreement in a positive fact, for nothing is asserted; but yet, from the absence of assertion, a presumption of such fact is conveyed to us by the separate narrative of each of the Evangelists.

X. JESUS IN THE SHIP

Matth. 13:2.—"And great multitudes were gathered together unto him, so that he went into *a ship* (εις το πλοιον), and sat."

'In this, and in some other places of the Evangelists,' says bishop Middleton, 'we have πλοιον with the article (*the* ship, not *a* ship); the force of which, however, is not immediately obvious. In the present instance the English version, Newcome, and Campbell, understand το πλοιον indefinitely; but that *any ship*, without reference, can be meant by this phrase, is grammatically impossible. Many philologists, indeed, have adduced this passage amongst others, to show that this article is sometimes without meaning: but this proves only that its meaning was sometimes unknown to them.

'Mr. Wakefield observes, in his New Testament, "a particular vessel is uniformly specified. It seems to have been kept on the lake for the use of Jesus and his apostles. It probably belonged to some of the fishermen (Matt. 4:22) who, I should think, occasionally at least, continued to follow their former occupation. See John 21:3." Thus far Mr. Wakefield, whose solution carried with it an air of strong probability: and when we look at Mark 3:9, which appears to have escaped him, this conjecture becomes absolute certainty. "And he spake to his disciples *that a small vessel should wait on him*," (constantly be waiting on him, προσκαρτερη αυτω) because of the multitude, lest they should throng him. Moreover, I think we may discover to whom the vessel belonged. In one Evangelist (Luke 5:3), we find a ship used by our Saviour for the very purpose here mentioned, declared expressly to be Simon's; and afterwards, in the same Evangelist (8:22), we have *the* ship, το πλοιον, definitely, as if it were intended that the reader should understand it of the ship already spoken of. It is therefore not improbable that in the other Evangelists also, the vessel so frequently used by our Saviour was that belonging to Peter and Andrew.' [Bishop Middleton on the Greek Article. p. 158.] Where bishop Middleton finds a philological solution, I find an undesigned coincidence. St. Matthew speaks of "*the* ship" (το πλοιον) into which Jesus went, as though referring to a well-known vessel. St. Mark tells us that he had "a *small vessel to wait on him*."

XI. HOW HEROD HEARD OF JESUS

Matth. 14:1.—"At that time Herod the tetrarch heard of the fame of Jesus, and said *unto his servants* (τοις παισιν αυτου), This is John the

Baptist, who is risen from the dead."

St. Matthew here declares that Herod delivered his opinion of Christ to *his servants*. There must have been some particular reason, one would imagine, to induce him to make such a communication to them above all other people. What could it have been? St. Mark does not help us to solve the question, for he contents himself with recording what Herod said. Neither does St. Luke in the parallel passage, tell us to whom he addressed himself—"he was desirous of seeing him, because he had *heard many things of him*." By referring, however, to the eighth chapter of this last Evangelist, the cause why Herod had *heard so much about Christ*, and why he talked to *his servants* about Him, is sufficiently explained, but it is most incidentally. We are there informed, "that Jesus went throughout every city and village, preaching and shewing the glad tidings of the kingdom of God; and the twelve were with him, and certain women who had been healed of evil spirits and infirmities: Mary, called Magdalene, out of whom went seven devils, and *Joanna the wife of Chuza, Herod's steward*, and Susanna, and many others, which ministered unto him of their substance."

And again, in chap. 13. ver. 1, of the Acts of the Apostles, we read, amongst other distinguished converts, of *"Manaen, which had been brought up with Herod the tetrarch,"* or, in other words, who was his foster-brother. We see, therefore, that Christ had followers from amongst the household of this very prince, and, accordingly, that Herod was very likely to discourse with *his servants* on a subject in which they were better informed than himself.

XII. THE LOAVES AND FISHES MIRACLES

1. Matth. 14:20.—In the miracle of feeding the five thousand with five loaves and two fishes, recorded by all four Evangelists, the disciples, we are told, took up δωδεκα κοφινους πληρεις (Matth. 14:20; Mark 6:43; Luke 9:17; John 6:13); in all these eases our translation renders the passages *"twelve baskets."*

In the miracle of feeding the four thousand with seven loaves and a few small fishes, recorded by two of the Evangelists, the disciples took up επτα σπυριδας (Matth. 15:37; Mark 8:8); in both these eases our translation renders the passages *"seven baskets;"* the term κοφινος, and σπυρις, being expressed both alike by *"basket."*

Yet there was, no doubt, a marked difference between these two vessels, whatever that difference might be, for κοφινος is invariably used when the miracle of the five thousand is spoken of; and σπυρις is invariable used when the miracle of the four thousand is spoken of. Moreover, such distinction is clearly suggested to us in Matth. 16:9, 10, where our Saviour cautions his disciples against the "leaven of the Pharisees and Sadducees;" and in so doing, alludes to each of these miracles thus: "Do ye not understand, neither remember the five loaves of the *five* thousand, and how many *baskets* (κοφινους) ye took up? neither the seven loaves of the *four* thousand, and how many *baskets* (σπυριδας) ye took up?" though here, again, the distinction is entirely lost in our translation, both κοφινους and σπυριδας being still rendered "baskets," alike.

The precise nature of the difference of these two kinds of baskets it may be difficult to determine; and the lexicographers and commentators do not enable us to do it with accuracy; though from the word σπυρις being used (Acts 9:25) for the basket in which St. Paul was let down over the wall, we may suppose that it was *capacious;* whereas from the κοφινοι, in this instance, being twelve in number, we may in like manner suppose that they were the provision-baskets carried by the twelve disciples, and were, consequently, *smaller.* But the point of the *coincidence* is independent of the precise difference of the vessels, and consists in the *uniform application* of the term κοφινος to the basket of the one miracle (wheresoever and by whomsoever told); and the as *uniform application* of the term σπυρις, to the basket of the other miracle; such uniformity marking very clearly the two miracles to be distinctly impressed on the minds of the Evangelists, as *real* events; the circumstantial peculiarities of each present to them, even to the shape of the baskets, as though they were themselves actual eye-witnesses; or at least had received their report from those who were so.

It is next to impossible that such coincidence in both cases, between the fragments and the receptacles, respectively, should have been preserved by chance; or by a teller of a tale at third or fourth hand; and accordingly we see that the coincidence is in fact entirely lost by our translators, who were not witnesses of the miracles; and whose attention did not happen to be drawn to the point.

2. There is another distinction perceptible in the narrative of these two miracles, which, like the last, seems to indicate a minute acquaintance with them, such as could only be the result of ocular testimony.

In Matt. 14:19, where the miracle of the five thousand is told, it is said, "And he commanded the multitude to sit down *on the grass*, and took the five loaves,"

In Mark 6:39, it is said, in the account of the same miracle, "And he commanded them to make all sit down by companies upon *the green grass.*"

In John 6:10, "And Jesus said, Make the men sit down. Now there was *much grass* in the place; so the men sat down."

St. Luke, 9:14, contenting himself with writing, "Make them sit down by fifties in a company."

But in the description of the corresponding miracle of the four thousand we find in

Matt. 15:35, "And he commanded the multitude to sit down on the ground."

And in the parallel passage of

Mark 8:6, "And he commanded the people to sit down on the ground."

The other two Evangelists not relating it.

It should seem, therefore, that the abundance of the grass was a feature in the scene of the miracle of the five thousand, which had impressed itself on the eye of the relator, as peculiar to it. It was a graphic trifle which had rendered the spectacle more vivid: and accordingly, unimportant as it is in itself, the incident finds a place in the narrative of three out of the four Evangelists, and in all the instances where they are speaking of the miracle of the five thousand. Whereas "the ground," and no more, is the term used in the nartive of the miracle of the four thousand by the two Evangelists who record it. The distinction seems to be of the same minute kind as that of the baskets; and, like that, marks the description to be from the life, and from the eye of the spectator.

3. There is still another indication of truth and accuracy in the account of the miracle of the five thousand, which presents itself on a comparison of St. John with St. Matthew; this also is a coincidence of a kind only discoverable in the Greek. In St. John 6:10, we read in our English version, "And Jesus said, Make the *men* sit down. Now there was much grass in the place; so the *men* sat down in number about five thousand;" "*men*" being the term used in both clauses of the verse. But in the Greek, ανθροπους stands in the first clause, ανδρες, in the second; as though Jesus had said, "Make the *people* sit down;" and, accordingly, the *men* amongst them did sit down in companies of fifty, as another Evangelist tells us (Luke 9:14), and were thus readily reckoned up; the women and children left, to be otherwise disposed of.

Such would be our inference from St. John's narrative.

Now let us turn to St. Matthew 14:21.

"They that had eaten were about five thousand men (ανδρες), *besides women and children.*"

Here the fact which we had only *inferred* from St. John, we find directly *asserted* by St. Matthew. Surely an instance this of concurrence without design, in the testimony of these writers; not the less valuable from being so delicate as to be lost in a translation.

On the whole, it seems most improbable that this miracle of the feeding the five thousand, as described by the Evanglists, should furnish so many arguments of veracity singly and alone, and yet be a fabrication after all.

XIII. THE LEAVEN OF HEROD AND THE SADDUCEES

We do not read a great deal respecting Herod the tetrarch in the Evangelists; but all that is said of him will be perceived, on examination (for it may not strike us at first sight) to be perfectly harmonious.

When the disciples had forgotten to take bread with them in the boat, our Lord warns them to "take heed and beware of the leaven of the Pharisees, and of *the leaven of Herod.*" So says St. Mark, 8:15. The charge which Jesus gives them on this occasion is thus worded by St. Matthew, "Take heed and beware of the leaven of the Pharisees and *of the Sadducees,* " 16:6. The obvious inference to be drawn from the two passages is, that Herod himself was a Sadducee. Let us turn to St. Luke, and though still we find no assertion to this effect, he would clearly lead us to the same conclusion. Chap. 9:7, "Now Herod the tetrarch heard of all that was done by him; *and he was perplexed, because that it was said of some, that John was risen from the dead;* and of some, that Elias had appeared; and of some, that one of the old prophets *was risen again.* And Herod said, *John have I beheaded*, but who is this of whom I hear such things? and he desired to see him."

The transmigration of the souls of good men was a popular belief at that time amongst the Pharisees (see Josephus, B. J. ii. 83.14); a Pharisee, therefore, would have found little difficulty in this resurrection of John, or of an old prophet; in fact, it was the Pharisees, no doubt, who started the idea: not so Herod; he was *perplexed* about it; he had "beheaded John," which was in his creed the termination of his existence; well then might he ask, "who is this of whom I hear such things?" Neither do I discover any objection in the parallel passage of St. Matthew, 14:1: "At that time Herod the tetrarch heard of the fame of Jesus, and said unto his servants, This is John the Baptist; he is risen from the dead; and therefore mighty works do show forth themselves in him." It is the language of a man (especially when taken in connection with St. Luke), who began to doubt whether he was right in his Sadducean notions: a guilty conscience awaking in him some apprehension that he whom he had murdered might be alive again— that there might, after all, be a "resurrection, and angel, and spirit."

XIV. THE DISCIPLES DID NOT FAST, AND THE DEMON DID NOT LEAVE

Matth. 17:19.—"Then came the disciples to Jesus apart, and said, Why could not we cast him out? And Jesus said unto them, Because of your unbelief ... Howbeit this kind goeth not out but by prayer and *fasting*."

Here, therefore, the words of Jesus imply that the disciples did not fast. Yet the observation is made in that incidental manner in which a fact familiar to the mind of the speaker so often comes out. It has not the smallest appearance of being introduced for the purpose of confirming any previous assertion to the same effect. Yet in chapter 9. ver. 14, we had been told that the disciples of John came to Jesus, saying, "Why do *we* and the Pharisees fast oft, but *thy disciples* fast not?" It may be remarked, too, that the former passage not only implies that the disciples of Jesus did not fast, but that Jesus himself did, and that the latter passage singularly enough implies the very same tiling; for it does not run, why do we and the Pharisees fast oft, but *Thou* and thy disciples fast not? (which would be the strict antithesis) but only, why do thy disciples fast not?

XV. DESTROY THIS TEMPLE AND IN THREE DAYS I WILL RAISE IT UP

Matth. 26:60.—"At the last came two false witnesses, and said, This fellow said, I am able to destroy the temple of God, and to build it in three days."

It is remarkable that though St. Matthew records the charge which was thus brought against Jesus, a charge very well calculated to mortify the pride of the Jews, and exasperate them against him, he does not give the least hint of the foundation on which it rested. It is introduced abruptly into the narrative, and left there without any explanation at all.

But if we turn to the 2nd chapter of the Gospel of St. John (v. 18), we shall find the conversation preserved which fastened this accusation on Jesus.

"Then answered the Jews and said unto him, What sign shewest thou unto us, seeing that thou doest these things?

"Jesus answered and said unto them, Destroy this temple, and in three days I will raise it up.

"Then said the Jews, Forty and six years was this temple in building, and wilt thou rear it up in three days?

"But he spake of the temple of his body."

It is evident that there is not the slightest intention in the two Evangelists to write with a reference to each other's narrative, so that the one may complete what in the other is left defective. Yet the coincidence between them is obvious. What can account for it but an independent knowledge of facts in both; truth, in short, in both?

It may be convenient to insert here some other examples of the same kind, rather than produce them separately elsewhere, according to their relative places in the order of the Gospels.

XVI. JESUS BEING TOLD, "PROPHESY … WHO SMOTE THEE?"

Matth. 26:67.—"Then did they spit in his face, and buffeted him; and others smote him with the palms of their hands, saying, *Prophesy unto us, thou Christ, who is he that smote thee?*"

I think undesignedness may be traced in this passage, both in what is expressed and what is omitted. It is usual for one who invents a story which he wishes should be believed, to be careful that its several parts hang well together—to make its conclusions follow from its premises—and to show how they follow. He naturally considers that he shall be suspected unless his account is probable and consistent, and he labours to provide against that suspicion. On the other hand, he who is telling the truth, is apt to state his facts and leave them to their fate; he speaks as one having authority, and cares not about the why or the wherefore, because it never occurs to him that such particulars are wanted to make his statement credible; and accordingly, if such particulars are discoverable at all, it is most commonly by inference, and incidentally.

Now in the verse of St. Matthew, placed at the head of this paragraph, it is written that "they smote him with the palms of their hands, saying, Prophesy unto us, thou Christ, who is he that smote thee?" Had it happened that the records of the other Evangelists had been lost, no critical acuteness could have possibly supplied by conjecture the omission which occurs in this passage, and yet, without that omission being supplied, the true meaning of the passage must for ever have lain hid; for where is the propriety of asking Christ to *prophesy* who smote Him, when He had the offender before his eyes? But when we learn from St. Luke (22:64) that "the men that held Jesus *blindfolded* him" before they asked Him to prophesy who it was that smote Him, we discover what St. Matthew intended to communicate, namely, that they proposed this test of his divine mission, whether, without the use of sight, He could tell who it was that struck Him. Such an oversight as this in St. Matthew it is difficult to account for on any other supposition than the truth of the history itself, which set its author above all solicitude about securing the reception of his conclusions by a cautious display of the grounds whereon they were built.

XVII. THE CHARGE ON WHICH THE JEWS CONDEMNED CHRIST

What was the charge on which the Jews condemned Christ to death [The following argument was suggested to me by reading Wilson's "Illustration of the Method of Explaining the New Testament by the Early Opinions of Jews and Christians concerning Christ."] ?

Familiar as this question may at first seem, the answer is not so obvious as might be supposed. By a careful perusal of the trial of our Lord, as described by the several Evangelists, it will be found that the charges were two, of a nature quite distinct, and *preferred with a most appropriate reference to the tribunals before which they were made.*

Thus the first hearing was before "*the Chief Priests and all the Council,* " a Jewish and ecclesiastical court; accordingly, Christ was then accused of *blasphemy.* "I adjure thee by the living God, that thou tell us whether thou be the *Son of God,* " said Caiaphas to Him, in the hope of convicting Him out of his own mouth. When Jesus in his reply answered that He was, "then the high-priest rent his clothes, saying, *He hath spoken blasphemy; what further need have we of witnesses? behold, now ye have heard his blasphemy.*" (Matt. 26:65.)

Shortly after, He is taken before *Pilate, the Roman governor*, and here the charge of blasphemy is altogether suppressed, and that of *sedition* substituted. "And the whole multitude of them arose, and led him unto Pilate: and they began to accuse him, saying, We found this fellow *perverting the nation, and forbidding bidding to give tribute to Cæsar, saying that he himself is Christ, a king.*" (Luke 23:2.) And on this plea it is that they press his conviction, reminding Pilate, that if he let Him go he was not Caesar's friend.

This difference in the nature of the accusation, according to the quality and characters of the judges, is not *forced* upon our notice by the Evangelists, as though they were anxious to give an air of probability to their narrative by such circumspection and attention to propriety; on the contrary, it is touched upon in so cursory and unemphatic a manner, as to be easily overlooked; and I venture to say, that it is actually overlooked by most readers of the Gospels. Indeed, how perfectly agreeable to the temper of the times, and of the parties concerned, such a proceeding was, can scarcely be perceived at first sight. The coincidence, therefore, will appear more striking if we examine it somewhat more closely. A charge of *blasphemy* was, of all others, the best fitted to detach the *multitude* from the cause of Christ; and it is only by a proper regard to this circumstance, that we can obtain the true key to the conflicting sentiments of the *people* towards Him; one while hailing Him, as they do, with rapture, and then again striving to put Him to death.

Thus, when Jesus walked in Solomon's Porch, the Jews came round about Him, and said unto Him, "If thou be the Christ tell us plainly.— Jesus answered them, I told you, and ye believed not." He then goes on to speak of the works which testified of Him, and adds, in conclusion, "I and my Father are one." The effect of which words was instantly this, that the *Jews* (*i.e.*, the people) took up stones to stone him, "for blasphemy, and because, being a man, he made himself God." (John 10:33.) Again, in the sixth chapter of St. John, we read of five thousand men, who, having witnessed his miracles, actually acknowledged Him as "that prophet that should come into the world," nay, even wished to take Him by force and make Him a king; yet the very next day, when Christ said to these same people, "This is that bread which came down from heaven," they murmured at Him, doubtless considering Him to lay claim to divinity; for He replies, "Doth this offend you? what and if ye shall see the Son of Man ascend up *where he was before?*" expressions, at which such serious offence was taken, that "from that time many of his disciples went back, and walked with him no more." So that it is not in these days only that men forsake Christ from a reluctance to acknowledge (as He demands of them) his Godhead. And again, when Jesus cured the impotent man on the Sabbath-day, and in defending Himself for having so done, said, "My Father worketh hitherto, and I work," we are told, "therefore the Jews sought the more to kill him, because he not only had broken the Sabbath, but said also that God was his Father, making himself equal with God." (John 5:18.) So, on another occasion, when Jesus had been speaking with much severity in the temple, we find Him unmolested, till He adds, "Verily, verily, I say unto you, Before Abraham was, *I am*" (John 8:58); but no sooner had He so said, than "they took up stones to cast at him." In like manner (to come to the last scene of his mortal life), when He entered Jerusalem He had the people in his favour, for the chief priests and scribes "feared them;" yet, very shortly after, the tide was so turned against Him, that the same people asked Barabbas rather than Jesus. And why? As *Messiah* they were anxious to receive Him, which was the character in which He had entered Jerusalem—but they rejected Him as the "*Son of God,* "which was the character in which He stood before them at his trial: facts which, taken in a *doctrinal* view, are of no small value, proving, as they do, that the Jews believed *Christ to lay claim to divinity*, however they might dispute or deny the right. It is consistent, therefore, with the whole tenor of the Gospel history, that the enemies of Christ, to gain their end with the Jews, should have actually accused Him of *blasphemy*, as they are represented to have done, and should have succeeded. Nor is it less consistent with that history, that they should have actually waived the charge of blasphemy, when they brought Him before a Roman magistrate, and substituted that of *sedition* in its stead; for the Roman governors, it is well known, were very indifferent about religious disputes—they had the toleration of men who had no creed of their own. Gallio, we hear in after-times, "cared for none of these things;" and, in the same spirit, Lysias writes to Felix about Paul, that "he perceived him to be accused *of questions concerning the law, but to have nothing laid to his charge worthy of death or of bonds.*" (Acts 23:29.)

Indeed, this case of Paul serves in a very remarkable manner to illustrate that of our Lord; and at the same time in itself furnishes a second coincidence, founded upon exactly the same facts. For the accusation brought against Paul by his enemies, when they had *Jews* to deal with, and, no doubt, that which was brought against him in the Jewish court, was *blasphemy:* "*Men of Israel*, this is the man that teacheth all men everywhere against the people, and *the law*, and this place." [Acts 21:28.] But when this same Paul, on the same occasion, was brought before Felix, the *Roman governor*, the charge became *sedition*, "We have found this man a pestilent fellow, and a mover of *sedition* among all the Jews throughout the world." [Acts 24:5. (See Biscoe on the Acts, p. 215.)]

It may be remarked, that this is not so much a casual coincidence between parallel passages of several Evangelists, as an instance of singular, but undesigned harmony, amongst the various component parts of one piece of history which they all record; the proceedings before two very different tribunals being represented in a manner the most agreeable to the known prejudices of all the parties concerned.

XVIII. THE MAID SAW PETER ON THE PORCH

Matth. 26:71.—"And when he was gone out *into the Porch* (τον πυλωνα), another maid saw him, and said unto them, This man was also with Jesus of Nazareth."

How came it to pass that Peter, a stranger, who had entered the house in the night, and under circumstances of some tumult and disorder, was thus singled out by the *maid in the Porch?*

Let us turn to St. John (ch. 18. ver. 16), and we shall find, that, after Jesus had entered, "Peter stood *at the door without*, till that other disciple went out which was known unto the high-priest, and *spake unto her that kept the door*, and brought in Peter." Thus was the attention of that girl directed to Peter (a fact of which St. Matthew gives no hint whatever), and thus we see how it happened that he was recognised in *the Porch*. Here is a minute indication of veracity in St. Matthew, which would have been lost upon us had not the Gospel of St. John come down to our times;—and how many similar indications may be hid, from a want of other contemporary histories with which to make a comparison, it is impossible to conjecture.

XIX. THE FEEDING OF THE FIVE THOUSAND

My next instance of coincidence without design is taken from the account of certain circumstances attending the feeding of the five thousand. And here, again, be it remarked, an indication of veracity is found, as formerly, *where the subject of the narrative is a miracle.*

In the sixth chapter of St. Mark we are told, that Jesus said to his disciples, "come ye yourselves apart into a desert place" (it was there where the miracle was wrought), "and *rest a while;* for there were many," adds the Evangelist, by way of accounting for this temporary seclusion, "*coming and going*, and they had no leisure so much as to eat." How it happened that so many were coming and going through Capernaum at that time, above all others, this Evangelist does not give us the slightest hint; neither how it came to pass that, by retiring for *a while*, Jesus and his disciples would escape the inconvenience. Turn we, then, to the parallel passage in St. John, and there we shall find the matter explained at once, though certainly this explanation could never have been given with a reference to the very casual expression of St. Mark. In St. John we do not meet with one word about Jesus retiring for *a while* into the desert, for the purpose of being apart, or that He would have been put to any inconvenience by staying at Capernaum, but we are told (what perfectly agrees with these two circumstances), "that *the Passover, a feast of the Jews, was nigh,*" 6:4. Hence, then, the "coming and going" through Capernaum was so unusually great, and hence, if Jesus and his disciples rested in the desert "a while," the crowd, which was pressing towards Jerusalem from every part of the country, would have subsided, and drawn off to the capital. For it may be observed that the desert place being at some distance from Capernaum, through which city the great road lay from the north to Jerusalem, the multitude could not follow Jesus there without some inconvenience and delay.

The confusion which prevailed throughout the Holy Land at this great festival we may easily imagine, when we read in Josephus [Bel. Jud. vi. 9. § 3.] , that, for the satisfaction of Nero, his officer, Cestius, on one occasion, endeavoured to reckon up the number of those who shared in the national rite at Jerusalem. By counting the victims sacrificed, and allowing a company of ten to each victim, he found that nearly two millions six hundred thousand souls were present; and it may be observed, that this method of calculation would not include the many persons who must have been disqualified from actually partaking of the sacrifice, by the places of their birth and the various causes of uncleanness.

I cannot forbear remarking another incident in the transaction we are now considering, in itself a trifle, but not, perhaps, on that account, less fit for corroborating the history. We read in St. John, that when Jesus had reached this desert place, He "lifted up his eyes and saw a great multitude come unto him, and he said unto *Philip*, Whence shall we buy bread that these may eat?" (6:5.) Why should this question have been directed to Philip in particular? If we had the Gospel of St. John and not the other Gospels, we should see no peculiar propriety in this choice, and should probably assign it to accident. If we had the other Gospels, and not that of St. John, we should not be put upon the inquiry, for they make no mention of the question having been addressed expressly to *Philip*. But, by comparing St. Luke with St. John, we discover the reason at once. By St. Luke, and by him alone, we are informed, that the desert place where the miracle was wrought *"was belonging to Bethsaida."* (9:10.) By St. John we are informed, (though not in the passage where he relates the miracle, which is worthy of remark, but in another chapter altogether independent of it, ch. 1:44,) that *"Philip was of Bethsaida."* To whom, then, could the question have been directed so properly as to him, who, being of the immediate neighbourhood, was the most likely to know where bread was to be bought? Here again, then, I maintain, we have strong indications of veracity in the case of a miracle itself; and I leave it to others, who may have ingenuity and inclination for the task, to weed out the falsehood of the miracle from the manifest reality of the circumstances which attend it, and to separate fiction from fact, which is in the very closest combination with it.

XX. SIMON THE CYRENIAN

Mark 15:21.—"And they compel one Simon, a Cyrenian, who passed by, coming out of the country, the father of Alexander and *Rufus*, to bear his cross."

Clement of Alexandria, who lived about the end of the second century, declares, that Mark wrote this Gospel on St. Peter's authority *at Rome*. Jerome, who lived in the fourth century, says, that Mark, the disciple and interpreter of St. Peter, being requested by his brethren *at Rome*, wrote a short Gospel.

Now this circumstance may account for his designating Simon as the *father of Rufus* at least; for we find that a disciple of that name, and of considerable note, was resident *at Rome*, when St. Paul wrote his Epistle to the Romans. "*Salute Rufus,* " says he, "*chosen in the Lord,* " 16:13. Thus, by mentioning a man living upon the spot where he was writing, and amongst the people whom he addressed, Mark was giving a reference for the truth of his narrative, which must have been accessible and satisfactory to all; since Rufus could not have failed knowing the particulars of the Crucifixion (the great event to which the Christians looked), when his father had been so intimately concerned in it as to have been the reluctant bearer of the cross.

Of course, the force of this argument depends on the identity of the Rufus of St. Mark and the Rufus of St. Paul, which I have no means of proving [See Michaelis, vol. iii. p. 213.] ; but admitting it to be probable that they were the same persons (which, I think, may be admitted, for St. Paul, we see, expressly speaks of a distinguished disciple of the name of Rufus at Rome, and St. Mark, writing for the Romans, mentions Rufus, the son of Simon, as well known to them)—admitting this, the coincidence is striking, and serves to account for what otherwise seems a piece of purely gratuitous and needless information offered by St. Mark to his readers, namely, that Simon was the father of Alexander and Rufus; a fact omitted by the other Evangelists, and apparently turned to no advantage by himself.

XXI. DARKNESS OVER THE LAND WHEN CHRIST IS CRUCIFIED

Mark 15:25.—"And it was the *third* hour, and they crucified him."

33.—"And when the *sixth* hour was come, there was darkness over the whole land until the *ninth* hour."

It has been observed to me by an intelligent friend, who has turned his attention to the internal evidence of the Gospels, that it will be found, on examination, that the scoffs and insults which were levelled at our Saviour on the cross, *were all during the early part of the Crucifixion*, and that a manifest change of feeling towards Him, arising, as it should seem, from a certain misgiving as to his character, is discoverable in the bystanders as the scene drew nearer to its close: I think the remark just and valuable. It is at the first that we read of those "who passed by railing on him and wagging their heads," Mark 15:29; of "the chief priests and scribes mocking him," 31; of "those that were crucified with him reviling him," 32; of the "soldiers mocking him and offering him vinegar," Luke 23:36, pointing out to Him, most likely, the "vessel of vinegar which was set," or holding a portion of it beyond his reach, by way of aggravating the pains of intense thirst, which must have attended this lingering mode of death:—that all this occurred at the beginning of the Passion is the natural conclusion to be drawn from the narratives of St. Matthew, St. Mark, and St. Luke.

But, during the latter part of it, we hear nothing of this kind; on the contrary, when Jesus cried, "I thirst," there was no mockery offered, but a sponge was filled with vinegar, and put on a reed and applied to his lips, with remarkable alacrity; "*one ran*" and did it, Mark 15:36: and, from the misunderstanding of the words "Eli, Eli," it is clear that the spectators had some suspicion that Elias might come to take Him down. Do not, then, these circumstances accord remarkably well with the alleged fact, that "*there was darkness over all the land from the sixth to the ninth hour?*" Matth. 27:45; Mark 15:33. Is not this change of conduct in the merciless crew that surrounded the cross very naturally explained, by the awe with which they contemplated the gloom as it took effect? and does it not strongly, though undesignedly, confirm the assertion, that such a fearful darkness there actually was?

XXII. JOSEPH OF ARIMATHAEA AND PILATE

Mark 15:43.—"And Joseph of Arimathæa, an honourable counsellor, which also waited for the kingdom of God, came, and went in *boldly* unto

Pilate, and craved the body of Jesus."

It is evident that the courage of Joseph on this occasion had impressed the mind of the Evangelist—he "went in *boldly*," τολμησας εισηλθε— he had the boldness to go in—he ventured to go in.

Now by comparing the parallel passage in St. John, we very distinctly trace the train of thought which was working in St. Mark's mind when he used this expression, but which would have entirely escaped us, together with the evidence it furnishes for the truth of the narrative, had not the gospel of St. John come down to us. For there we read (19:38), "And after this Joseph of Arimathæa, being a disciple of Jesus, *but secretly for fear of the Jews*, besought Pilate that he might take away the body of Jesus."

It appears, therefore, that Joseph was known to be a *timid* disciple; which made his conduct on the present occasion seem to St. Mark remarkable, and at variance with his ordinary character; for there might be supposed some risk in manifesting an interest in the corpse of Jesus, whom the Jews had just persecuted to the death.

Moreover, it may be observed that St. John, in the passage before us, continues, "And there came also Nicodemus, which *at the first came to Jesus by night*, and brought a mixture of myrrh and aloes"—as though the timid character of Joseph was uppermost in his thoughts too (though he says nothing of his going in *boldly*), and suggested to him Nicodemus, and what he did; another disciple of the same class as Joseph; and whose constitutional failing, he does intimate, had occurred to him at the moment, by the notice that it was the same person who had come to Jesus by night.

I will add, that both these cases of Joseph and Nicodemus bear upon the coincidence in the last Number; for whence did these fearful men derive their courage on this occasion, but from having witnessed the circumstances which attended the Crucifixion?

XXIII. THE SECOND SABBATH AFTER THE FIRST

Luke 6:1, 2.—"And it came to pass on the *second Sabbath after the first* (εν σαββατω δευτεροπρωτω,) that he went through the *corn-fields;* and his disciples plucked the ears of *corn*, and did eat, rubbing them in their hands. And certain of the Pharisees said," &c.

This transaction occurred on the first Sabbath after the second day of unleavened bread; on which day the *wave sheaf was offered*, as the first-fruits of the harvest; [Lev. 23:10–12.] and from which day the fifty days were reckoned to the Pentecost.

Is it not, therefore, very natural that this conversation should have taken place at this time, and that St. Luke should have especially given the date of the conversation, as well as the conversation itself?

It being the first Sabbath after the day when the first-fruits of the corn were cut, accords perfectly with the fact that the disciples should be walking through fields of standing corn at that season.

The Rite which had just then been celebrated, an epoch in the *church*, as well as an epoch in the year, naturally turned the minds of all the parties here concerned to the subject of *corn*—the Pharisees, to find cause for cavil in it—Jesus, to find cause for instruction in it—St. Luke, to find cause for especially naming the *second Sabbath after the first*, as the period of the incident. And yet, be it observed, no connection is pointed out between the time and the transaction, either in the conversation itself, or in the Evangelist's history of it. That is, there is coincidence without design in both.

XXIV. JESUS GOING TO THE PASSOVER AT JERUSALEM

Luke 9:53.—"And they did not receive him, because his *face was as though he would go to Jerusalem.*"

Jesus was then going to the Passover at Jerusalem, and was, therefore, plainly acknowledging that men ought to worship *there*, contrary to the practice of the Samaritans, who had set up the Temple at Gerizim, in opposition to that of the Holy City. That this was the cause of irritation is implied in the expression, that they would not receive Him, *"because his face was as though he would go to Jerusalem."* Let us observe, then, how perfectly this account harmonizes with that which St. John gives of Jesus' interview with the woman of Samaria at the well. Then Jesus was coming *from* Judæa, and at a season of the year when no suspicion could attach to Him of having been at Jerusalem for devotional purposes, for it wanted "four months before the harvest should come," and with it the Passover. Accordingly, on this occasion, Jesus and his disciples were treated with civility and hospitality by the Samaritans. They purchased bread in the town without being exposed to any insults, and they were even requested to tarry with them.

I cannot but think that the stamp of truth is very visible in all this. It was natural, that at certain seasons of the year (at the great feasts) this jealous spirit should be excited, which at others might be dormant; and though it is not expressly stated by the one Evangelist, that the insult of the villagers was at a season when it might be expected, yet, from a casual expression (ver. 51), such may be inferred to have been the case. And though it is not expressly stated by the other Evangelist, that the hospitality of the Samaritans was exercised at a more propitious season of the year, yet by an equally casual expression in the course of the chapter (ver. 35), that, too, is ascertained to have been the fact. Surely, it is beyond the reach of the most artful imposture to observe so strict a propriety even in the subordinate parts of the scheme, especially where less distinctness of detail would scarcely have excited suspicion; and surely it is a circumstance most satisfactory to every reasonable mind to discover, that the evidence of the truth of that Gospel (on which our hopes are anchored) is, not only the more conspicuous the more minutely it is examined, but that, without such examination, full justice cannot be done to the variety and pregnancy of its proofs.

XXV. WATER INTO WINE

John 2:7.—"Jesus saith unto them, *Fill* the water-pots with water."
There appears to me to be in this passage an undesigned coincidence, very slight and trivial indeed in its character, but not on that account less valuable as a mark of truth. These water-pots had to be *filled* before Jesus could perform the miracle. It follows, therefore, that they had been emptied of their contents—the water had been drawn out of them. But for what purpose was it used, and why were these vessels here? It was for purifying. For "all the Jews," as St. Mark tells us more at large (7:3), "except they wash their hands oft, eat not, holding the tradition of the elders." The vessels, therefore, being now empty, indicates that the guests had done with them—that the meal, therefore, was advanced; for it was before they sat down to it that they performed their ablutions—a circumstance which accords with the moment when our Lord is represented as doing this miracle; for the governor of the feast said to the bridegroom, "Every man at the beginning doth set forth good wine ... but thou hast kept the good wine *until now*." It is satisfactory, that in the record of a great miracle, like this, the minor circumstances in connection with it should be in keeping with one another.

XXVI. NICODEMUS AND JESUS

John 3:1, 2.—"There was a man of the Pharisees, named Nicodemus, a ruler of the Jews: The same came to Jesus by *night*, and said unto him, Rabbi," &c.

It is a remarkable and characteristic feature of the discourses of our Lord, that they are often prompted, or shaped, or illustrated, by the event of the moment; by some scene or incident that presented itself to him at the time he was speaking. It is scarcely necessary to give examples of a fact so undisputed. Thus it was the day after the miracle of the loaves, and it was to the persons who had witnessed that miracle, and profited by it, that Jesus said, "Labour not for the meat which perisheth, but for that meat which endureth unto everlasting life," [John 6:27.] &c.; and much more to the same effect. It was at Jacob's well, and in reply to the question of the woman, "How is it that thou, being a Jew, askest drink of me, which am a woman of Samaria?" [John. 4:9] that Jesus spake so much at large of the water whereof "whosoever drank should never thirst," &c. It was whilst tarrying in this same rural spot, that, calling the attention of his disciples to the scene around them, he said, "Say not ye, There are yet four months, and then cometh harvest? behold, I say unto you, Lift up your eyes, and look on the fields; for they are white already to harvest;" [John 4:35.] and he then goes on to remind them of sowing and reaping to be done in another and higher sense. These are a few instances out of many which might be produced, where the incident that gave rise to the remarks is actually related; and by which the habit of our Lord's discourse is proved to be such as I have described. But in other places, the incident itself is omitted, and but for some casual expression which is let fall, it would be impossible to connect the discourse with it; by means, however, of some such expression, apparently intended to serve no such purpose, we are enabled to get at the incident, and so discover the propriety of the discourse. In such cases we are furnished once more with the argument of coincidence without design—as in the following passage: "*In the last day,* that great day of the feast, Jesus stood and cried, saying, If any man thirst, let him come unto me, and drink. He that believeth on me, as the Scripture hath said, out of his belly shall flow *rivers* of living *water,*" [John 7:37, 38.] &c. Now, but for the expression, "In the last day, that great day of the feast," we should have been at a loss to know the circumstances in which that speech of our Lord originated. But the day when it was delivered being named, we are enabled to gather from other sources, that on that day, the eighth of the Feast of Tabernacles, it was a custom to offer to God a pot of water drawn from the pool of Siloam. Coupling this fact, therefore, with our Lord's practice, already established by other evidence, of allowing the spectacle before him to give the turn to his address, we may conclude that he spake these words whilst he happened to be observing the ceremony of the water-pot. And an argument thus arises, that the speech here reported is genuine, and was really delivered by our Lord.

The passage, then, in St. John, with which I have headed this paragraph, furnishes testimony of the same kind. It describes Nicodemus as coming to Jesus *by night*—fear, no doubt, prompting him to use this secrecy. Now observe a good deal of the language which Jesus directs to him—"And this is the condemnation, that *light* is come into the world, and men loved *darkness* rather than *light*, because their deeds were evil. For every one that doeth evil hateth the *light*, neither cometh to the *light*, lest his deeds should be reproved. But he that doeth truth, cometh to the *light*, that his deeds may be made manifest, that they are wrought in God." (3:19–21.) When we remember that the interview was a *nocturnal* one, and that Jesus was accustomed to speak with a reference to the circumstances about him at the instant, what more natural than the turn of this discourse? What more satisfactory evidence could we have, than this casual evidence, that the visit was paid, and the speech spoken as St. John describes? that his narrative, in short, is true [I was put upon this coincidence by a passage which I heard in one of Mr. Marden's Hulsean Lectures.] ?

XXVII. SYCHARA CITY OF SAMARIA

John 4:5.—"Then cometh he to a city of Samaria, which is called Sychar."

Here Jesus converses with the woman at the well. She perceives that he is a prophet. She suspects that he may be the Christ. She spreads her report of him through the city. The inhabitants are awakened to a lively interest about him. Jesus is induced to tarry there two days; and it was probably the favourable disposition towards him which he found to prevail there that drew from him at that very time the observation to his disciples, "Say not ye, There are yet four months, and then cometh harvest? behold, I say unto you, Lift up your eyes, and look on the fields; for *they are white already to harvest*. And he that reapeth receiveth wages, and gathereth fruit unto life eternal: that both he that soweth and he that reapeth may rejoice together. And herein is that saying true, One soweth and another reapeth. I sent you to reap that whereon ye bestowed no labour: other men laboured, and ye are entered into their labours." It is the favourable state of Samaria for the reception of the Gospel that suggests these reflections to Jesus; he, no doubt, perceiving that God had much "people in that city."

Such is the picture of the religious state of Sychar presented in the narrative of St. John.

Now the author of the Acts of the Apostles confirms the truth of this statement in a remarkable but most unintentional manner. From him we learn that, at a period a few years later than this, and after the death of Jesus, Philip, one of the deacons, "went down to the city of Samaria" (the emphatic expression marks it to have been *Sychar*, the capital), "and preached Christ unto them." (Acts 8:5.) His success was just what might have been expected from the account we have read in St. John of the previous state of public opinion at Sychar. "The people with one accord gave heed unto those things which Philip spake" (ver. 6); and "when they believed Philip preaching the things concerning the kingdom of God and the name of Jesus Christ, they were baptized, both men and women" (ver. 12). It is evident that these histories are not got up to corroborate one another. It is not at all an obvious thought, or one likely to present itself to an impostor, that it might be prudent to fix upon Sychar as the imaginary scene of Philip's successful labours, seeing that Jesus had been well received there some years before; at least in such a case some allusion or reference would have been made to this disposition previously evinced; it would not have been left to the reader to discover it or not, as it might happen, where the chance was so great that it would be overlooked. Moreover, his recollection of the passage in St. John would probably have been studiously arrested by the use of the same word "Sychar," rather than "the city of Samaria," as designating the field of Philip's labours.

XXVIII. JESUS WALKING ON WATER

John 6:16.—"And when even was now come, his disciples went down into the sea, and entered into a ship, and went over the sea toward Capernaum. And it was now dark, and Jesus was not come to them. And *the sea arose by reason of a great wind that blew.* So when they had rowed about five-and-twenty or thirty furlongs, they see Jesus walking on the sea, and drawing nigh unto the ship: and they were afraid. But he saith unto them, It is I; be not afraid. Then they willingly received him into the ship: and immediately the ship was at the land whither they went. *The day following, when the people which stood on the other side of the sea saw that there was none other boat there, save that one whereinto his disciples were entered, and that Jesus went not with his disciples into the boat, but that his disciples were gone away alone; (howbeit there came other boats from Tiberias nigh unto the place where they did eat bread, after that the Lord had given thanks:)* when the people therefore saw that Jesus was not there, neither his disciples, they also took shipping, and came to Capernaum, seeking for Jesus. And when they had found him on the other side of the sea, they said unto him, *Rabbi, when camest thou hither?*"

Matth. 14:22.—"And straightway Jesus constrained his disciples to get into a ship, and to go before him unto the other side, while he sent the multitudes away. And when he had sent the multitudes away, he went up into a mountain apart to pray: and when the evening was come, he was there alone. But the ship was now in the midst of the sea, tossed with waves: *for the wind was contrary.*"

It appears from St. John, that the people thought that Jesus was still on the side of the lake where the miracle had been wrought. And this they inferred because there was no other boat on the preceding evening, except that in which the disciples had gone over to Capernaum on the other side, and they had observed that Jesus went not with them. It is added, however, that, "*there came other boats from Tiberias*" (which was on the same side as Capernaum), nigh unto the place where the Lord had given thanks. Now why might they not have supposed that Jesus had availed himself of one of these return-boats, and so made his escape in the night? St. John gives no reason why they did not make this obvious inference. Let us turn to St. Matthew's account of the same transaction (which I have placed at the head of this paragraph), and we speedily learn why they *could* not. In this account we find it recorded, not simply that the disciples were in distress in consequence of the sea arising "by reason of a great wind that blew," but it is further stated, that "*the wind was contrary,*" *i.e.*, the wind was blowing *from* Capernaum and Tiberias, and therefore not only might the ships readily come from Tiberias (the incident mentioned by St. John), a course for which the wind (though violent) was fair, but the multitude might well conclude that with such a wind Jesus *could* not have used one of those return-boats, and therefore must still be amongst them.

Indeed, nothing can be more probable than that these ships from Tiberias were fishing vessels, which, having been overtaken by the storm, suffered themselves to be driven before the gale, to the opposite coast, where they might find shelter for the night; for what could such a number of boats, as sufficed to convey the people across (v. 24), have been doing at this desert place, neither port, nor town, nor market? so that here again is another instance of undesigned consistency in the narrative; the very fact of a number of boats resorting to this "desert place," at the close of day, strongly indicating (though most incidentally) that the sea actually was rising (as St. John asserts), "by reason of a great wind that blew."

I further think this to be the correct view of a passage of some intricacy, from considering, first, the question which the people put to Jesus on finding him at Capernaum the next day. Full as they must have been of the miracle which they had lately witnessed, and anxious to see the repetition of works so wonderful, their first inquiry is, "*Rabbi, when camest thou hither?*" surely an inquiry not of mere form, but manifestly implying that, under the circumstances, it could only have been by some extraordinary means that he had passed across; and, second, from observing the satisfactory explanation it affords of the parenthesis of St. John, "*howbeit there came other boats from Tiberias,*" ... which no longer seems a piece of purely gratuitous and irrelevant information, but turns out to be equivalent with the expression in St. Matthew, that the "*wind was contrary;*" though the point is not directly asserted, but only a fact is mentioned from which such an assertion naturally follows.

It might indeed be said, that the circumstance of the ships coming from Tiberias was mentioned for the purpose of explaining how the people could take shipping (as they are stated to have done to go to Capernaum), when it had been before affirmed that there was no other boat there save that into which the disciples were entered. Such caution, however, I do not think at all agreeable to the spirit of the writings of the Evangelists, who are always very careless about consequences, not troubling themselves to obviate or explain the difficulties of their narrative. But, whatever may be judged of this matter, the main argument remains the same; and a minute coincidence between St. John and St. Matthew is made out, of such a nature as precludes all suspicion of collusion, and shows consistency in the two histories without the smallest design.

And here again I will repeat the observation which I have already had occasion more than once to make—that the truth of the general narrative in some degree involves the truth of a *miracle*. For if we are satisfied by the undesigned coincidence that St. Matthew was certainly speaking truth when he said, the wind was "boisterous," how shall we presume to assert, that he speaks truth no longer, when he tells us in the same breath that Jesus "walked on the sea," in the midst of that very storm, and that when "he came into the ship the wind ceased?"

Doubtless, the one fact does not absolutely *prove* the others; but in all *ordinary* cases, where one or two particulars in a body of evidence are so corroborated as to be placed above suspicion, the rest, though not admitting of the like corroboration, are nevertheless received without dispute.

XXIX. THE SIX DAYS OF JESUS AT BETHANY

The events of the last week of our Saviour's earthly life, as recorded by the Evangelists, will furnish us with several arguments of the kind we are collecting.

1. John 12:1.—"Then Jesus, *six days* before the Passover, came to *Bethany*, where Lazarus was."

Bethany was a village at the mount of Olives (Mark 11:1), near Jerusalem; and it was in his approach to that city, to keep the last Passover and die, that Jesus now lodged there for the night, meaning to enter the capital the next day. (John 12:12.)

St. John tells us no more of the movements of Jesus on this occasion with precision; however, this one date will suffice to verify his narrative, as well as that of St. Mark. Turn we, then, to the latter, who gives us an account of the proceedings of Jesus immediately before his crucifixion in more detail; or rather, enables us to infer for ourselves what they were, from phrases which escape from him; and we shall find that the two narratives are very consistent with respect to them, though it is very evident that neither narrative is at all dressed by the other, but that both are so constructed as to argue independent knowledge of the facts in the Evangelists themselves.

In Mark 11:1, we read, "And when they came nigh to Jerusalem, unto Bethphage and *Bethany*, at the mount of Olives, He sendeth forth two of his disciples, and saith unto them, Go your way into the village over against you," &c. The internal evidence of this whole transaction implies, that the disciples were despatched on this errand the morning after they had arrived at Bethany, where Jesus had lodged for *the night*, and not the evening before, on the instant of his arrival; the events of the day being much too numerous to be crowded into the latter period of time—the procuring the ass, the triumphant procession to Jerusalem, the visit to the temple, all filling up that day; and its being expressly said, when all these transactions were concluded, that "the even-tide was come" (ver. 11); and this internal evidence entirely accords with the direct assertion of St. John (12:12) that it was "the *next* day." Accordingly, this day closed with Jesus "looking round about upon all things," in the temple (ver. 11), and then "when the eventide was come, going out unto *Bethany* with the twelve." This, then, was the *second* day Jesus lodged at Bethany, as we gather from St. Mark. "On the morrow, as they were coming from *Bethany*, " Jesus cursed the fig-tree (ver. 13); proceeded to Jerusalem; spent the day, as before, in Jerusalem and the temple, casting out of it the moneychangers; and again, "when even was come He went out of the city" (ver. 19), certainly returning to Bethany; for though this is not said, the fact is clear, from the tenor of the next paragraph. This was the *third* day Jesus lodged at Bethany, according to St. Mark. "In the morning, as they passed by, they saw the fig-tree dried up from the roots" (ver. 20), *i. e.*, they were proceeding by the same road as the morning before, and therefore from

Bethany, again to spend the day at Jerusalem, and in the temple (ver. 27; 12:41); Jesus employing himself there in enunciating parables and answering cavils. After this "he went out of the temple" (13:1), to return once more, no doubt, the evening being come, to Bethany; for though this again is not asserted, it is clearly to be inferred, which is better, since we immediately afterwards find Jesus sitting with the disciples, and talking with several of them privately, "on the mount of Olives" (ver. 3), which lay in his road to Bethany. This was the *fourth* day, according to St. Mark. St. Mark next says, "After *two days* was the feast of the Passover." (14:1.)

This, then, makes up the interval of the *six days* since Jesus came to Bethany, according to St. Mark, which tallies exactly with the direct assertion of St. John, that "Jesus *six days* before the Passover came to Bethany."

But how unconcerted is this agreement between the Evangelists! St. John's declaration of the date of the arrival of Jesus at Bethany is indeed unambiguous; but the corresponding relation of St. Mark, though proved to be in perfect accordance with St. John, has to be traced with pains and difficulty; some of the steps necessary for arriving at the conclusion altogether inferential. How extremely improbable is a concurrence of this nature upon any other supposition than the truth of the incident related, and the independent knowledge of it of the witnesses: and how infallibly would that be the impression it would produce on the minds of a jury, supposing it to be an ingredient in a case of circumstantial evidence presented to them.

2. A second slight coincidence, which offers itself to our notice on the events of Bethany, is the following:—

It is in the *evening* that the Evangelists represent Jesus as returning from the city to Bethany: "And now the *even-tide* was come, he went out unto Bethany with the twelve." (Mark 11:11.) "And when *even* was come, he went out of the city" (ver. 19), says St. Mark. "And he left them, and went out of the city into Bethany; and he *lodged* there. Now in the *morning*, as he returned," &c. (Matth. 21:17), says St. Matthew.

St. John does not speak directly of Jesus going in the evening to Bethany. But there is an incidental expression in him which implies that such was his own conviction, though nothing can be less studied than it is. For he tells us, that at Bethany, "they made him a *supper*," δειπνον, a term, as now used, indicating an *evening* meal. Had St. John happened to employ the same phrase St. Mark does when relating this same event (κατακειμενου αυτου, "as he sat at meat,") the argument would have been lost; as it is, the mention of the meal by St. John (who takes no notice of the fact that Jesus *lodged* at Bethany, though he spent the day at Jerusalem), and such meal being an *evening* meal, is tantamount to St.

Mark's statement, that he passed his evenings in this village.

3 The same fact coincides with several other particulars, though our attention is not drawn to them by the Evangelists. It is obvious, from the history, that the danger to Jesus did not arise from the multitude, but from the priests. The multitude were with Him, until, as I have said in a former paragraph, they were persuaded that he assumed to Himself the character of God, and spake blasphemy, when they turned against Him: but till then they were on his side. Judas "promised, and sought opportunity to betray Him in the *absence of the multitude*." (Luke 22:6.) The chief priests and elders, in consulting on his death, said, "Not on the feast-day, lest there be an *uproar among the people*." (Matth. 26:5.) Jesus, therefore, felt Himself safe, nay, powerful, so that he could even clear the temple of its profaners by force, in the day; but not so in the night. In the night, the chief priests might use stratagem, as they eventually did; and the fact appears to be, that the very first night Jesus did not retire to Bethany, but remained in and about Jerusalem, He was actually betrayed and seized. There is a consistency, I say, of the most artless kind in the several parts of this narrative; a consistency, however, such as we have to detect for ourselves; and so latent and unobtrusive, that no forgery could reach it [Several of the thoughts in this Number are suggested to me by Mr. A. Johnson's "Christus Crucifixus."] .

XXX. "HE STEDFASTLY SET HIS FACE TO GO TO JERUSALEM"

It appears to me that there is a coincidence in the following particulars, relating to this same locality, not the less valuable from being in some degree intricate and involved.

1. Luke 9:51.—"And it came to pass, when the time was come that he should be received up, he stedfastly *set his face to go to Jerusalem*."

Expressions occur in the remainder of this and in the following chapter, which show that the mind of St. Luke was contemplating the events which happened on this journey, though he does not make it his business to trace it step by step: thus (ver. 52), "And they *went, and entered* into a village of the Samaritans." And again (vet. 57), "And it came to pass, that, *as they went in the way*, a certain man said unto him," &c. And again (10:38), "Now it came to pass, *as they went*, that he entered into a *certain village:* and a certain woman named Martha received him into her house. And she had a sister called Mary." The line of march, therefore, which St. Luke was pursuing in his own mind in the narrative, was that which was leading

Jesus through Samaria to Jerusalem; and in the last of the verses I have quoted, he brings him to this "certain village," which he does not name, but he tells us it was the abode of Martha and Mary.

Accordingly, on comparing this passage with John (11:1), we are led to the conclusion that the village was *Bethany;* for it is there said, that Bethany was "the town of Mary and her sister Martha."

But on looking at St. Mark's account of a similar journey of Jesus, for probably it was not the same [See Luke 13:22; 17:11; 18:31; where a subsequent journey is perhaps spoken of.] , we find that the preceding stage which he made before coming to Bethany was from *Jericho* (Mark 10:46). "And they came to *Jericho:* and as he went out of *Jericho* with his disciples and a great number of people," &c. And then it follows (11:1), "And when they came nigh to Jerusalem, unto Bethphage and *Bethany,* " &c. This, therefore, brings us to the same point as St. Luke. Thus, to reca-pitulate: we learn, from St. Luke, that Jesus, in a journey from Galilee to Jerusalem, arrived at the village of Martha and Mary.

We learn from St. John, that this village was Bethany.

And we learn from St. Mark, that the last town Jesus left before he came to Bethany, on a similar journey, if not the same, was Jericho.

Now let us turn once more to St. Luke (10:30), and we shall there discover Jesus giving utterance to a parable on this occasion, which is placed in immediate juxtaposition with the history of his reaching Bethany, as though it had been spoken just before. For, as soon as it is ended, the narrative proceeds, "Now it came to pass, as they went, that he entered into a *certain village:* and a certain woman named Martha received him into her house" (10:38). And what was this parable? That of "a certain man who went down from *Jerusalem* to *Jericho*, and fell among thieves," &c. It seems, then, highly probable, that Jesus was actually trav-elling from *Jericho* to *Jerusalem* (Bethany being just short of Jerusalem) when he delivered it. What can be more like reality than this? Yet how circuitously do we get at our conclusion!

2. Nor is even this all. The parable represents a priest and Levite as on the road. This again is entirely in keeping with the scene: for whether it was that the school of the prophets established from of old at Jericho [2 Kings 2:5.] had given a sacerdotal character to the town; or whether it was its comparative proximity to Jerusalem, that had invited the priests and Levites to settle there; certain it is that a very large portion of the courses that waited at the temple resided at Jericho, ready to take their turn at Jerusalem when duty called them [See Lightfoot, vol. ii. p. 45, fol.] ; so that it was more than probable that Jesus, on coming from Jericho to Jerusalem, on this occasion, with his disciples, would meet many of this

order. How vivid a colouring of truth does all this give to the fact of the parable having been spoken as St. Luke says!

3. Nay more still—I can believe that there may be discovered a reason coincident with the circumstances of the time, in Jesus choosing to imagine a *Samaritan* for the benefactor at this particular moment—for it had only been shortly before, at least it was upon this same journey, that James and John had proposed, when the *Samaritans* would not receive him, to call down fire from heaven and consume them (Luke 9:54). Could the spirit they were of be more gracefully rebuked than thus? Again, how real is all this! [Comp. No. XII. of the Appendix.]

XXXI. MALCHUS AND PETER

John 18:10.—"Then Simon Peter having a sword drew it, and smote the high-priest's servant, and cut off his right ear. *The servant's name was Malchus.*"

15.—"And Simon Peter followed Jesus, and so did another disciple: *that disciple was known unto the high-priest,* and went in with Jesus into the palace of the high-priest.

16.—"But Peter stood at the door without. Then went out that other disciple, which was known unto the high-priest, *and spake unto her that kept the door, and brought in Peter.*"

In my present argument, it will be needful to show, in the first instance, that "the disciple who was known unto the high-priest," mentioned in ver. 15, was probably the Evangelist himself. This I conclude from three considerations:—

1. From the testimony of the fathers, Chrysostom, Theophylact, and Jerome [See Lardner's History of the Apostles and Evangelists, ch. ix.] .

2. From the circumstance that St. John often unquestionably speaks of himself in the third person in a similar manner. Thus, chap. 20:2, "Then she runneth, and *cometh to Simon Peter, and to rite other disciple whom Jesus loved;*" and yet. 3. "Peter therefore went forth, and *that other disciple.*" The like phrase is repeated several times in the same chapter and elsewhere.

3. Moreover, it may be thought, as Bishop Middleton has argued, that St. John has a distinctive claim to the title of "*the* other disciple" (o αλλος μαθητης, not "another," as our version has it), where St. Peter is the colleague: for that a closer relation subsisted between Peter and John than between any other of the disciples. They constantly act together. Peter and John are sent to prepare the last Passover (Luke 22:8). Peter and

John run together to the sepulchre. John apprizes Peter that the stranger at the sea of Tiberias is Jesus (John 21:7). Peter is anxious to learn of Jesus what is to become of John (ver. 21). After the ascension they are associated together in all the early history of the Acts of the Apostles.

4. The narrative of the motions of "that disciple who was known unto the high-priest," his coming out and going in, is so express and circumstantial, that it bears every appearance of having been written by the *party himself.* Nor in fact do any other of the Evangelists mention a syllable about "that other disciple;" they tell us, indeed, that Peter did enter the high-priest's house, but they take no notice of the particulars of his admission, nor how it was effected, nor of any obstacles thrown in the way.

For these reasons, I understand the disciple known unto the high-priest to have been St. John. My argument now stands thus:—The assault committed by Peter is mentioned by all the Evangelists, *but the name of the servant is given by St. John only.* How does this happen? Most naturally: for it seems that by some chance or other St. John as known not only unto the high-priest, but also to his household—that the servants were acquainted with him, and he with them, since he was permitted to enter into the high-priest's house, whilst Peter was shut out, and no sooner did he "speak unto her that kept the door," than Peter was admitted. So again, in further proof of the same thing, when another of the servants charges Peter with being one of Christ's disciples, St. John adds a circumstance peculiar to himself, and marking his knowledge of the family, that *"it was his kinsman whose ear Peter cut off."*

These facts, I conceive, show that St. John (on the supposition that St. John and "the other disciple" are one and the same) was personally acquainted with the servants of the high-priest. How natural, therefore, was it, that in mentioning such an incident as Peter's attack upon one of those servants, he should mention the man by name, and the *"servant's name was Malchus;"* whilst the other Evangelists, to whom the sufferer was an individual in whom they took no extraordinary interest, were satisfied with a general designation of him, as "one of the servants of the high-priest."

This incident also, in some degree, though not in the same degree perhaps as certain others which have been mentioned, supports the miracle which ensues. For if the argument shows that the Evangelists are uttering the truth when they say that such an event occurred as the blow with the sword—if it shows *that there actually was such a blow struck*—then is there not additional ground for believing that they continue to tell the truth, when they say in the same passage that the effects of the blow were miraculously removed, and that the ear was healed?

I am aware that there are those who argue for the superior rank and station of St. John, from his being known unto the high-priest; and who may, therefore, think him degraded by this implied familiarity with his servants. Suffice it however to say,—that as, on the one hand, to be known to the high-priest does not determine that he was his equal, so, on the other, to be known to his servants does not determine that he was not their superior; furthermore, that the relation in which servants stood towards their betters was, in ancient times, one of much less distance than at present; and, lastly, that the Scriptures themselves lay no claim to dignity of birth for this Apostle, when they represent of him and of St. Peter (Acts 4:13), that Annas and the elders, after hearing their defence, "perceived them to be unlearned and ignorant men."

XXXII. "THEN WOULD MY SERVANTS FIGHT"

John 18:36.—"Jesus answered, My kingdom is not of this world: if my kingdom were of this world, *then would my servants fight*, that I should not be delivered to the Jews."

Nothing could have been more natural than for his enemies to have reminded our Lord that in one instance at least, and that too of very recent occurrence, his *servants did fight*. Indeed Jesus himself might here be almost thought to challenge inquiry into the assault Peter had so lately committed upon the servant of the high-priest. Assuredly there was no disposition on the part of his accusers to spare him. The council *sought* for witness against Jesus, and where could it be found more readily than in the high-priest's own house? Frivolous and unfounded calumnies of all sorts were brought forward, which agreed not together; but this act of violence, indisputably committed by one of his companions in his Master's cause, and, as they would not have scrupled to assert, under his Master's eye, is altogether and intentionally, as it should seem, kept out of sight.

The suppression of the charge is the more remarkable, from the fact, that a relation of Malchus was actually present at the time, and evidently aware of the violence which had been done his kinsman, though not quite able to identify the offender. "One of the servants of the high-priest, being his kinsman whose ear Peter cut off, said, Did I not see thee in the garden with him?" (ver. 26.) Surely nothing could have been more natural than for this man to be clamorous for redress.

Had the Gospel of St. Luke never come down to us, it would have remained a difficulty (one of the many difficulties of Scripture arising from the conciseness and desultory nature of the narrative), to have accounted for the suppression of a charge against Jesus, which of all others would have been the most likely to suggest itself to his prosecutors, from the offence having been just committed, and from the sufferer being one of the high-priest's own family; a charge, moreover, which would have had the advantage of being founded in truth, and would therefore have been far more effective than accusations which could not be sustained. Let us hear, however, St. Luke. He tells us, and he only, that when the blow had been struck, Jesus said, "Suffer ye thus far: and *he touched his ear and healed him."*—(22:51.)

The miracle satisfactorily explains the suppression of the charge—to have advanced it would naturally have led to an investigation that would have more than frustrated the malicious purpose it was meant to serve. It would have proved too much. It might have furnished indeed an argument against the peaceable professions of Jesus's party, but, at the same time, it would have made manifest his own compassionate nature, submission to the laws, and extraordinary powers. Pilate, who sought occasion to release him, might have readily found it in a circumstance so well calculated to convince him of the innocence of the prisoner, and of his being (what he evidently suspected and feared) something more than human.

XXXIII. HOW DID JOHN OUTRUN PETER TO THE TOMB?

John 20:4.—"So they ran both together: and *the other disciple did outrun Peter*, and came first to the sepulchre.

5.—"And he stooping down, and looking in, saw the linen clothes lying; yet *went he not in.*

6.—"Then cometh Simon Peter following him, *and went into the sepulchre*, and seeth the linen clothes lie.

7.—"And the napkin, that was about his head, not lying with the linen clothes, but wrapped together in a place by itself.

8.—*"Then went in also that other disciple*, which came first to the sepulchre."

How express and circumstantial is this narrative! How difficult it is to read it and doubt for a moment of its perfect truth! My more immediate concern, however, with the passage is this, that it affords two coincidences, certainly very trifling in themselves, but still signs of veracity:—

1. *St. John outran St. Peter.* It is universally agreed by ecclesiastical writers of antiquity, that John was the *youngest* of all the Apostles. That Peter was at this time past the vigour of his age, may perhaps be inferred from an expression in the twenty-first chapter of St. John—"Verily, verily, I say unto thee," says Jesus to Peter, "*when thou wast young*, thou girdedst

thyself, and walkedst whither thou wouldst: but when thou shalt be old, thou shalt stretch forth thy hands, and another shalt gird thee, and carry thee whither thou wouldst not."—ver. 18. Or (what may be more satisfactory) there being every reason to believe that St. John survived St. Peter six or seven and thirty years [See Lardner's History of the Apostles and Evangelists, ch. ix. sect. 6, and ch. xviii, sect. 5.] , it almost necessarily follows, that he must have been much the younger man of the two, since the term of St. Peter's natural life was probably not very much forestalled by his martyrdom [Consult 2 Peter 1:14, and John 21:18.] . Accordingly, when they ran both together to the sepulchre, it was to be expected that John should *outrun his more aged companion and come there first.*

I do not propose this as a new light, but I am not aware that it has been brought so prominently forward as it deserves. An incident thus trivial and minute disarms suspicion. The most sceptical cannot see cunning or contrivance in it; and it is no small point gained over such persons, to lead them to distrust and re-examine their bold conclusions. This little fact may be the sharp end of the wedge that shall, by degrees, cleave their doubts asunder. Seeing this, they may by and by "see greater things than these." But this is not all:—for, 2ndly, though John came first to the sepulchre, *he did not venture to go in till Peter set him the example.* Peter did not pause "to stoop down" and "look in," but boldly entered at once—he was not troubled for fear of seeing a spirit, which was probably the feeling that withheld St. John from entering, as it was the feeling which, on a former occasion, caused the disciples (Matth. 14:26) to cry out. Peter was anxiously impatient to satisfy himself of the truth of the women's report, and to meet once more his crucified Master; all other considerations were with him absorbed in this one. Now such is precisely the conduct we should have expected from a man, who seldom or never is offered to our notice in the course of the New Testament (and it is very often that our attention is directed to him), without some indication being given of his possessing a fearless, spirited, and impetuous character. Slight as this trait is, it marks the same individual who ventured to commit himself to the deep and "walk upon the water," whilst the other disciples remained in the boat; who "drew his sword and smote the high-priest's servant," whilst they were confounded and dismayed; who "girt his fisher's coat about him and cast himself into the sea" to greet his Master when he appeared again, whilst his companions came in a little ship, dragging the net with fishes; who was ever most obnoxious to the civil power, so that when any of the disciples are cast into prison, there are we sure to find St. Peter. (See Acts 5:18, 29; 12:3.) Again, I say, I cannot imagine that designing persons, however wary they might have been, however much upon their guard, could possibly have given their fictitious narrative this singular air of truth, by the introduction of circumstances so unimportant, yet so consistent and harmonious.

XXXIV. THE ASCENSION OF JESUS

The Gospel of St. John contains no history whatever of the *Ascension* of Jesus; indeed, the narrative termimates before it comes to that point. Yet there are passages in it from which we may *incidentally* gather that the ascension was considered by him as a notorious fact. Passages which perfectly coincide with the *direct description* of that event, contained in Acts 1:3–13.

Thus, John 3:13.—"And no man hath *ascended* up to heaven, but he that came down from heaven, even the Son of man which is in heaven."

Again, 6:62.—"What and if ye shall see the Son of man *ascend up* where he was before?"

Again, 20:17.—"Jesus saith unto her, Touch me not; for I am not yet *ascended* to my Father: but go to my brethren, and say unto them, I *ascend* unto my Father, and your Father; and to my God, and your God."

Had the Gospel of St. John been the only portion of the New Testament which had descended to our times, and all record of the Ascension had perished, these casual allusions to it might have been lost upon us; but when coupled with such record, a record quite independent of the Gospel of St. John, they convey to us, far more strongly than any account he might have given of it in detail could have done, the testimony of that Apostle to the truth of this last marvellous act of the marvellous life of our blessed Lord; and of which He was himself a spectator.

XXXV. THE PHARISEES AND THE SADDUCEES

There is a difference in the quarter from which opposition to the Gospel of Christ proceeded, as represented in the Gospels and in the Acts, most characteristic of truth, though most unobtrusive in itself. Indeed, these two portions of the New Testament might be read many times over without the feature I allude to happening to present itself.

Throughout the *Gospels*, the hostility to the Christian cause manifested itself almost exclusively from the *Pharisees*. Jesus evidently considers them as a sect systematically adverse to it—"Woe unto you, Scribes and *Pharisees*, hypocrites!.... Ye are the children of them which killed the prophets ... Fill ye up then the measure of your fathers." [Matt. 23:29. 32.] And before Jesus came up to the last passover, "the chief priests and *Pharisees*," we read, "gave commandment, that, if any man knew where he were, he should shew it, that they might take him:" [John 11:57.] and that when Judas proposed to betray him, "he received a band of men and officers from the chief priests and *Pharisees*." [John. 18:3.] On the other hand, throughout the *Acts*, the like hostility is discovered to proceed from the *Sadducees*. Thus, "And as they" (Peter and John) "spake unto the people, the priests, and the captain of the temple, and the *Sadducees* came upon them." [Acts 4:1.] And again, on another occasion, "The high-priest rose up, and all that were with him, which is the sect of the *Sadducees*, and were filled with indignation; and laid their hands on the Apostles, and put them in the common prison." [Acts 5:17.] And again, in a still more remarkable case: when Paul was maltreated before Ananias, and there was danger perhaps to his life, he "perceiving," we read, "that the one part were *Sadducees*, and the other *Pharisees*, cried out in the council, Men and brethren, I am a Pharisee, the son of a Pharisee;" [Acts 23:6.] evidently considering the Pharisees now to be the friendly faction, and soliciting their support against the *Sadducees*, whom he equally regarded as a hostile one; nor was he disappointed in his appeal.

Whence, then, this extraordinary change in the relations of these parties respectively to the Christians? No doubt, because the doctrine of *the resurrection of the dead*, which before Christ's own resurrection, *i. e.* during the period comprised in the Gospels, had been so far from dispersed by the disciples, that they scarcely knew what it meant (Mark 9:10), *had now become a leading doctrine with them;* as any body may satisfy themselves was the case by reading the several speeches of St. Peter, which are given in the early chapters of the Acts; in each and all of which the resurrection is a prominent feature—in that which he delivers, on providing a successor for Judas (Acts 1:22); at the feast of Pentecost (2:32); at the Beautiful Gate (3:12); the next day, before the priests (4:10); again, before the council (5:31); once more, on the conversion of Cornelius (10:40). The *coincidence* here lies in the Pharisees and Sadducees acting on this occasion consistently with their respective tenets: "For the Sadducees say that there is no resurrection, neither angel nor spirit: but the Pharisees confess both." [Acts 23:6.] The *undesigned-ness* of the coincidence consists in its being left to the readers of the Gospels and Acts to discover for themselves that there was this change of the persecuting sect after the Lord's resurrection, their attention not drawn to it by any direct notice in the documents themselves.

XXXVI. BARNABAS OF THE COUNTRY OF CYPRUS

Acts 4:36.—"And Joses, who by the Apostles was surnamed *Barnabas*, a Levite, and *of the country of Cyprus*, having land, sold it, and brought the money, and laid it at the Apostles' feet."

I have often thought that there is a harmony pervading everything connected with Barnabas, enough in itself to stamp the Acts of the Apostles as a history of perfect fidelity. In the verse which I have placed at the head of this paragraph, we see that he was a native of *Cyprus;* a circumstance upon which a good deal of what I have to say respecting him will be found to turn.

1. First, then, we discover him coming forward in behalf of Paul, whose conversion was suspected by the disciples at Jerusalem, with the air of a man who could vouch for his sincerity, by previous personal knowledge of him. How it was that he was better acquainted with the Apostle than the rest, the author of the Acts does not inform us. Cyprus, however, *the country of Barnabas,* was usually annexed to Cilicia, and formed an integral part of that province, whereof *Tarsus, the counting of Paul,* was the chief city [Cicer. Epist. Familiar. Lib. i. ep. vii. See also Maffei Verona Illustrata, Vol. i. p. 352.] . It may seem fanciful, however, to suppose that at Tarsus, which was famous for its schools and the facilities it afforded for education [See Wetstein on Acts ix. 11.] , the two Christian teachers might have laid the foundation of t heir friendship in the years of their boyhood. Yet I cannot think this improbable. That Paul collected his Greek learning (of which he had no inconsiderable share) in his native place, before he was removed to the feet of Gamaliel, is very credible; nor less so, that Barnabas should have been sent there from Cyprus, a distance of seventy miles only, as to the nearest school of note in those parts. Be that, however, as it may, what could be more natural than for an intimacy to be formed between them subsequently in Jerusalem, whither they had both resorted? They were, as we have seen, all but compatriots, and, under the circumstances, were likely to have their common friends. Neither may it be thought wholly irrelevant to observe, that when it was judged safe for Paul to return from Tarsus, where he had been living for a time to avoid the Greeks, Barnabas seized the opportunity of visiting that town in person, "to seek him," and bring him to Antioch; a journey, which, as it does not seem to be necessary, was possibly undertaken by Barnabas partly for the purpose of renewing his intercourse with his early acquaintance.

2. Again, in another place we read, "And some of them were *men of Cyprus* and Cyrene, which, when they were come to Antioch, spake unto the Grecians, preaching the Lord Jesus. And the hand of the Lord was

with them: and a great number believed, and turned unto the Lord. Then tidings of these things came unto the ears of the church which was at Jerusalem. *And they sent forth Barnabas, that he should go as far as Antioch.*" (Acts 9:20.) Here no reason is assigned why Barnabas should have been chosen to go to Antioch, and acquaint himself with the progress these new teachers were making amongst the Grecians; but we may observe, that *"some of them were men of Cyprus;"* and having learned elsewhere that *Barnabas was of that country also,* we at once discover the propriety of despatching him, above all others, to confer with them on the part of the church at Jerusalem.

3. Again, when, at a subsequent period, Paul and Barnabas went forth together to preach unto the Gentiles, we perceive that "they departed unto Seleucia, *and from thence sailed to Cyprus.*" (13:4.) And further, in a second journey, after Paul in some heat had parted company with them, we read that Barnabas and Mark again *"sailed unto Cyprus."* (15:32.) This was precisely what we might expect. Barnabas naturally enough chose to visit his own land before he turned his steps to strangers. Yet all this, satisfactory as it is in evidence of the truth of the history, we are left by the author of the Acts of the Apostles to gather for ourselves, by the apposition of several perfectly unconnected passages.

4. Nor is this all. "And some days after (so we read, ch. 15) Paul said unto Barnabas, Let us go again and visit our brethren in every city where we have preached the word of the Lord, and see how they do. And Barnabas determined to take with them John, whose surname was Mark. But Paul thought not good to take him with them, *who departed from them from Pamphylia,* and went not with them to the work. And the contention was so sharp between them, that they departed asunder one from the other: and *so Barnabas took Mark, and sailed unto Cyprus.*"

A curious chain of consistent narrative may be traced throughout the whole of this passage. The cause of the contention between Paul and Barnabas has been already noticed by Dr. Paley; I need not, therefore, do more than call to my reader's mind (as that excellent advocate of the truth of Christianity has done) the passage in the Epistle to the Colossians, 4:10, where it is casually said, that *"Marcus was sister's son to Barnabas"*—a relationship most satisfactorily accounting for the otherwise extraordinary pertinacity with which Barnabas takes up Mark's cause in this dispute with Paul. Though anticipated in this coincidence, I was unwilling to pass it over in silence, because it is one of a series which attach to the life of Barnabas, and render it, as a whole, a most consistent and complete testimony to the veracity of the Acts.

One circumstance more remains still to be noticed. Mark, it seems, in the former journey, "departed from them from Pamphylia, and went not with them to the work." How did this happen? The explanation, I think, is not difficult. Paul and Barnabas are appointed to go forth and preach. Accordingly they hasten to Seleucia, the nearest sea-port to Antioch, where they were staying, and taking with them John or Mark, "*sail to Cyprus*." (13:4.) Since Barnabas was a Cypriote, it is probable that his nephew Mark was the same, or, at any rate, that he had friends and relations in that island. His mother, it is true, had a house in Jerusalem, where the disciples met, and where some of them perhaps lodged (12:12); but so had Mnason, who was nevertheless of Cyprus (21:16). How reasonable then is it to suppose, that in joining himself to Paul and Barnabas in the outset of their journey, he was partly influenced by a very innocent desire to visit his kindred, his connections, or perhaps his birth-place, and that having achieved this object, he landed with his two companions in Pamphylia, and so returned forthwith to Jerusalem. And this supposition (it may be added) is strengthened by the expression applied by St. Paul to Mark, "that he went not with them *to the work*"—as if in the particular case the voyage to Cyprus did not deserve to be considered even the beginning of their labours, being more properly a visit of choice to kinsfolk and acquaintance, or to a place at least having strong local charms for Mark.

XXXVII. THE MURMURING OF THE GRECIANS

Acts 6:1.—"And in those days, when the number of the disciples was multiplied, there arose a murmuring of *the Grecians against the Hebrews*, because their widows were neglected in the daily ministration."

2.—"Then the twelve called the multitude of the disciples unto them, and said, It is not reason that we should leave the word of God and serve tables. Wherefore, brethren, look ye out among you seven men, of honest report, full of the Holy Ghost and wisdom, whom we may appoint over this business."

5.—"And the saying pleased the whole multitude: and they chose *Stephen*, a man full of faith and of the Holy Ghost, and *Philip*, and *Prochorus*, and *Nicanor*, and *Timon*, and *Parmenas*, and *Nicolas*, a proselyte of Antioch."

In this passage, I perceive a remarkable instance of consistency without design. There is a murmuring of the *Grecians* against the *Hebrews*, on account of what they considered an unfair distribution of the alms of the church. Seven men are appointed to redress the grievance. No mention is made of their country or connections. The multitude of the disciples is called together, and by them the choice is made. No other limitation is spoken of in the commission they had to fulfil, than that the men should be of honest report, full of the Holy Ghost. Yet it is probable (and here lies the coincidence,) that these deacons were all of the party aggrieved, *for their names are all Grecian.*

It is difficult to suppose this accidental. There must have been Hebrews enough fitted for the office. Yet Grecians alone seem to have been appointed. Why this should be so, St. Luke does not say, does not even hint. We gather from him that the Grecians thought themselves the injured party; and we then draw our own conclusions, that the church, having a sincere wish to maintain harmony, and remove all reasonable ground of complaint, chose, as advocates for the Greeks, those who would naturally feel for them the greatest interest, and protect their rights with a zeal that should be above suspicion.

XXXVIII. CORNELIUS AND PETER

Acts 10.—"I think the narrative of this chapter, which is very circum-stantial, will supply a coincidence of dates so casual and inartificial as to be strongly characteristic of truth."

Cornelius sees a vision at Cæsarea about the ninth hour of a certain day. In obedience to this vision he sends men to Joppa, to Peter, despatching them thither on the same day he saw the vision. (v. 5. 8.) They reach Joppa the next day, "on the morrow." (v. 9.) They lodge with Peter at Joppa that night. (v. 23.) They set out with Peter on the next day, "on the morrow," (τη επαυριον) from Joppa to return to Cornelius at Cæsarea (v. 23): and on "the morrow after" (τη επαυριον) they arrive at Cæsarea again. (v. 24.)

Cornelius now proceeds to inform Peter how it happened that he had sent for him; and begins with telling him very incidentally, "*Four days ago* I was fasting until this hour" (v. 30), and so on. Now this date exactly tallies with the time which his messengers had been in going to and returning from Joppa, as we gather it piece-meal from the previous narra-tive—a narrative which is so far from thrusting the time upon our notice, that it requires a little attention to make it out. Indeed, in the Greek, "the morrow" and "the morrow *after* (v. 23)," as it is properly expressed in the translation, are both simply τη επαυριον, the writer not perceiving or thinking about the ambiguity of the term; and consequently careless about impressing his reader with the fact (familiar to himself), that the messen-gers were two days on their return from Joppa, as they were two days in going there; and never dreaming about making the time consumed in the journey coincide with the date incidentally assigned by Cornelius to his vision. And here again, be it observed, we detect the marks of truth in a transaction of which the supernatural forms a fundamental part.

XXXIX. THE CHRISTIANS IN ANTIOCH

Acts 11:26.—"And the disciples were called *Christians* first in Antioch."

The mention of this fact as a remarkable one, and worthy of being recorded, is natural, and coincides with the circumstances of the case as gathered from other passages of the Acts. For it should seem, from the various phrases and circumlocutions resorted to in that book, by which to express Christians and Christianity, that for a long time no very distinctive term was applied to either. We read of "all that believed" (οι πιστευοντες, ii. 44); of "the disciples" (οιμαθηται, vi. 1); of "any of this way" (οι της οδου, ix. 2); and again, of "the way of God" (η του Θεου οδος, xviii. 26); or simply of "that way" (η οδος, xix. 9); or of "this way" (αυτη η οδος, xxii. 4). Indeed, the name *Christian* occurs but in two other places in the New Testament. (Acts 26:28; 1 Pet. 4:16.) A title therefore which characterized the new sect succinctly and in a word, and which saved so much inconvenient and ambiguous periphrasis, was memorable; and, even if given in the first instance as a reproach, was sure to be soon adopted and rendered familiar. On the supposition that the book of the Acts of the Apostles was a fiction, is it possible to imagine that this unobtrusive evidence of the progress of a name would have been found in it [My attention was drawn to this coincidence by a passage in Bishop Pearson. Minor Theolog. Works, i.p. 367.] ?

XXXL. BOOK BURNING AT EPHESUS

Acts 19:19.—"Many of them also which used curious arts brought their books together, and burned them before all men: and they counted the price of them, and found it fifty thousand pieces of silver."

It was at *Ephesus* where the effect of St. Paul's ministry was thus powerful—and where, therefore, it seems that these magical arts very greatly prevailed.

Now it was at *Ephesus* that Timothy was residing when St. Paul wrote to him, "But evil men and *seducers* (γοητες, conjurors) shall wax worse and worse, *deceiving, and being deceived* (cheats and cheated); but continue thou in the things which thou hast learned," &c. (2 Tim. 3:13.) These were the men who dealt in curious arts—the trade of the place in such impostures not having altogether ceased, it should seem, when a bonfire was made of the books [This coincidence is suggested by Dr. Burton's Bampton Lectures, iv. p. 103.] .

XLI. THE CENTURION WHO KEPT PAUL

Acts 24:23.—"And he commanded *a centurion* to keep Paul, and to let him have liberty."

Rather, "he commanded *the* centurion," τω εκατονταρχη.

It should seem, therefore, that St. Luke had in his mind some particular centurion. Is there anything in the narrative which would enable us to identify him?

It will be remembered, that in the preceding chapter (23:23) the chief captain "called unto him *two* centurions, saying, Make ready two hundred soldiers to go to Cæsarea, and horsemen threescore and ten, and spearmen two hundred, at the third hour of the night; and provide them beasts that they may set Paul on, and bring him safe unto Felix the governor."

This escort, having arrived with their prisoner at Antipatris (v. 32), divided; the infantry returning to Jerusalem, and of course the centurion who commanded them; the horsemen and the other centurion proceeding with Paul to Cæsarea.

When, therefore, St. Luke tells us that Felix commanded *the* centurion to keep Paul, he no doubt meant the commander of the horse who had conveyed him to Cæsarea; whose fidelity having been already proved, he consigned to him this further trust.

This is very natural: but the neglect or non-detection of this touch of truth in our version, shows how delicate a thing the translation of the Scripture is; and how favourable to the evidence of its veracity is the strict and accurate, nay, even grammatical investigation of it [Bp. Middleton, on the Greek Article, p. 298, finds a subject for philology, here again, where I find one for evidence.] .

XLII. FELIX AND PAUL

Acts 24:26.—"He (Felix) hoped also *that money should have been given him of Paul*, that he might loose him: wherefore he sent for him the oftener, and communed with him."

It is observed by Lardner [Vol. i. p. 27, 8vo. edition.] , that Felix (it might be thought) could have small hopes of receiving money from such a prisoner as Paul, had he not recollected his telling him, on a former interview, that "after many years he *came to bring alms to his nation, and offerings*."—Hence he probably supposed, that the alms might not yet be all distributed, or if they were, that a public benefactor would soon find friends to release him.

The observation is curious, and in confirmation of its truth, I will add, that the personal appearance of Paul, when he was brought before Felix, was certainly not such as would give the governor reason to believe that he had wherewithal to purchase his own freedom, but quite the contrary. For a passage in the Acts (22:28) certainly conveys very satisfactory, though indirect, evidence, that the Apostle wore poverty in his looks at the very period in question. When Lysias, the chief captain at Jerusalem, had been apprized that he was a Roman, he could scarcely give credit to the fact; and, being further assured of it by Paul himself, he said, "With a great sum obtained I this freedom," manifestly implying a suspicion of Paul's veracity, whose appearance bespoke no such means of procuring citizenship. The cupidity, therefore, of Felix was no doubt excited, as has been said, by his recollecting the errand on which his prisoner had come so lately to Jerusalem.

And this, moreover, furnishes the true explanation of the orders which Felix (very far from a merciful or indulgent officer) gave to the keeper of Paul, "to let him have liberty, *and to forbid none of his acquaintance to minister or come unto him;*" a free admission of his friends being necessary, in order that they might furnish him with the ransom.

It is true that there is no coincidence here between independent writers, but surely every unprejudiced mind must admit that there is an extremely nice, minute, and undesigned harmony between the speech of Paul and the subsequent conduct of Felix; though the cause and effect are so far from being traced by the author of the Acts, that it may be doubted whether he saw any connection subsisting between them. Surely, I repeat, such a harmony must convince us that it is no fictitious or forged narrative that we are reading, but a true and very accurate detail of an actual occurrence.

XLIII. "A SHIP OF ALEXANDRIA"

Acts 27:5.—"And when we had sailed over the sea of Cilicia and Pamphylia, we came to Myra, a city of Lycia. And there the centurion found a *ship of Alexandria sailing into Italy.*"

10.—"Sirs, I perceive that this voyage will be with hurt and much damage, not only of the *lading* (τοῦ φόρτου) and ship, but also of our lives."

38.—"And when they had eaten enough, they lightened the ship, and cast out *the wheat* (τον σιτον) into the sea."

It has been remarked, I think with justice, that the circumstantial details contained in this chapter of the shipwreck cannot be read without a conviction of their truth. I have never seen, however, the following coincidence in some of these particulars taken notice of in the manner it deserves. In my opinion it is very satisfactory, and when combined with a paragraph on the same subject, which will be found in the Appendix, (No. XXII.) establishes the fact of St. Paul's voyage beyond all reasonable doubt.

The ship into which the centurion removed Paul and the other prisoners at Myra, was a *ship of Alexandria* that was *sailing into Italy.* It was evidently a merchant-vessel, for mention is made of its *lading.* The nature of the lading, however, is not *directly* stated. It was capable of receiving Julius and his company, and was bound right for them. This was enough, and this was all that St. Luke cares to tell. Yet, in verse 38, we find, but most casually, of what its cargo consisted. The furniture of the ship, or its "tackling," as it is called, was thrown overboard in the early part of the storm; but the freight was naturally enough kept till it could be kept no longer, and then we discover, for the first time, that it was *wheat—"the wheat* was cast into the sea."

Now it is a notorious fact that Rome was in a great measure supplied with corn from Alexandria—that in times of scarcity the vessels coming from that port were watched with intense anxiety as they approached the coast of Italy [See Sueton. Nero. § 45.] —that they were of a size not inferior to our line of battle ships [See Wetstein, Acts 27:6.] , a thing by no means usual in the vessels of that day—and accordingly, that such an one might well accommodate the centurion and his numerous party, in addition to its own crew and lading.

There is a very singular air of truth in all this. The several detached verses at the head of this Number tell a continuous story, but it is not perceived till they are brought together. The circumstances drop out one by one at intervals in the course of the narrative, unarranged, unpremeditated, thoroughly incidental; so that the chapter might be read twenty times, and their agreement with one another and with contemporary history be still overlooked. I confess, it seems to me the most unlikely thing in the world, that a mere inventor of St. Paul's voyage should have been able to arrange it all, try how he would. It is possible that he might have affected some circumstantial detail, and so have made St. Paul and his companions change their ship at Myra; he might have said that it was a ship of Alexandria bound for Italy; but that he should have added, some thirty verses afterwards, and then quite incidentally, that its cargo was wheat, a fact so curiously agreeing with his former assertion that the vessel was Alexandrian, and was sailing to Italy, argues a subtlety of invention quite incredible. But if the account of the voyage, as far as relates to the change of ship, the tempest, the disastrous consequences, &c. is found, on being tried by a test which the writer of the Acts could never have contemplated, to be an unquestionable fact, how can the rest, which does not admit of the same scrutiny, be set aside as unworthy of credit?—for instance, that Paul actually foretold the danger—that again, in the midst of it, he foretold the final escape, and that an angel had declared to him God's pleasure, that for his sake not a soul should perish? I see no alternative but to receive all this, nothing doubting; unless we consider St. Luke to have mixed up fact and fiction in a manner the most artful and insidious. Yet who can read the Acts of the Apostles and come to such a conclusion?

Undesigned Coincidences Between the Gospels and Acts, and Josephus

It will not be out of place, if to a work which has had for its object to establish the veracity of the Scriptures in general, and in the last Part, that of the Gospels and Acts in particular, on the evidence of undesigned coincidences found in them, when compared with themselves or one another, I subjoin as a cognate argument, some other instances of undesigned coincidence between those latter writings and Josephus. The subject has been treated, but not exhausted, by Lardner and Paley; the latter of whom, indeed, did not profess to do more than epitomise that part of the "Credibility of the Gospel history" which considers the works of the Jewish historian. Josephus was born a.d. 37, and therefore must have been long the contemporary of some of the Apostles. For my purpose it matters little, or nothing, whether we reckon him a believer in Christianity or not; whether he had, or had not, seen the records of the Evangelists; since the examples of agreement between him and them, which I shall produce, will be such as are evidently without contrivance, the result of veracity in both.

If we allow him to be a Christian, if we even allow him to have seen the writings of the Evangelists, he will nevertheless be an independent witness, as far as he goes, provided his corroborations of the Gospel be clearly unpremeditated and incidental. In short, he will then be received like St. Mark or St. John, as a partisan indeed; but yet as a partisan who, upon cross-examination, confirms both his own statements and those of his colleagues.

I. JOSEPHUS AND THE EVANGELISTS

Before I bring forward *individual* examples of coincidence between Josephus and the Evangelists, I cannot help remarking the effect which the writings of the former have, when *taken together and as a whole*, in convincing us of the truth of the Gospel history. No man, I think, could rise from a perusal of the latter books of the Antiquities, and the account of the Jewish War, without a very strong impression, that the state of Judæa, civil, political and moral, as far as it can be gathered from the Gospels and Acts of the Apostles, is portrayed in these latter with the greatest accuracy, with the strictest attention to all the circumstances of the place and the times. It is impossible to impart this conviction to my readers in a paragraph; the nature of the case does not admit of it; it is the result of a thousand little facts, which it would be difficult to detach from the general narrative, and which, considered separately, might seem frivolous and fanciful. We close the pages of Josephus with the feeling that we have been reading of a country, which, for many years before its final fall, had been the scene of miserable anarchy and confusion. Everywhere we meet with open acts of petty violence, or the secret workings of plots, conspiracies, and frauds;—the laws ineffectual, or very partially observed, and very wretchedly administered;—oppression on the part of the rulers; amongst the people, faction, discontent, seditions, tumults;—robbers infesting the very streets, and most public places of resort, wandering about in arms, thirsting for blood no less than spoil, assembling in troops to the dismay of the more peaceable citizens, and with difficulty put down by military force;—society, in fact, altogether out of joint. Such would be our view of the condition of Judæa, as collected from Josephus.

Now let us turn to the New Testament, which, without professing to treat about Judæa at all, nevertheless, by glimpses, by notices scattered, uncombined, never intended for such a purpose, actually conveys to us the very counterpart of the picture in Josephus. For instance, let us observe the character of the parables; stories evidently in many cases, and probably in most cases, taken from passing events, and adapted to the occasions on which they were delivered. In how many may be traced scenes of disorder, of rapine, of craft, of injustice, as if such scenes were but too familiar to the experience of those to whom they were addressed! We hear of a "man going down from Jerusalem to Jericho, and falling among thieves, which stripped him of his raiment, and wounded him, and departed, leaving him half dead." (Luke 10:30.) Of another who planted a vineyard, and sent his servants to receive the fruits; but the "husbandmen

took those servants, and beat one, and killed another, and stoned another."
(Matth. 21:35.) Of a "judge which feared not God nor regarded man," and
who avenged the widow only "lest by her continual coming she should
weary him." (Luke 18:2.) Of a steward who was accused unto the rich
man of having wasted his goods," and who by taking further liberties with
his master's property, secured himself a retreat into the houses of his
lord's debtors, "when he should be put out of the stewardship." (Luke
16:1.) Of "the coming of the Son of man, like that of a thief in the night,"
whose approach was to be watched, if the master would "not suffer his
house to be broken up." (Matth. 24:43.) Of a "kingdom divided against
itself being brought to desolation." Of a "city or house divided against
itself not being able to stand." (Matth. 12:25.) Of the necessity of "binding the strong man" before "entering into his house and spoiling his
goods." (Matth. 12:29.) Of the folly of "laying up for ourselves treasures
upon earth, where moth and rust doth corrupt, and where thieves break
through and steal." (Matth. 6:19.) Of the enemy who had maliciously
sown tares amongst his neighbour's wheat, "and went his way." (Matth.
13:25.) Of the man who found a treasure in another's field, and cunningly
sold all that he had, and "bought that field." (13:44.) These instances may
suffice. Neither is it to the parables only that we must look for our proofs.
Many historical incidents in the Gospels and Acts speak the same
language. Thus, when Jesus would "have entered into a village of the
Samaritans," they would not receive Him, upon which his disciples,
James and John, who no doubt partook in the temper of the times,
proposed "that fire should be commanded to come down from heaven and
consume them." (Luke 9:52.) Again, when Jesus had offended the people
of Nazareth by his preaching, they made no scruple "of rising up and
thrusting him out of the city, and leading him unto the brow of the hill
whereon the city was built, that they might cast him down headlong"
(Luke 4:29); and, on another occasion, after He had been speaking in the
temple at Jerusalem, "the Jews took up stones to stone him," but he
"escaped out of their hand." (John 10:31.) Again, we are told of certain
"Galilæans whose blood Pilate had mingled with their sacrifices." (Luke
13:1.) And when our Lord was at last seized, it was "by a great multitude
with swords and staves" (Matth. 26:47), as in a country where nothing but
brute force could avail to carry a warrant into execution. So again,
Barabbas, whom the Jews would have released instead of Jesus, was one
"who lay bound with them that had made insurrection with him, who had
committed murder in the insurrection." (Mark 15:7.) And when he was at
length crucified, it was between two *thieves*. Let us trace the times somewhat further, and we shall discover no amendment, but rather the

contrary; as we learn from Josephus was the case on the nearer approach to the breaking out of the war. Thus Stephen is tumultuously stoned to death. (Acts 7:58.) And "Saul made havoc of the church, entering into every house, and taking men and women, committed them to prison." (8:3.) But when Saul's own turn came that he should be persecuted, what a continued scene of violence and outrage is presented to us! Turn we to the 21st, 22nd, and 23rd chapters of the Acts. It might be Josephus that is speaking in them. Paul, on his coming to Jerusalem, is obliged to have recourse to a stratagem to conciliate the people, because "the multitude would needs come together, for they would hear that he was come." Still it was in vain. A hue and cry is raised against him by a few persons who had known him in Asia, and forthwith "all the city is moved, and the people run together and take Paul, and draw him out of the temple." The Roman garrison gets under arms, and hastens to rescue Paul; but still it is needful that he be "borne of the soldiers, for the violence of the people." He makes his defence. They, however, "cry out, and cast off their clothes, and throw dust in the air." He is brought before the council, and the "high-priest commands them that stand by him to strike him on the mouth." He now, with much dexterity, divides his enemies, by declaring himself a Pharisee and a believer in the resurrection. This was enough to set them again at strife; for then there arose a dissension between the Pharisees and Sadducees—and such was its fury, that "the captain, fearing Paul should be pulled in pieces by them, commands his soldiers to go down and take him by force from among them." No sooner is he rescued from the multitude, than forty persons and more "bind themselves by a curse to kill him" when he should be next brought before the council. Intelligence of this plot, however, is conveyed to the captain of the guard, who determines to send him to Cæsarea, to Felix the governor. The escort necessary to attend this single prisoner to his place of destination is no less than four hundred and seventy men, horse and foot, and, as a further measure of safety and precaution, they are ordered to set out at the third hour of the night. All these things, I say, are in strict agreement with the state of Judæa as it is represented by Josephus. And it might be added, that independently of such consideration, an argument for the truth of the Gospels and Acts results from the harmony upon this point which prevails throughout them all: a circumstance which I might have dwelt upon in the former section, but which it will be enough to have noticed here.

But further, a perusal of the writings of Josephus leaves another impression upon our minds—*that there was a very considerable intercourse between Judæa and Rome.* To Rome we find causes and litigations very constantly referred—thither are the Jews perpetually resorting in search of titles and offices—there it is that they make known their grievances, explain their errors, supplicate pardons, set forth their claims to favour, and return their thanks. Neither are there wanting passages in the New Testament which would lead us to the same conclusion; rather, however, casually, by allusion, by an expression incidentally presenting itself, than by any direct communication on the subject. Hence may we discover, for instance, the propriety of that phrase so often occurring in the parables and elsewhere, of men going for various purposes "*into a far country.*"

Thus we read that "the Son of man is as a man taking a *far journey*, who left his house and gave authority to his servants, and to every man his work, and commanded the porter to watch." (Mark 13:34.) And again, that "a certain nobleman *went into a far country to receive for himself a kingdom, and to return.*" (Luke 19:12.) And again, that the prodigal son, "gathered all together, and took his *journey into a far country*, and there wasted his substance in riotous living." (Luke 15:13.) And again, that "a certain householder planted a vineyard, and hedged it round about, and digged a winepress in it, and built a tower, and let it out to husbandmen, and *went into a far country.*" (Matth. 21:33.) Moreover, it is probable that this political relationship of Judæa to Rome, the seat of government, from whence all the honours and gainful posts were distributed, suggested the use of those metaphors, which abound in the New Testament, of the "kingdom of heaven," of "seeking the kingdom of heaven," of "giving the kingdom of heaven," and the like. All I mean to affirm is this, that such allusions and such figures of speech would very naturally present themselves to a Teacher situated as the Gospel represents Jesus to have been—and therefore go to prove that such representation is the truth.

II. HEROD AND THE BIRTH OF CHRIST

Matth. 2:3.—"When Herod the king had heard these things, he was troubled, and all Jerusalem with him. And when he had gathered all the chief priests and scribes of the people together, he demanded of them where Christ should be born."

Nor was he yet satisfied; for he "*privily* called the wise men, and enquired of them *diligently* what time the star appeared." (ver. 7.) And when they did not return from Bethlehem, as he expected, he seems to have been still more apprehensive,—"exceeding wroth." (ver. 16.)

Such a transaction as this is perfectly agreeable to the character of Herod, as we may gather it from Josephus. He was always in fear for the stability of his throne, and anxious to pry into futurity that he might discover whether it was likely to endure.

Thus we read in Josephus of a certain Essene, Manahem by name, who had foretold, whilst Herod was yet a boy, that he was destined to be a king. Accordingly, "when he was actually advanced to that dignity, and in the plenitude of his power, he sent for Manahem and *inquired of him how long he should reign?* Manahem did not tell him the precise period. Whereupon he questioned him further, whether he should reign ten years or not? He replied, Yes, twenty, nay, thirty years; but he did not assign a limit to the continuance of his empire. With these answers Herod was satisfied, and giving Manahem his hand, dismissed him, and from that time he never ceased to honour all the Essenes." (Antiq. xv. 10. § 5.)

III. JOSEPH AND ARCHELAUS, SON OF HEROD

Matth. 2:22.—"But when he heard that Archelaus did reign in Judæa in the room of his father Herod, he was afraid to go thither."

On the death of Herod, Joseph was commanded to return to the land of Israel, and "he arose and took the young child" and went. However, before he began his journey, or whilst he was yet in the way, he was told that Archelaus did reign in Judæa in the room of his father Herod; on which he was afraid to go thither. Archelaus, therefore, must have been notorious for his cruelty (it should seem) *very soon indeed after coming to his throne.* Nothing short of this could account for the sudden resolution of Joseph to avoid him with so much speed.

Now it is remarkable enough, *that at the very first passover after Herod's death, even before Archelaus had yet had time to set out for Rome* to obtain the ratification of his authority from the emperor, he was guilty of an act of outrage and bloodshed, under circumstances above all others fitted to make it generally and immediately known. One of the last deeds of his father, Herod, had been to put to death Judas and Matthias, two persons who had instigated some young men to pull down a golden eagle, which Herod had fixed over the gate of the Temple, contrary, as they conceived, to the law of Moses. The hapless fate of these martyrs to the law excited great commiseration at the Passover which ensued. The parties, however, who uttered their lamentations aloud were silenced by Archelaus, the new king, in the following manner:—

"He sent out all the troops against them, and ordered the horsemen to prevent those who had their tents outside the temple from rendering assistance to those who were within it, and to put to death such as might escape from the foot. The cavalry slew nearly *three thousand men;* the rest betook themselves for safety to the neighbouring mountains. Then Archelaus commanded proclamation to be made, that they should all retire to their own homes. So they went away, and *left the festival out of fear lest somewhat worse should ensue.*" (Antiq. xvii. 9. § 3.)

We must bear in mind that, at the Passover, Jews from all parts of the world were assembled; so that any event which occurred at Jerusalem during that great feast would be speedily reported on their return to the countries where they dwelt. Such a massacre, therefore, at such a season, would at once stamp the character of Archelaus. The fear of him would naturally enough spread itself wherever a Jew was to be found; and, in fact, so well remembered was this his first essay at governing the people, that several years afterwards it was brought against him with great effect on his appearance before Cæsar at Rome.

It is the more probable that this act of cruelty inspired Joseph with his dread of Archelaus, because that prince could not have been much known before he came to the throne, never having had any public employment, or, indeed, future destination, like his half-brother, Antipater, whereby he might have discovered himself to the nation at large [Lardner briefly alludes to this transaction, but has not made the best of his argument.— Vol. i. p. 14, 8vo. ed.] .

IV. THE DIDRACHMA

Matth. 17:24.—"And when they were come to Capernaum, they that received *tribute-money* came to Peter, and said, Doth not your master pay tribute? He saith, Yes."

The word which is translated *tribute-money* is in the original *"the didrachma,"* of which indeed notice is given in the margin of our version; and it is worthy of remark, that this tax seems not to have been designated by any *general* name, such for instance as tribute, custom, &c., but actually had the specific appellation of *"the didrachma."* Thus Josephus writes: "Nisibis, too, is a city surrounded by the same river (the Euphrates); wherefore the Jews, trusting to the nature of its position, deposited there the *didrachma,* which it is customary for each individual to pay to God, as well as their other offerings."—(Antiq. xviii. 10. § 1.)

There is something which indicates veracity in the Evangelist, to be correct in a trifle like this. He makes no mistake in the sum paid to the temple, nor does he express himself by a general term, such as would have concealed his ignorance, but hits upon the exact payment that was made, and the name that was given it.

It may be added, that St. Matthew uses the word *didrachma* without the smallest explanation, which is not the case, as we have seen, with Josephus; yet the argument of Jesus which follows would be quite unintelligible to those who did not know for whose service this tribute-money was paid. It is evident, therefore, that the Evangelist thought there could be no obscurity in the term; that it was much too familiar with his readers to need a comment. Now the use of it probably ceased with the destruction of the temple; after which but few years would elapse before some interpretation would be necessary, more especially as the term itself does not in the least imply the nature of the tax, but only its individual amount. The undesigned omission of everything of this kind, on the part of St. Matthew, pretty clearly proves the Gospel to have been written before the temple was destroyed.

V. THE SADDUCEES AND THE RESURRECTION

Matth. 22:23.—"The same day came to him the Sadducees, *which say that there is no resurrection*, and asked him," &c.

It is very unusual to find in St. Matthew a paragraph like this, explanatory of *Jewish* opinions or practices. In general it is quite characteristic of him, and a circumstance which distinguishes him from the other Evangelists, that he presumes upon his readers being perfectly familiar with Judæa and all that pertains to it. St. Mark, in treating the same subjects, is generally found to enlarge upon them much more, as though conscious that he had those to deal with who were not thoroughly conversant with Jewish affairs.

Compare the following parallel passages in these two Evangelists.

Matth. 9:14.—"Then came to him the disciples of John, saying, Why do we and the Pharisees fast oft, but thy disciples fast not?"

Mark 2:18.—"*And the disciples of John and of the Pharisees used to fast:* and they come and say unto him, Why do the disciples of John and of the Pharisees fast, but thy disciples fast not?"

Matth. 15:1.—"Then came to Jesus Scribes and Pharisees, which were of Jerusalem, saying, Why do thy disciples transgress the tradition of the Elders? for they wash not their hands when they eat bread. But he answered and said unto them," &c.

Mark 7:1.—"Then came together unto him the Pharisees, and certain of the Scribes, which came from Jerusalem. And when they saw some of his disciples eat bread with defiled, that is to say, with unwashen, hands, they found fault. *For the Pharisees, and all the Jews, except they wash their hands oft, eat not, holding the tradition of the Elders. And when they come from the market, except they wash, they eat not. And many other things there be, which they have received to hold, as the washing of cups, and pots, brazen vessels, and of tables.* Then the Pharisees and Scribes asked him, Why walk not thy disciples according to the tradition of the Elders, but eat bread with unwashen hands?" &c.

Matth. 27:62.—"Now the next day, that followed the day of the Preparation, the Chief Priests and Pharisees came together," &c.

Mark 15:42.—"And now when the even was come, because it was the Preparation, *that is, the day before the Sabbath,* " &c.

These examples (to which many more might be added, may suffice to show the manner of St. Matthew as compared with that of another of the Evangelists; that it dealt little in explanation. How then does it happen, that in the instance before us he deviates from his ordinary, almost his uniform, practice; and whilst writing for Jews, thinks it necessary to inform them of so notorious a tenet of the Sadducees (for such we might suppose it) as their disbelief in a resurrection? Would not his Jewish readers have known at once, and on the mere mention of the name of this sect, that he was speaking of persons who denied that doctrine?

Let us turn to Josephus (Antiq. xviii. 1. § 4), and we shall find him throwing some light upon our inquiry.

"The doctrine of the Sadducees is, that the soul and body perish together. The law is all that they are concerned to observe. They consider it commendable to controvert the opinions of masters even of their own school of philosophy. This doctrine, however, *has not many followers, but those persons of the highest rank—next to nothing of public business falls into their hands.*" Thus, we see, it was very possible for the people of Judæa, though well acquainted with most of the local peculiarities of their country, to be ignorant, or at least ill-informed, of the dogmas of a sect, insignificant in numbers, removed from them by station, and seldom or never brought into contact with them by office; and therefore that St. Matthew was not wasting words, when he explained in this instance, though in so many other instances he had withheld explanation [See Hug's Introduction to the New Testament, Vol. ii. p. 7. Translation by the Rev. D. G. Wait.] .

VI. "LEST THERE BE AN UPROAR"

Matth. 26:5.—"But they said, Not on the *feast* day, lest there *be an uproar among the people.*"

I have already alluded to the insubordinate condition of *Judæa* in general, about the period of our Lord's ministry. We have here an example of the feverish and irritable state of the *capital* itself, in particular, during the feast of the Passover.

"The feast of the Passover," says Josephus (who relates an event that happened some few years after Christ's death), "being at hand, wherein it is our custom to use unleavened bread, and a great multitude being drawn together from all parts to the feast, Cumanus (the governor) *fearing that some disturbance might fall out amongst them, commands one cohort of soldiers to arm themselves and stand in the porticoes of the temple, to suppress any riot which might occur; and this precaution the governors of Judæa before him had adopted."*—(Antiq. xx. 4. § 3.)

In spite, however, of these prudent measures, a tumult arose on this very occasion, in which, according to Josephus, twenty thousand Jews perished.

VII. JEWS AND SWINE?

Mark 5:1.—"And they came over unto the other side of the sea, into the *country of the Gadarenes,* " &c.

11.—"Now there was there nigh unto the mountains a great herd of *swine* feeding."

Here it might at first seem that St. Mark had been betrayed into an over-sight—for since swine were held in abhorrence by the Jews as unclean, how (it might be asked) did it happen that a herd of them were feeding on the side of the sea of Tiberias?

The objection, however, only serves to prove yet more the accuracy of the Evangelist, and his intimate knowledge of the local circumstances of Judæa; for on turning to Josephus (Antiq. xvii. 13. § 4), we find that "Turris Stratonis, and Sebaste, and Joppa, and Jerusalem, were made subject to Archelaus, but that Gaza, *Gadara*, and Hippos, *being Grecian cities*, were annexed by Cæsar to Syria." This fact, therefore, is enough to account for swine being found amongst the Gadarenes.

VIII. HEROD'S BIRTHDAY

Mark 6:21.—"And when a convenient day was come, *that Herod on his birth-day made a supper to his lords, high captains, and chief estates of Galilee;* and when the daughter of the said Herodias came in, and danced," &c.

It is curious and worthy of remark, that a feast, under exactly similar circumstances, is incidentally described by Josephus as made by Herod, the brother of Herodias, and successor of this prince in his government. *"Having made a feast on his birth-day* (writes Josephus), *when all under his command partook of the mirth,* he sent for Silas" (an officer whom he had cast into prison for taking liberties with him), "and offered him a seat at the banquet." (Antiq. xix. 7. § 1). This, I say, is a coincidence worth notice, because it proves that these *birth-day feasts* were observed in the family of Herod, and that it was customary to assemble the officers of government to share in them.

IX. THE GUEST CHAMABER FOR JESUS AND THE DISCIPLES AT PASSOVER

Mark 14:13.—"And he sendeth forth two of his disciples, and saith unto them, Go ye into the city, and there shall meet you a man bearing a pitcher of water: follow him. And wheresoever he shall go in, say ye to the good man of the house, The Master saith, *Where is the guest-chamber, where I shall eat the Passover with my disciples?*"

When Cestius wished to inform Nero of the numbers which attended the Passover at Jerusalem, he counted the victims and allowed *ten persons* to each head, "because a company not less than *ten* belong to every sacrifice (for it is not lawful for them to feast singly by themselves), and many are *twenty* in company."—Bell. Jud. c. vi. 9. § 3.

Accordingly, the Gospel narrative is in strict conformity with this custom. When Christ goes up to Jerusalem to attend the Passover for the last time, He is not described as running the chance of hospitality in the houses of any of his friends, because, on this occasion, the parties would be made up, and the addition of thirteen guests might be inconvenient, but He sends forth beforehand, from Bethany most probably, two of his disciples to the city, with orders to engage a room (a precaution very necessary where so many companies would be seeking accommodation), and there eats the Passover with his followers, a party of thirteen, which it appears was about the usual number [See Whiston's Note upon Joseph. B. J. vi. 9. 3.]

X. JESUS GOING TO JERUSALEM AT TWELVE YEARS OLD

Luke 2:42.—"And when *he was twelve years old,* they went up to Jerusalem after the custom of the feast."

I am aware that commentators upon this text quote the Rabbins, to show that children of twelve years old amongst the Jews were considered to be entering the estate of manhood (see Wetstein), and that on this account it was that Jesus was taken at that age to the Passover. Such may be the true interpretation of the passage. I cannot, however, forbear offering a conjecture which occurred to me in reading the history of Archelaus.

The birth of Christ probably preceded the death of Herod by a year and a half, or thereabout. (See Lardher, Vol. i. p. 352.8vo. edit.) Archelaus succeeded Herod, and governed the country, it should seem, about ten years. "In the *tenth year* of Archelaus' reign, the chief governors among the Jews and Samaritans, unable any longer to endure his cruelty and tyranny, accused him before Cæsar." Cæsar upon this sent for him to Rome, and "as soon as he came to Rome, when the Emperor had heard his accusers, and his defence, he banished him to Vienne, in France, and confiscated his goods."—Antiq. xvii. c. 15. The removal, therefore, of this obnoxious governor, appears to have been effected in our Lord's twelfth year. Might not this circumstance account for the parents of the child Jesus venturing to take Him to Jerusalem at the Passover when He was *twelve years old*, and not before? It was only because "Archelaus reigned in Judæa in the room of his father Herod," that Joseph was afraid to go thither on his return from Egypt; influenced not merely by motives of personal safety, but by the consideration that the same jealousy which had urged Herod to take away the young child's life, might also prevail with his successor; for we do not find that any fears about himself or Mary withheld him from subsequently going to the Passover, even during the reign of Archelaus, since it is recorded that "they went every year." I submit it, therefore, to my readers' decision, whether the same apprehensions for the life of the infant Jesus, which prevented Joseph from taking Him into Judæa, on hearing that Archelaus was king, did not, very probably, prevent him from taking Him up to Jerusalem till he heard that Archelaus was deposed?

XI. THE TWELVE AND THE SEVENTY CHOSEN BY CHRIST

Luke 6:13.—"And when it was day, he called unto him his disciples: and of them he chose *twelve*, whom also he named Apostles."

10:1.—"After these things the Lord appointed other *seventy* also, and sent them two and two before his face," &c.

There is something in the selection of these numbers which indicates veracity in the narrative. They were, on several accounts, favourite numbers amongst the Jews; the one (to name no other reason) being that of the Tribes, the other (taken roundly) that of the Elders. Accordingly we read in Josephus, that Varus, who held a post in the government under Agrippa, "called to him *twelve* Jews of Cæsarea, of the best character, and ordered them to go to Ecbatana, and bear this message to their country-men who dwelt there: 'Varus hath heard that you intend to march against the king; but not believing the report, he hath sent us to persuade you to lay down your arms, counting such compliance to be a sign that he did well not to give credit to those who so spake concerning you.' " "He also enjoined those Jews of Ecbatana to send *seventy* of their *principal* men to make a defence for them touching the accusation laid against them. So when the *twelve* messengers came to their countrymen at Ecbatana, and found that they had no designs of innovation at all, they persuaded them to send the *seventy* also. Then went these *seventy* down to Cæsarea together with the *twelve* ambassadors."—(Life of Josephus, § 11.)

This is a very slight matter, to be sure, but it is still something to find the *subordinate* parts of a history in strict keeping with the habits of the people and of the age to which it professes to belong. The Evangelist might have fixed upon any other indifferent number for the Apostles and first Disciples of Jesus, without thereby incurring any impeachment of a want of veracity; and therefore it is the more satisfactory to discover marks of truth, where the absence of such marks would not have occa-sioned the least suspicion of falsehood.

XII. THE CITY CALLED NAIN

Luke 7:1.—"Now when he had ended all his sayings in the audience of the people, he entered into Capernaum."

11.—"And it came to pass the day after, that he went into a city called *Nain;* and many of his disciples went with him, and much people."

Jesus comes to Capernaum—He goes on to Nain—fame precedes Him as He approaches Judæa—He arrives in the neighbourhood of the Baptist—He travels still further south to the vicinity of the Holy City, near which the Magdalen dwelt—St. Luke, therefore, it will be perceived, is here describing a journey of Jesus from Galilee to Jerusalem.

Now let us hear Josephus (Antiq. xx. 5. § 1): "A quarrel sprung up between the Samaritans and the Jews, and this was the cause of it. The Galilæans, when they resorted to the Holy City at the feasts, had to pass through the country of the Samaritans. Now it happened that certain inhabitants of a *place on the road, Nain by name,* situated on the borders of Samaria and the Great Plain, rose upon them and slew many." [Hudson reads κωμγς Γιναιας λεγομενης, instead of Ναις, the common reading; but see Hug's Introduction to the New Testament, Vol. i. p. 23 (translation), where the coincidence is suggested, and the reasons given for abiding by the ordinary text.]

Jesus, therefore, in this his journey southwards, (a journey, be it observed, which the Evangelist does not formally lay down, but the general direction of which we gather from an incident or two occurring in the course of it, and from the point to which it tended,)—Jesus, in this his journey, is found to come to a city which, it appears, did actually lie in the way of those who travelled from Galilee to Jerusalem. This is as it should be. A part of the story is certainly matter of fact. There is every reason to believe the Evangelist when he says that Jesus "went into a city called Nain." What reason is there to disbelieve him when he goes on to say, that he met a dead man at the gate; that he touched the bier; bade the young man arise; and that the dead sat up and spake?

XIII. HEROD AT JERUSALEM

Luke 23:6.—"When Pilate heard of Galilee, he asked whether the man were a Galilgæan. And as soon as he knew that he belonged unto Herod's jurisdiction, he sent him to Herod, *who himself* Also *was at Jerusalem at that time.*"

The fair inference from this last clause is, that Jerusalem was not the common place of abode either of *Herod* or *Pilate*. Such is certainly the force of the emphatic expression, "who himself *also* was at Jerusalem at that time," applied, as it is, directly to Herod, but with a reference to the person of whom mention had been made in the former part of the sentence. The more circuitous this insinuation is, the stronger does it make for the argument. Now that Herod did not reside at Jerusalem, may be inferred from the following passage in Josephus.

"This king" (says he, meaning the Herod who killed James, the brother of John, Acts 12.) "was *not at all like that Herod who reigned before him*" (meaning the Herod to whom Christ was sent by Pilate), "for the latter was stern and severe in his punishments, and had no mercy on those he hated: confessedly better disposed towards the Greeks than the Jews: accordingly, of the cities of the strangers, some he beautified at his own expense with baths and theatres, and others with temples and corridors; but upon no Jewish city did he bestow the smallest decoration or the most trifling present. Whereas the latter Herod (Agrippa) was of a mild and gentle disposition, and good to all men. To strangers he was beneficent, but yet more kind to the Jews, his countrymen, with whom he sympathised in all their troubles. *He took pleasure, therefore, in constantly living at Jerusalem*, and strictly observed all the customs of his nation."—Antiq. xix. 7. § 3. Thus does it appear from the Jewish historian, that the Herod of the Acts was a *contrast* to the Herod in question, inas-much as he loved the Jews and *dwelt at Jerusalem*. Nor is St. Luke less accurate in representing *Pilate* to have been not resident at Jerusalem. Cæsarea seems to have been the place of abode of the Roman governors of Judæa in general. (See Antiq. xviii. 4. § 1.— xx. 4. § 4.) Of Pilate it certainly was; for when the Jews had to complain to him of the profanation which had been offered to their temple by the introduction of Cæsar's image into it, it was to Cæsarea that they carried their remonstrance. (Bell. Jud. ii. c. 9. § 2.)

It was probably the business of the Passover which had brought Pilate to Jerusalem for a few days, the presence of the Governor being never more needful in the capital than on such an occasion.

XIV. SYCHAR WITHOUT WATER

John 4:15.—"The woman saith unto him, Sir, give me this water, that I thirst not, neither come hither to draw."

It seems, therefore, that there was no water in Sychar, and that the inhabitants had to come to this well to draw. Most likely it was at some little distance from the town, for the woman speaks of the labour of fetching the water as considerable; and Jesus stopped short of the town at the well, because He "was wearied with his journey," whilst his disciples went on to buy bread.

Now, on the breaking out of the war with the Romans, some of the Samaritans assembled on Mount Gerizim, *close to the foot of which* (be it observed) *was the city of Sychar placed* [Σικιμα κειμενην προς τω Γαριζειν ορει—*Joseph. Antiq.* ii. 8. 6.] Upon this Vespasian determined to put some troops in motion against them. "For, although all Samaria was provided with garrisons, yet did the number and evil spirit of those who had come together at Mount Gerizim give ground for apprehension; therefore he sent Cerealis, the commander of the fifth Legion, with six hundred horse, and three thousand foot. Not thinking it safe, however, to go up the mountain and give them battle, because many of the enemy were on the higher ground, he encompassed all the circuit (υπωρειαν) of the mountain with his army, and watched them all that day. But it came to pass, that whilst the *Samaritans were now without water*, a terrible heat came on, for it was summer, and the people were unprovided with necessaries, *so that some of them died of thirst that same day*, and many others, preferring slavery to such a death, fled to the Romans."—Bell. Jud. iii. 7. § 32.

The troops of Cerealis, no doubt, cut them off from the well of Sychar, which, we perceive from St. John, was the place to which the neighbourhood were compelled to resort. This is the more likely, inasmuch as the soldiers of the Roman general do not appear to have suffered from thirst at all on this occasion.

XV. PILATE AT THE PAVEMENT

John 19:13.—"When Pilate therefore heard that saying, he brought Jesus forth, and sat down in the judgment seat in a place that is called the *Pavement*." (Λιθόστρωτον.)

According to St. John, therefore (he being the only one of the Evangelists who mentions this incident), Pilate comes out of his own hall to his judgment-seat on the *Pavement*. The hall and the Pavement, then, were near or contiguous.

Now let us turn to Josephus. "The City was strengthened by the palace in which he (Herod) dwelt, and the Temple by the fortifications attached to the bastion called Antonia." (Antiq. xv. 8. § 5.) Hence we conclude that the temple was near the Castle of Antonia.

"On the western side of the court (of the temple) were four gates, one looking to the *palace*." (Antiq. xv. 11. § 5.) Hence we conclude that the temple was near the *palace* of Herod. Therefore the palace was near the Castle of Antonia.

But if Pilate's hall was a part of the palace, as it was (that being the residence of the Roman governor when he was at Jerusalem), then Pilate's hall was near the Castle of Antonia.

Here let us pause a moment, and direct our attention to a passage in the Jewish War (vi. 1. § 8) where Josephus records the prowess of a centurion in the Roman army, Julianus by name, in an assault upon Jerusalem.

"This man had posted himself near Titus, at the Castle of Antonia, when, observing that the Romans were giving way, and defending themselves but indifferently, he rushed forward and drove back the victorious Jews to the corner of the inner temple, single-handed, for the whole multitude fled before him, scarcely believing such strength and spirit to belong to a mere mortal. But he, dashing through the crowd, smote them on every side, as many as he could lay hands upon. It was a sight which struck Cæsar with astonishment, and seemed terrific to all. Nevertheless, his fate overtook him—as how could it be otherwise, unless he had been more than man?—for having many sharp nails in his shoes, after the soldier's fashion, he slipped as he was running upon the *Pavement* (κατα Λιθοστρωτου), and fell upon his back. The clatter of his arms caused the fugitives to turn about: and now a cry was set up by the Romans in the Castle of *Antonia*, who were in alarm for the man."

From this passage it appears that *a pavement* was near the Castle of Antonia; but we have already seen that the Castle of Antonia was near the palace (or Pilate's hall); therefore this pavement was near Pilate's hall. This then is proved from Josephus, though very circuitously, which is not the worse, that very near Pilate's residence a pavement (Λιθοστρωτον) there was; that it gave its name to that spot is not proved, yet nothing can be more probable than that it did; and consequently nothing more probable than that St. John is speaking with truth and accuracy when he makes Pilate bring Jesus forth and sit down in his judgment-seat in a place called the *Pavement* [See Hug's Intro. to the New Testament, Vol. i. p. 18] .

XVI. NO KING BUT CAESAR

John 19:15.—"The chief priests answered, We have no *king* but *Cæsar*."
Although the Roman emperors never took the title of kings [For this remark I am indebted to Whiston.] , yet it appears from Josephus that they were so called by the Jews; and in further accordance with the writers of the New Testament, that historian commonly employs the term *Cæsar*, as sufficient to designate the reigning prince. Thus, when speaking of Titus, he says, "many did not so much as know that *the king* was in any danger." And again, shortly after, "the enemy indeed made a great shout at the boldness of *Cæsar*, and exhorted one another to rush upon him."—Bell. Jud. v. 2. § 2.

This is a curious coincidence in popular phraseology, and such as bespeaks the writers of the New Testament to have been familiar with the scenes they describe, and the parties they introduce.

XVII. SOLOMON'S PORCH AND THE BEAUTIFUL GATE

Acts 3:1, 2.—"Now Peter and John went up together into the temple at the hour of prayer, being the ninth hour. And a certain man lame from his mother's womb was carried, whom they laid daily at the gate of the temple which is called *Beautiful*, to ask alms of them that entered into the temple."

Peter recovers the cripple. The fame of his miraculous cure is instantly spread abroad.

"And as the lame man which was healed held Peter and John, all the people ran together unto them *in the porch that is called Solomon's*, greatly wondering."—ver. 11.

There is a propriety in the localities of this miracle which is favourable to a belief in its truth.

Josephus speaks of a great outer gate (that of the Porch), "opening into the court of the women *on the East*, and opposite to the gate of the temple, in size surpassing the others, being fifty cubits high and forty wide; and more finished in its decorations, by reason of the thick plates of silver and gold which were upon it."—(Bell. Jud. v. 5. § 3.)

But in another passage of the same author we read as follows:—"They persuaded the king (Agrippa) to restore the *Eastern Porch*. This was a porch of the outer temple, situated upon the edge of a deep abyss, resting upon a wall four hundred cubits high, constructed of quadrangular stones, quite white, each stone twenty cubits by six, the work of King *Solomon*, the original builder of the temple." (Antiq. xx. 8. § 7.) Thus it appears that a gate, more highly ornamented than the rest, looked to the East; that a porch, of which Solomon was the founder, looked also to the East; that both, therefore, were on the same side of the temple, and accordingly that it was very natural for the people, hearing that a cripple who usually lay at the *Beautiful* Gate, and who had been cured as he lay there,—it was very natural for them to run to *Solomon's Porch*, to satisfy themselves of the truth of the report [See Hug, Vol. i. p. 19.]

XVIII. THE DISCIPLE NAMED TABITHA, CALLED DORCAS

Acts 9:36.—"Now there was at Joppa a certain disciple named Tabitha, *which by interpretation is called Dorcas*."

It may be remarked, that Josephus, who (like St. Luke) wrote in Greek of things which happened in a country where Syriac was the common language, thinks fit to add a similar explanation when he alludes to this same proper name.

"They sent one John, who was the most bloody-minded of them all, to do that execution. This man was *also called the son of Dorcas in the language of our country*."—Bell. Jud. iv. 3. § 5.

XIX. THE GRECIANS AND THE HEBREWS

Acts 6:1.—"And in those days, when the number of the disciples was multiplied, there arose *a murmuring of the Grecians against the Hebrews*, because their widows were neglected in the daily ministration."

In the first section I found an instance of consistency without design in this passage, on comparing it with the context; I now find a second like instance, on comparing it with Josephus. It seems that when the disciples became more numerous, a jealousy began to discover itself between the Grecians and the Hebrews. The circumstance is casually mentioned by St. Luke, as the accident which gave occasion to the appointment of deacons; yet how strictly characteristic is it of the country and times in which it is said to have happened.

"There was a disturbance at Cæsarea," writes Josephus, "between the *Jews* and *Syrians* respecting the equal enjoyment of civil rights; the Jews laying claim to precedence because Herod, who was a Jew, had founded the city; the Syrians, on the other hand, admitting this, but maintaining that Cæsarea was originally called the Tower of Straton, and did not then contain a single Jew."—Antiq. xx. 7. § 7. In the end the two parties broke out into open war. This was when Felix was governor. On another occasion, under Florus, we read of 20,000 Jews perishing at Cæsarea by the hands of the Greek or Syrian part of the population.—Bell. Jud. ii. 18.1. And again, we are told that "fearful troubles prevailed throughout all Syria, *each city dividing itself into two armies*, and the safety of the one consisted in forestalling the violence of the other. Thus the people passed their days in blood and their nights in terror."—Bell. Jud. ii. 15. 2.

It is most improbable that the writer of the Acts, if he were making up a story, should have bethought himself of a circumstance at once so unimportant as this murmuring of the Grecians against the Hebrews, and yet so truly descriptive of the people where his scene was laid. This little incident (the more trifling the better for our purpose) carries with it the strongest marks of truth; and, like the single watch-word, is a voucher for the general honesty of the party that utters it. Indeed, the establishment of one fact may be thought in itself to entail the credibility of many more. If it be *certain* that there was a murmuring of the Grecians against the Hebrews because their widows were neglected in the daily ministration, then it is *probable* that there was a common fund out of which widows were maintained; that many sold their possessions to contribute to this fund; that it must have been a strong motive which could urge to such a disposal of their property; that no motive could be so likely as their conviction of the truth of Christianity; and that such a conviction could spring out of nothing so surely as the evidence of miracles. I do not say that all these matters *necessarily* follow from the certainty of the first simple fact, but I say that, admitting it, they all follow in a train of very natural consequence.

XX. KING AGRIPPA AND BERNICE SALUTE FESTUS

Acts 25:13.—*"And after certain days King Agrippa and Bernice came unto Cæsarea to salute Festus."*

This Agrippa (Agrippa Minor) had succeeded, by permission of Claudius, to the territories of his uncle Herod; at least, Trachonitis, Batanæa, and Abilene, were confirmed to him. From this passage in the Acts it appears, as might be expected, that he was anxious to be well with the Roman Government, and accordingly that he lost no time in paying his respects to Festus, the new representative of that government in Judæa. It is a singular and minute coincidence well worth our notice, that Josephus records instances of this same Agrippa's obsequiousness to Roman authorities, of precisely the same kind. "About this time," says he, *"King Agrippa went to Alexandria, to salute Alexander, who had been sent by Nero to govern Egypt."*—Bell. Jud. ii. 15. § 1.

And again (what is yet more to our purpose) we read on another occasion, *that Bernice accompanied Agrippa in one of these visits of ceremony;* for having appointed Varus to take care of their kingdom in their absence, *"they went to Berytus with the intention of meeting Gessius (Florus), the Roman governor of Judæa."*—Josephus's Life, § 11.

This is a case singularly parallel to that in the Acts: for Gessius Florus held the very same office, in the same country, as Felix.

XXI. KING AGRIPPA AND BERNICE

Acts 25:23.—"And on the morrow, when Agrippa was come, and *Bernice*, with great pomp, and was entered into the place of hearing, with the chief captains, and principal men of the city, at Festus' commandment Paul was brought forth."

It might seem extraordinary that *Bernice* should be present on such an occasion—that a woman should take any share in an affair, one would have supposed, foreign to her, and exclusively belonging to the other sex. But here again we have another proof of the veracity and accuracy of the sacred writings. For when Agrippa (*the same Agrippa*) endeavoured to combat the spirit of rebellion which was beginning to show itself amongst the Jews, and addressed them in that famous speech, given in Josephus, which throws so much light on the power and provincial polity of the Romans, he first of all "*placed his sister Bernice* (the same Bernice) *in a conspicuous situation*, upon the house of the Asamonæans, which was above the gallery, at the passage to the upper city, where the bridge joins the temple to the gallery;" and then he spoke to the people. And when his oration was ended, we read that "*both he and Iris sister shed tears*, and so repressed much violence in the multitude."—(Bell. Jud. ii. 16. § 3.)

There is another passage, occurring in the life of Josephus, which is no less valuable; for it serves to show yet further the political importance of Bernice, and how much she was in the habit of acting with Agrippa on all public occasions. One Philip, who was governor of Gamala, and the country about it, under Agrippa, had occasion to communicate with the latter, probably on the subject of his escape from Jerusalem, where he had been recently in danger, and of his return to his own station. The transaction is thus described:—

"He wrote to *Agrippa and Bernice*, and gave the letters to one of his freedmen to carry to Varus, who at that time was procurator of the kingdom, which *the sovereigns* (*i.e.*, the king and his sister-wife) had entrusted him withal, while *they* were gone to Berytus to meet Gessius. When Varus had received these letters of Philip, and had learned that he was in safety, he was very uneasy at it, supposing that he should appear useless to the *sovereigns* (βασιλευσιν) now Philip was come."—(Josephus's Life, § 11.)

XXII. ALEXANDRIA AND PUTEOLI

Acts 28:11, 12, 13.—"And after three months we departed in a ship of Alexandria, which had wintered in the isle, whose sign was Castor and Pollux. And landing at Syracuse, we tarried there three days. And from thence we fetched a compass, and came to Rhegium: and after one day the south wind blew, and *we came the next day to Puteoli*."

Puteoli then, it should seem, was the destination of this vessel from *Alexandria*. Now, we may collect, from the independent testimony of the Jewish historian, *that this was the port of Italy to which ships from Egypt and the Levant in those times commonly sailed*. Thus, when Herod Agrippa went from Judæa to Rome, for the purpose of paying his court to Tiberius, and bettering his fortune, he directed his course first to *Alexandria*, for the sake of visiting a friend, and then crossing the Mediterranean, *he landed at Puteoli*. (Antiq. xviii. 7. § 4.) Again, when

Herod the Tetrarch, at the instigation of Herodias, undertook a voyage to Rome, to solicit from Caligula a higher title, which might put him upon a level with his brother-in-law, Herod Agrippa, the latter pursued him to Italy, and *both of them* (says Josephus) *landed at Dichæarchia* (Puteoli), and found Caius at Baiæ. (Antiq. xviii. 8. § 2.)

Take a third instance. Josephus had himself occasion, when a young man, to go to Rome. On his passage the vessel in which he sailed foundered, but a ship from Cyrene picked him up, together with eighty of his companions; *"and having safely arrived* (says he) *at Dichæarchia, which the Italians called Puteoli*, I became acquainted with Aliturus, &c." (Josephus's Life, § 3.)

In the last passage there is a singular resemblance to the circumstances of St. Paul's voyage. Josephus, though not going to Rome as a prisoner who had himself appealed from Felix to Cæsar, was going to Rome on account of two friends, whom Felix thought proper to send to Cæsar's judgment-seat—he suffered ship wreck—he was forwarded by another vessel coming from Africa—and finally he landed at Puteoli.

CPSIA information can be obtained at www.ICGtesting.com
Printed in the USA
BVOW04s2205301015

424526BV00002B/149/P

9 781597 812740